CALIFORNIA JOE

Moses Embree Milner, better known as "California Joe," was never without his briar pipe. Courtesy of the Kansas State Historical Society.

California Joe

Noted Scout *and*
Indian Fighter By JOE E. MILNER, his Grandson, and EARLE R. FORREST

With an
Authentic Account
of Custer's Last Fight

By COLONEL WILLIAM H. C. BOWEN

Foreword by Joseph G. Rosa

University of Nebraska Press
Lincoln and London

First Bison Book printing: 1987
Most recent printing indicated by the first digit below:
1   2   3   4   5   6   7   8   9   10

Library of Congress Cataloging-in-Publication Data
Milner, Joe E., d. 1936
    California Joe.

    Reprint. Originally published: Caldwell, Idaho:
Caxton Printers, 1935.
    Bibliography: p.
    1. Milner, Moses Embree, 1829–1876. 2. Custer,
George Armstrong, 1839–1876. 3. Frontier and
pioneer life—West (U.S.) 4. Little Big Horn, Battle of
the, 1876. 5. Scouts and scouting—West (U.S.)—
Biography. 6. West (U.S.)—History—1848–1950.
7. West (U.S.)—Biography. I. Forrest, Earle Robert,
1883–   . II. Bowen, William H. C. Custer's last
fight. 1987. III. Title.
F594.M654   1987   978'.02'0922   87-5908
ISBN 0-8032-3121-0
ISBN 0-8032-8150-1 (pbk.)

Reprinted by arrangement with The Caxton Printers, Ltd.

To
NANCY EMMA MILNER,
who, as the bride of California Joe, spent her
honeymoon in a covered wagon, crossing
the plains to California in 1850.

TABLE OF CONTENTS

*C*ALIFORNIA JOE is the story of Moses Embree Milner, whose frontier reputation as an Indian fighter, scout, guide and rifle shot, won him the respect of his fellow plainsmen, army officers, and indeed almost everybody with whom he came in contact. Although few of his contemporaries knew his real name, or much about him, they readily accepted "California Joe" as an equal, for he was the kind of man who inspired adulation. His life was one long adventure, and his many exploits make exciting reading. This Bison edition of a long out-of-print book will be welcomed by a new and larger audience.

Unlike some of his fellow scouts and guides, California Joe has not received the fame and recognition that I think was his due. Rather, he has been neglected in favor of other frontier personalities — a situation that is not new. In their preface to the 1935 edition of *California Joe,* Joe E. Milner and Earle R. Forrest admitted that "to the present generation he is scarcely more than a name." Today, more than one hundred years after his death, California Joe remains obscure to all but the scholar and the western buff, and no serious attempt, to my knowledge, has been made to up-

date the book or to learn more about its subject. This, I
think, is a mistake, for Moses Embree Milner commands
our attention and demands a rehearing.

Some might argue that he lacked the press coverage or
"color" of a Hickok or a Cody, but I suspect Joe contributed to his own obscurity, for then as now this noted Indian fighter and scout was shrouded in mystery. "Who was
California Joe?" asked J. W. Buel in 1882. He suggested
that his real name was either "Joseph Milmer" (according
to Buffalo Bill Cody) or "Joseph Hawkins" (as recalled by
Captain D. L. Payne). Cody was closest, but without offer-
ing any proof, Payne added that California Joe was his own
third cousin and distantly related to Daniel Boone. And
perhaps it was Buel, unaware that there was more than one
"California Joe," who first confused Moses Embree Milner
with Truman Head, the celebrated "California Joe" of Colonel Hiram Berdan's Civil War sharpshooters.[1] When
Head died at San Francisco in 1875, the *Alta California*
reported that a "bogus California Joe" was operating as a
"desperado" in Wyoming.[2] This was obviously a reference
to Moses Milner, who, on the plains, was generally called
"California Joe." "No other name seemed ever to have
been given him, and no other name ever seemed necessary," wrote his erstwhile commander, General George A.
Custer.[3]

A desperado California Joe was not, but a colorful
character he certainly was. "He was a queer sort, most of
the time wandering about alone except for his dog—seldom rode—just tramped over the country, rarely stayed
long in one place," wrote Julia McGillicuddy.[4] That he
"seldom rode" is incorrect. His favorite plains mount was

an army mule, but by the mid-1870s he also owned a very fast horse that he raced with some success.

General Custer was fascinated by California Joe, whose "dingy-looking brierwood pipe in full blast" was a constant source of interest—and alarm. The "endurance of his smoking powers was only surpassed by his loquacity," for he could hold conversations on almost any subject and never lacked an audience.[5]

Just as strong was California Joe's appetite for strong drink, particularly home-brewed whiskey, although this was hardly mentioned by Milner and Forrest. Custer, who promoted Milner chief of scouts for the Washita campaign, promptly demoted him when he celebrated by getting drunk and causing pandemonium. The pair remained friends, however, and corresponded infrequently until Joe's death. (Curiously, Milner and Forrest ignored, or perhaps were unaware of, Joe's rapid demotion and imply that he remained chief of scouts throughout the Washita campaign.)[6] In February 1870, Joe further enhanced his alcoholic reputation when he caused some inconvenience to his old friend, General Phil Sheridan, whom he had known since the 1850s when "Little Phil" had soldiered in Oregon. Joe got hopelessly drunk at Fort Arbuckle and was incapable of guiding Sheridan to Camp Wichita. Sheridan lost a day while he sobered up, and a still "gloriously tipsy" Joe was bundled into a wagon for the return trip. Sheridan was angered but awed both by Joe's ability to find liquor and by his massive consumption.[7]

Despite his reputation as a "loner," Moses Milner had several partners during his scouting career, the most prominent being Jack Corbin, a shadowy character who was later lynched by vigilantes who claimed that he was a horse thief.[8] And he had a wife. On May 8, 1850, his twenty-first birthday, he married Nancy Emma Watts and took his bride to California, and later Oregon, where he built a home at Corvallis. The couple had four sons. Nancy proved to be a remarkable woman—she had to be to let her husband disappear for months at a time—yet she never complained, and his family adored him. For his part, Moses was proud of his sons and on occasion allowed the older boys to accompany him on his western wanderings.

By the early years of this century, there were still many people who had either known California Joe personally or by reputation, but few knew his real name. One who did was Dr. Valentine T. McGillycuddy (sometimes spelled McGillicuddy or M'Gillycuddy), post surgeon at Fort Robinson, Nebraska, when Joe was murdered in 1876. The doctor found papers on him stating that his name was Moses Embree Milner and that he had been born in Kentucky in 1829. It was the early 1920s, however, before any serious attempt was made to establish the truth about California Joe, and this was due largely to his grandson, Joseph (he apparently preferred to be called "Joe") E. Milner.

The Milner family, then living in Portland, Oregon, placed letters and other material at Joe's disposal. How long it took him to draft the original manuscript of *California Joe* is not clear, for he apparently spent some time seeking a coauthor. The late Raymond W. Thorp told me in 1959 that he had been asked "back in the 20s to write that book." He refused, however, because he was too busy writing magazine articles at the time to get involved.[9]

Joe Milner later had the good fortune to enlist the aid

of Earle R. Forrest. Forrest, a trained newspaperman, was the ideal choice. As a young man he had worked as a cowboy in Arizona, and his own western wanderings (while armed with a camera) had covered much of the territory that had known California Joe. Forrest contributed graphic descriptions of some of the places associated with Milner and an appendix devoted to the Custer Battlefield National Cemetery. This material was boosted by an account of the Battle of the Little Big Horn by Colonel William H. C. Bowen, whose version of the fight was the most accurate available in 1935, although some critics have seen it as unnecessary padding. Perhaps, but in hindsight I think that the authors were right to include it. Even with today's high-powered Custer industry, the serious student should still cover old ground.

My own involvement with California Joe began in 1956 when I was researching for my biography of Wild Bill Hickok. Joe E. Milner had died on August 8, 1936, at Portland, Oregon,[10] but his coauthor was still alive. Although Earle R. Forrest was anxious to help, and did (through correspondence he became a personal friend), he died on August 29, 1969, only weeks before we were to meet for the first time. Hickok aside, I suspect that if Forrest had been the sole author of *California Joe* he would have paid more attention to documented sources and relied less upon family recollections and hearsay, although he never said as much. As it now stands, only a careful reexamination of Joe Milner's sources might reveal how the fiction crept in. Two hearsay stories, in particular, highlight the problem.

On page 236 it is claimed that on November 2, 1875,

California Joe left the Red Cloud Agency to act as a guide
for thirty soldiers sent to aid Major E. W. Wynkoop—the
same Wynkoop who had once hired him at Fort Larned
during the Civil War. Now, however, he was in command
of the Black Hills Rangers. The date of Joe's departure has
a bearing on the events surrounding his death (which we
shall examine later). On page 235 the authors reproduce a
letter dated November 1 from Joe to his sons in which he
mentions the soldiers but not Wynkoop, which is not sur-
prising. Wynkoop was not commissioned in the regular
army, but during the Civil War had served as a major in
the First Colorado Cavalry and for a time had commanded
Fort Lyon. His appearance in the Black Hills was as a civilian with the so-called "Rangers," who had no connection
with the thirty regular troops guided by Milner. The authors then allege that Wynkoop persuaded Joe to make a
seven-hundred-mile trek to Fort Abraham Lincoln to carry
dispatches to General Custer. Custer did not return to the
fort from New York until March 13, 1876, and Joe's
actual movements are easily followed. In January 1876, he
was at Golden City, where he was engaged to guide some
miners to Bismark, arriving there on the 23rd. Further
trips to the Hills kept him busy until May, so he missed
Custer entirely. (It is strange how many attempts have
been made to place Custer's former scouts and guides in a
position to assist him or "save" him from his "Last Stand,"
only to be frustrated at the last moment. I recall an absurd
story that has Custer telegraphing Wild Bill Hickok at
Cheyenne and ordering him to report to Fort Lincoln, but
Western Union lost the message!)[11]

The second yarn concerns Joe's alleged rescue of a little

girl named Maggie Reynolds from Indians in 1864. He accomplished this single-handed, and her elder brother later became a scout, immortalized as "Lonesome Charlie" Reynolds. Both claims are nonsense, of course, but they inspired Jack Crawford, the self-styled "Poet Scout of the Black Hills," to produce one of his "epic" poems, which is reproduced in full on pages 118–24. As one eminent historian quite rightly pointed out, the result is "an interminable and lachrymose poem that defies description."[12]

The Milner family's recollections of California Joe's military service, however, appears to be based upon much firmer evidence. I suspect that, concerning this period in his life, they were better informed than some other sources. When I asked the National Archives for a synopsis of Moses Milner's service for the Quartermaster's Department, there was some confusion concerning his real name. They found a "M. E. Milliner," a "M. E. Williams," and a "J. M. Milner," all of whom were concluded to be "California Joe." The first was listed as a scout at Fort Harker, Kansas, during the period September 1868 to April 1869; the second as a guide on the Black Hills Expedition, July to October 1875; and the third as a guide in the field, Wyoming Territory, October 1876. No record was found of Joe's service in the Mexican War (1846–48); but it was admitted that because "of the nature of the extant records in our custody and the various ways in which civilians were hired by the Army during the 19th century, it is possible that M. E. Milner was hired at other times."[13]

Milner and Forrest placed much emphasis upon Joe's skill with firearms—a feature of many western biographies published during the 1920s and 1930s. No serious

student doubts the contemporary opinion that California
Joe was an excellent rifle shot, possibly one of the best on
the plains, but one questions some of the "pistoliferous"
feats credited to him and to others. I personally doubt that
he was as good a revolver shot as Hickok, or Frank North,
and certainly had no contemporary reputation as a
gunfighter. Therefore, the inclusion of a particularly un-
savory story on page 156 leads me to think that the authors
fell into the trap of sensationalism rather than recorded
fact. They describe how, when drunk, Joe was robbed by a
gambler at Newton, Kansas. When Joe sobered up and demanded his money back, the fellow fled. Joe pursued him
and, when he refused to stop, shot him in the back five
times and then prepared to stand off his companions.
They, naturally, would not face Joe. Had the incident really happened, it would have involved Joe with the law, and
left him with a reputation as a "backshooter," which he
never was.

It was also at Newton that Joe is reported to have first
met Wild Bill Hickok, and the narrative suggests that was
in 1866. Newton, however, was not founded until March
1871, by which time deputy U.S. Marshal Hickok was
based at Junction City, and Joe was still out on the plains
with the army. I think that the two probably first met at
Fort Riley, Kansas, late in 1866 or early in 1867.

California Joe's relationship with Hickok was tenuous
but genuine. On August 2, 1876, Hickok was shot
through the back of the head by John ("Jack") McCall as he
played poker in Saloon No. 10 (the authors mistakenly call
it the Sixty-Six). On the 26th the *Cheyenne Daily Leader*
reported that Wild Bill had had a premonition of his

approaching death, but said that he had "two trusty friends. One is my six-shooter and the other is California Joe." Joe, unfortunately, was out of town when Hickok was killed; but when he returned to learn that a kangaroo court and a bought jury had turned McCall loose, he was fighting mad. He grabbed his rifle and advanced on McCall's cabin. Jack's "cheeks blanched" when he was confronted by the angry giant, and he slunk away rather than face him. Later, McCall was arrested, legally tried for murder, and hanged on March 1, 1877.

When news of California Joe's own death swept the West, it shocked his many friends—especially the manner of it. Like Hickok, he was shot from behind without a chance to defend himself. On November 5, 1876, the *New York Herald* carried a piece (datelined Fort Laramie, November 4) which claimed that one Tom Newcomb shot Joe in retaliation for his alleged "connection with the killing of John Richard the father of Louis Richard, one of General Crook's scouts on the Big Horn Expedition."

John Richard (sometimes called "Reshaw") was a Frenchman who had moved west from Missouri in the 1840s. His marriage to a part-Indian woman was blessed with a number of children, of whom John, Jr., and Louis were the best known. By the mid-1870s, however, there was hostility between the family and the Sioux. In November 1875, John Richard and Alfred Palladay (said to be a nephew) were found murdered. Moccasin prints and other Indian "sign" made it clear who was responsible, but Thomas Newcomb, an employee in the Quartermaster's butcher shop at Fort Robinson, blamed Moses Milner, voicing his opinion to anyone who would listen to him. He even made his views known in Deadwood the following spring. Joe reportedly threatened to kill him if he did not stop his lies. Newcomb, however, simply bided his time. [14]

Evidence furnished (see pages 279–82) fifty years later by the ubiquitous Dr. McGillycuddy reveals that, following a brief confrontation in the sutler's store at Fort Robinson on October 29, 1876, Newcomb and California Joe pulled their pistols, but Joe persuaded Newcomb to put up his "darn gun" and have a drink. Onlookers thought the feud to be over, but later Newcomb appeared with a Winchester rifle and shot Joe in the back as he stood talking to friends. [15]

Newcomb was arrested but released when no civil charges were preferred. He later disappeared, some said to the Pacific Coast. In 1906 it was claimed that some weeks after Joe's death two of his sons appeared at the fort anxious to see his grave and to seek out Newcomb. They later returned, claiming that their mission had been "accomplished," which was understood to mean that Joe had been avenged. It was also reported that Newcomb was a "lightheaded individual" anxious for a reputation and that he had killed Joe because Joe had blamed *him* for Richard's murder! Later, in 1910 or 1911, Dr. McGillycuddy was visited by a friend who had recently been in Montana, where he met a man who said: "If you see him [McGillycuddy] you might mention you met Tom Newcomb; but he won't be pleased to hear of me." [16]

California Joe's involvement in Richard's murder is soon refuted. He was a guide for the Jenney Expedition from May 25, 1875, until it returned to Fort Laramie on October 14 of that year. He then headed *north* to the Black

Hills by way of the Red Cloud Agency (as previously
noted), rather than *south* to Richard's home on the Niobrara River, which meant that he was well on his way to the
Hills when the murder took place.

Despite its fictional lapses, I am delighted that *California Joe* is again available. For too long it has been out of the
reach of all but the scholar and Western Americana collector. I also hope that its reappearance will inspire a dedi-
cated student to reexamine its content—the clues are all
there—and make a determined effort to track down the
original manuscript and the family's papers. These,
together with the benefit of hindsight and modern research, will provide a fresh interpretation of the material.
Then, perhaps, the *real* California Joe Milner can take his
rightful place alongside the other great frontiersmen of his
time. In the meantime, I recommend *California Joe* to all
western buffs and to the general public. It is good reading
and a sympathetic study of one of the truly colorful characters of the Old West.

Notes

1. J. W. Buel, *Heroes of the Plains* (New York and St. Louis: N. D.
Thompson & Co., 1882), 419.

2. Head was the author, under his own name and his alias, of *Hope of a
Civiliation Yet to Be. With Direction How to Take Beaver, Otter, etc. etc.*, published in San Francisco in 1867 (Arthur Woodward, "Historical Sidelights on
California Joe," *The Westerners, Los Angeles Corral, Eighth Brand Book* [1959],
208–9.)

3. Gen. G. A. Custer, *Life on the Plains* (New York: Sheldon & Co.,
1876). 131.

4. Julia B. McGillycuddy, *McGillycuddy Agent: A Biography of Dr. Valentine T. McGillycuddy* (Stanford, Calif.: Stanford University Press, 1941), 29–
30.

5. Custer, *Life on the Plains,* 131.

6. Ibid., 134–35.

7. Paul Andrew Hutton, *Phil Sheridan and His Army* (Lincoln: University of Nebraska Press, 1985), 105–6.

8. Early in November 1870, while in pursuit of a man wanted by the military, Corbin made the fatal mistake of spending the night with Lewis and George Booth, both accused of horse stealing by the Butler County Vigilantes. The vigilantes surprised the three men: the Booth brothers were both shot dead and Corbin, protesting his innocence, was dragged to a sycamore tree and hanged. His guilt or otherwise has yet to be established (James D. Drees to Joseph G. Rosa, December 12, 1986; *Leavenworth* [Kans.] *Daily Times,* November 16, 1870).

9. Raymond W. Thorp to Joseph G. Rosa, June 12, 1959.

10. Christian Frazza, Manuscripts Librarian, Washington State University, to Joseph G. Rosa, December 9, 1986. The university now houses all the original publisher's collection of material, including reviews and correspondence concerning *California Joe.*

11. John S. Gray, "A Triple Play," *The Westerners Brand Book,* vol. 26, no. 3 (Chicago: May 1969): 19; Robert M. Utley, ed., *Life in Custer's Cavalry: Diaries and Letters of Albert and Jennie Barnitz, 1867–1868* (New Haven, Conn.: Yale University Press, 1977; reprinted Lincoln: University of Nebraska Press, 1987), 282–83.

12. Gray, "A Triple Play," 19.

13. Michael E. Pilgrim, Military Archives Division, National Archives, to Joseph G. Rosa, October 21, 1986.

14. Brian Jones, "Those Wild Reshaw Boys," *Sidelights of the Sioux Wars* (London: The English Westerners' Society, 1967), 33. Mr. Jones's account of the Richard family is the most complete and accurate to date. See also Woodward, "Historical Sidelights on California Joe," 207–11.

15. Gray, "A Triple Play," 18; Woodward, "Historical Sidelights on California Joe," 207–11.

16. Eli Seavey Ricker, interviews with Magloire Alexis Mosseau, Pine Ridge, S. D., October 30, 1906, and Frank Salaway, Allen, S. D., November 4, 1906 (Microfilm copy, the Ricker Papers, Kansas State Historical Society, Topeka, Kansas); McGillycuddy, *McGillycuddy Agent,* 67.

O F all the Indian fighters, army scouts, and frontiersmen produced by the old West of three-quarters of a century ago, none were better known in their day than Moses E. Milner, famous from the Missouri to the Pacific as "California Joe." He ranked with such men as Kit Carson, Wild Bill Hickok, Buffalo Bill Cody, Captain Jack Crawford, the North brothers, Billy Comstock, Jack Corbin, and Charley Reynolds; but to the present generation he is scarcely more than a name. Although he has been dead for more than fifty years there are still living a few of the old-timers, scattered here and there, who knew California Joe when he was one of the greatest scouts in all the West.

A halo of mystery has long hovered about the identity of California Joe. Few of the old plainsmen knew his real name. Buffalo Bill was nearer correct than any when he gave it as Joseph Milmer, while Captain D. L. Payne, the Cimarron scout, was far from the truth when he declared that it was Joseph Hawkins. As will be seen, his first name was not Joseph but Moses.

The reason for this is easily explained. Moses Milner made no attempt to conceal his real name; but, like most frontiersmen of note, he had been given a nickname. This was a custom of the times, and as "California Joe" he was known from the Black Hills to Texas. The men of the Old West were not concerned with a man's past; that was his own business. Moses Milner had nothing in his past life to conceal, but as family history was of no interest to frontiersmen of that day he told little or nothing, and to all, even his best friends, he was just "California Joe." Franklin W. Hall, now living at Houlton, Maine, was well acquainted with him during the early Black Hills days, but even he did not know the real name of his old friend for many years after the scout's death.

Even General Custer, under whom California Joe served as chief of scouts, did not know his real name, at least not before the Washita campaign of 1868. In his *Wild Life on the Plains* the general has this to say in speaking of the names applied to scouts in general: "Who they are, whence they come from, or whither they go, their names even, except such as they choose to adopt or which may be given them, are all questions which none but themselves can answer."

In this biography of Moses Milner the authors have related for the first time a complete and authentic history of the famous scout, California Joe. Joe E. Milner, one of the authors, is a grandson of this

Indian fighter of the Old West, and he has given family records and adventures of California Joe never before published. Their authenticity is beyond question, for they have been records in the Milner family for three generations. Before her death in 1915, Joe Milner's grandmother gave him much accurate and valuable information on the life of her Indian-fighting husband. Mr. Milner carefully preserved all facts related to him by this woman of the old frontier, whose journey across the plains to California in that golden, romantic year of 1850 was her honeymoon.

The task of writing the story of Moses Milner has not been easy, for his was a life of many thrills and adventures in the days when the Old West was young. In recording his history the authors have adhered to these facts as handed down in the Milner family. His army service as a scout has been verified from War Department records. Therefore we feel that we are presenting the first and only authentic history of California Joe, mountain man, Mexican War veteran, Forty-niner, Oregon pioneer, gold-seeker in California, Idaho, and Montana, Indian fighter, and army scout.

In addition to the family records, this life of one of the Old West's most famous scouts and Indian fighters is the result of careful research and gathering of historical data during a period of thirty-five years by Joe E. Milner, who has spent his entire life wandering over the West. In earlier years he met many of the noted characters of the wild, free days that are

now gone forever, and was fortunate in a personal
acquaintance with a number of old-timers who knew
and rode side by side with his grandfather, California
Joe, on many a long journey; men who took an active
part with him in Indian battles. Mr. Milner is in
possession of several hundred letters from old-timers
and army officers from the four corners of the United
States, who knew the famous scout, Moses E. Milner.

The only previous attempt ever made at a biography of California Joe is found in J. W. Buel's
Heroes of the Plains, a book that had a wide circula-
tion in the eighties and nineties of the last century,
and at the time was accepted as authentic; for the
author gave the impression that he was on intimate
terms with, or had known personally, every plainsman mentioned in his work. Nevertheless Buel's book
must be ranked with the dime novel literature of that
period. It is now a well-known fact that few of the
adventures attributed to his various heroes ever took
place. His accounts of Wild Bill and Buffalo Bill are
not founded on facts; and his life of California Joe
is pure fiction from beginning to end. Even his version of Joe's murder is false, as will appear later. If
Buel's life of California Joe had appeared in dime
novel form it could be understood and forgiven; but
since it was published in a book purporting to be a
history of noted plainsmen, it must be exposed as the
most outrageous piece of fiction ever crammed down
the throats of a gullible public as historical fact.

The so-called mystery around the life of California Joe had its origin with Buel, who began his biography with the following:

"The man in the Iron Mask and the author of the Junius letters are the great unsolved personalities of history; but while a comparison between these and California Joe would appear, in some degree, ridiculous to the æsthetic student of human nature, yet insofar as identity alone is concerned they were not altogether unlike; though the character of the Wandering Jew would afford an altogether more appropriate resemblance when considering alone the odd traits and singular adventures of this great plainsman.

"Who was California Joe? This question many may consider themselves able to answer, but no one, perhaps, can distinguish between the California Joes who have figured in so many escapades attributed to this enigmatic character, for there has been more than one person to adopt this title. Where was he born? No one will attempt to answer. The California Joe who hunted, trailed, fought and slept beside General Custer and Buffalo Bill is believed to have been a native of Kentucky. Buffalo Bill maintains that his real name was Joseph Milmer, while Captain Payne declares that his real name was Joseph Hawkins, and, as further proof of the claim, asserts that Joe was a distant relative of Daniel Boone, and also his (Payne's) third cousin. We are only able to say, therefore, that California Joe was singularly reticent concerning his early life, and died at last with his full identity unsolved. For what facts I here present concerning his life I am indebted to Buffalo Bill and Capt. Payne, and it is this reason that has prompted me to respect the opinions of each by giving their assertions, not, however, with any desire to involve them in any further discussion concerning Joe's real name."

As a matter of fact there was but one "California Joe" in the history of the West. Throughout our book will be found frequent references to Buel's errors. In 1862 he places Joe in the Union army during the first siege of Richmond, but in that year California Joe was in the gold camps of Idaho and Montana, and he did not at any time serve in the Union army during the Civil War. There was no mystery about his past life, and he never made any attempt to conceal anything.

Custer's description of California Joe, found in the general's book, *Wild Life on the Plains,* is interesting and well worth recording, for it comes down to us from one who knew him:

"He was a man about forty years of age, perhaps older, over six feet in height, and possessing a well-proportioned frame. His head was covered with a luxurious crop of long, almost black hair, strongly inclined to curl, and so long as to fall carelessly over his shoulders. His face, at least as much of it as was not concealed by the long, waving brown beard and moustache, was full of intelligence and pleasant to look upon. His eye was undoubtedly handsome, black

and lustrous, with an expression of kindness and mild-
ness combined. On his head was generally to be seen,
whether asleep or awake, a huge sombrero, or black
slouch hat. A soldier's overcoat with its long, circular cape, a pair of trousers with the legs tucked in
the tops of his boots, usually constituted the outside
makeup of the man whom I selected as chief scout.
He was known by the euphonious title of 'California
Joe'; no other name ever seemed to have been given
him, and no other name ever seemed necessary. His
military armament consisted of a long Springfield
breech-loading musket, from which he was insepar-
able, and a revolver and hunting knife, both the latter
being carried in his waist-belt. His mount completed
his equipment for the field, being instead of a horse
a finely-formed mule, in whose speed and endurance
he had every confidence.

"California Joe was an inveterate smoker and was
rarely seen without his stubby, dingy-looking brierwood pipe in full blast. The endurance of his smoking powers was only surpassed by his loquacity. His
pipe frequently became exhausted and required re-
filling, but California Joe never seemed to lack for
material or disposition to carry on a conversation,
principally composed of personal adventures among
the Indians, episodes in mining life, or experience in
overland journeyings before the days of steam engines
and palace cars rendered a trip across the plains a
comparatively uneventful one. It was evident from
the scraps of information volunteered from time to

time, that there was but little of the Western country
from the Pacific to the Missouri river with which
California Joe was not intimately acquainted. He
had lived in Oregon years before, and had become acquainted from time to time with most of the officers
who had served on the plains or on the Pacific coast.
I once inquired of him if he had ever seen General
Sheridan. 'What, Gineral Shuridun? Why, bless my
soul, I knowed Shuridun way up in Oregon more'n
fifteen years ago, an' he was only a second lootenant
uv infantry. He wuz quartermaster of the foot or
something uv that sort, an' I had the contract uv
furnishin' wood to the post, and, would ye b'leve it?
I had a kind of sneakin' notion then that he'd hurt
somebody ef they'd ever turn him loose. Lord, but
ain't he old lightnin'?' This was the man whom upon
a short acquaintance I decided to appoint as chief of
scouts."

Custer paid a high tribute to California Joe's
military ability by saying that he generally had the
correct idea of how to conduct an Indian campaign.

Colonel Henry Inman, an old-time army officer
on the frontier and author of *The Old Santa Fe Trail*
and *The Great Salt Lake Trail*, classified California
Joe as a scout of the old regime, and the best all-
around shot on the plains. Dr. V. T. McGillycuddy,
another old-timer, still living at Berkeley, California,
was a personal friend of this noted scout.

The authors have deemed it fitting that the life
story of California Joe should close with an account

of the last fight of his old commander, General George A. Custer. By a strange coincidence, both of these famous frontiersmen passed over their last trail in that year of 1876.

"Custer's Last Fight," which forms the closing chapter of this book, was written by the late Colonel William H. C. Bowen, a retired officer of the old regular army. We have been very fortunate in securing from such an authority this account of one of the greatest Indian battles of all the centuries of Indian warfare. Colonel Bowen, in his last years as instructor of history at the Hill Military Academy of Portland, Oregon, was especially well qualified to write on Custer's last fight. In 1884 he was stationed as a young lieutenant of infantry, at Fort Custer, Montana, only ten miles from the Custer battlefield. That was eight years after Custer's historic last stand; and there were still many officers and men in the regular army who had fought with Reno and Benteen, or who had arrived in the relief column with General Terry.

While at Fort Custer, young Lieutenant Bowen, in company with officers of the Second Cavalry who had been with General Terry when he rescued Reno on June 27, 1876, often visited the scene of this most famous of all Indian battles. On the occasion of the tenth anniversary of the fight in 1886, Company K, Fifth infantry, commanded by Captain Frank D. Baldwin, acted as hosts to the survivors of the old Seventh Cavalry.

The first lieutenant of Company K was William H. C. Bowen. Few men ever had like opportunity to secure first-hand information of events of the campaign against the Northwest tribes in 1876 from men who had taken part, and he took advantage of it. Benteen, Godfrey, McDougal, and others of the Seventh Cavalry, and several of the Second Cavalry who had been with Terry, together with Gall, Hump, White Bull, and other Sioux and Cheyenne chiefs were there that day in reunion.

Four years later when Lieutenant Bowen was stationed at New Haven, Connecticut, on recruiting duty, he became interested in the Connecticut National Guard. As soon as it became known that he had served on the frontier he was asked so many questions on the Custer fight that he prepared a lecture on the subject, and collected over one hundred and fifty pictures and maps. In 1894 he had risen to the rank of captain and was stationed at Atlanta, Georgia. At that time Colonel Benteen, a former captain of the Seventh Cavalry and the hero of Reno's fight of June 25, 1876, had been retired from active service and was living at Atlanta. He kindly revised the manuscript of Captain Bowen's lecture, and when completed pronounced it "the best account of the Custer fight ever written." It was from this revised manuscript that the chapter on "Custer's Last Fight" was written by Colonel Bowen.

California Joe will live in history as one of the most noted scouts of the Old West. He was not of the braggart type, in spite of Buel's statements; but was the direct opposite, always quiet and unassuming, making little of his achievements. Of a kindly disposition, he had but few enemies. A quick temper was his greatest fault, but when wrong he was always ready to admit it. Generous to a fault, he would share his last dollar with a comrade. Six feet two inches tall and weighing one hundred and ninety pounds, he was known as one of the strongest men on the frontier; and with nerves of steel and the strength of a lion, he never knew the meaning of fear.

California Joe was a Kentuckian by birth. He liked his whisky and he drank it "a little at a time but often," but he was seldom intoxicated. A big majority of frontiersmen, army officers, and soldiers drank, most of them heavily, in those days. This was a fault of the period in which they lived, for drinking and gambling were the principal sources of amusement on the old frontier.

In conclusion we will say that California Joe's wife and four sons remembered him as an affectionate husband and good father.

JOE E. MILNER,
EARLE R. FORREST.

INTRODUCTION BY FRANKLIN W. HALL

A Seventy-six Pioneer of the Black Hills

CALIFORNIA JOE! What a world of memories those two words arouse, when we recall that in the time of California Joe there was not a railroad west of the Missouri river, and every pound of freight, every emigrant, every letter, and every message had to be carried by wagon or on horseback, and at the risk of life and hardships untold. At that time Kansas City consisted of a warehouse; and there was not a single private residence of civilized man between the Missouri river and San Francisco. When these conditions are known it can well be understood that the man who could "carry on" in a successful way was no ordinary individual.

It is fortunate for the preservation of frontier history that such a biographical task as the life of California Joe should be undertaken by one so well qualified for the work as his grandson, Joe E. Milner, upon whom I have many times urged the necessity of such an attempt. Mr. Milner has been fortunate in securing the collaboration of Earle R. Forrest, an authority on frontier history and an author who has contributed much to the history of the Old West.

Insofar as it would be possible for a boy to know a man of middle age, I may say that I knew California Joe, he being a frequent visitor at the cabin of the Hall boys at Rapid Creek, Dakota Territory, where Joe had a fine ranch, and was trying to induce newcomers to settle and build a town.

Strange as it may seem I never knew the real name of California Joe until years after his death. To his friends and neighbors, and to the world in general, he was known as California Joe. As to who he was, or what his name was, nobody knew and nobody seemed to care, for it was an accepted unwritten law of the time and region for people to mind their own business, and considerably safer.

California Joe has been variously described by different writers as odd and eccentric, so foreign to every-day life, as to be almost a freak. I would like to say that he was badly misunderstood, but he took no pains to rectify the misconception. He hunted, trailed, fought, ate, and slept with such men as General Custer and Buffalo Bill, and was the friend and contemporary of "Jim" Bridger, "Jim" Baker, "Jim" Beckwourth, "Kit" Carson, Alex Majors, "Wild Bill" Hickok, Charles Utter, and dozens more of the same type. The relied-upon man of every general who went to the frontier posts was no oddity, but a real man of nature, nothing assumed, no polish. An extremely quiet, modest man, with long, flowing hair and full brown beard, bashful as a boy if women

were present; it was hard to get him to speak when
one was within hearing. But among men his independence was commanding, standing out in striking contrast to the deference and respect for rank
instilled in a soldier. He looked upon the commanding officer with no more awe than he would the
meanest awkward-squad man of the troopers. One
peculiarity of the man was his inability to show surprise. Occurrences that would make others gasp in
astonishment made no more impression upon him
than the most trivial circumstance.

He seemed to have a personal knowledge of the
whole territory from the Missouri river to the Pacific ocean. His wide acquaintance with noted hunters, and his roaming disposition had given him an
experience vastly superior to that of the common
plainsman.

His quaint vocabulary and droll expression placed
him in a class unique unto himself. His stories of adventure, his wit, his fearless and original exposition
carried a strong appeal to the younger men who
were fortunate enough to enjoy his friendship. It
was generally conceded that he sometimes "drew a
long bow," but his tales were startling enough without any necessity for exaggeration. "Where he and
Bridger had been"; or "what he and Baker had seen";
or "what he and Carson had done"; or "he and Beckwourth had heard" were always entertaining.

One story he delighted in telling was of a family,
consisting of a mother and several strapping daugh-

ters who lived in a cabin on the Bozeman road. They kept a few cows, and Joe stopped at their cabin one morning to get some milk. While he was waiting for the milking to be done, the shriveled old mother bent over the fire-place, stolid and silent, diligently puffing away at her clay pipe. Then one of the "gals," according to Joe, came in barefooted and wet from running through the wet grass, and stood by the fire to dry her wet homespun dress. Without raising her head or moving a muscle, the mother said, "Sal, there's a coal under your foot."

With no more emotion and without moving, the daughter asked, "Which foot, mammy?"

The girl had run barefooted all her life, and the shale and rough ground had made her soles so tough that the red-hot coal was some time making its way through to a tissue with any sense of pain.

In conclusion, I will say that California Joe was noted for his wonderful marksmanship at long range. He had few, if any superiors, and mighty few equals. His trusty old Sharps rifle and inevitable brier-root pipe were his constant companions.

FRANKLIN W. HALL.

THE MAKING OF A
FRONTIERSMAN

I

MOSES EMBREE MILNER, famous in the old West as California Joe, was born in a log cabin on his father's plantation near Standford, Kentucky, May 8, 1829, the oldest of a family of four children. His brother George was the second child; Eliza came next, and Jenny was the youngest.

The family has been in America for two hundred and fifty years; for it was about 1683 that two brothers by this name landed on the shore of Virginia. They came from Yorkshire, England, where the name had been known for centuries; but they were of a roving, adventurous disposition, and answered the call to the new world that was then sweeping through England. Virginia was a wild land at that time, populated by a mere handful of Englishmen, wild beasts and wilder men.

Soon after landing the Milner brothers married; and during the next two centuries their descendants helped make American history, pioneering in new lands, fighting Indians, and battling for liberty and independence throughout the dark days of the Revo-

lution and again in the War of 1812. The hero of
this book was a descendant of those first Milners,
and Joe E. Milner, one of the authors, has the honor
of being another.

Moses Embree Milner, better known as California
Joe, was given the middle name of Embree after his
father whose name was Embree Armstead Milner.
His mother's name was Sarah Ann Milner. Embree
Armstead Milner had fought against the British in
1812, and his father was one of General Washington's
soldiers during the Revolutionary War. It will be
readily seen that Moses Milner inherited fighting traits
from his ancestors.

When a boy Moses Milner attended school in a
log cabin in the Kentucky wilderness. He was a
bright pupil, and always at the head of his class; but
the forest in which he lived was always calling him.
Rarely did he miss a day that he did not take his
father's long-barreled Kentucky rifle to school, and
in this way he gained much practice shooting at
birds and small animals. When not at school he spent
his time hunting, and although only a lad he kept
the household well supplied with wild meat. It was
his proud boast that he killed his first deer when only
twelve years of age.

He quickly learned the arts of woodcraft, and at
the age of fourteen he was known as one of the best
shots in that part of the country. In those days his
rifle was of the muzzle-loading variety; but it gave
him the practice that in years to come made him one

of the greatest all-around shots in the West. Even today with modern high-powered rifles only experts could duplicate some of the remarkable long shots which he made during his eventful life on the frontier. He began his wandering life at the tender age of fourteen when he quit school much against his parents' wishes; but the wilderness was calling. One day in August, 1843, he shouldered his Kentucky rifle, and, telling his parents that he was going hunting for a few days, started out through the forest. That was the last they saw of their son for five years; and then one day in 1848 he appeared at their new home in Warren County, Missouri, Embree Milner having emigrated to that state because Kentucky was getting too thickly populated to suit him and he wanted a little more elbow room.

It is not definitely known whether young Milner intended to leave home when he started on that hunting trip; but he wandered on and on until finally he reached St. Louis, the first large city he had ever seen. In those days it was headquarters for the American fur trade and the gateway to the Far West. In a few days the boy met and joined a party of trappers on their way to Independence, then only a trading post, to outfit themselves for a hunting trip on the Platte and its tributaries. Milner was the youngest of the party of twelve.

With their pack horses laden down with supplies and traps the little band left Independence on Sep-

tember 5, 1843; and in a few weeks was in the Platte
Valley, at that time the heart of the game and trapping country of the Far West. A winter camp was
established on the North Platte, and several months
were spent in trapping beaver and other fur-bearing
animals.

Young Milner quickly became one of the best
trappers in the outfit, and his ready rifle supplied all
kinds of game; for in those days that section was alive
with deer, buffalo, wild turkeys, and prairie chicken.
The winter was one of many hardships; but the experience and knowledge gained by the youthful
trapper was the groundwork of a long career not
surpassed by any frontiersman who ever roamed the
Old West. During the days of that long winter the
boy was always out with his rifle; and at night he
listened with close attention to the campfire tales of
wild adventure told by veteran trappers. He was the
favorite of the camp. Always pleasant, he never
shirked his duty, and was the first to volunteer for
any task.

In the early spring of 1844 a wandering trapper
from Fort Laramie, Wyoming, stumbled upon the
camp, and informed the men that they could dispose
of their furs at that post and secure employment from
the American Fur Company, its proprietor. As this
would save a long journey back to Independence,
they all agreed to go to Fort Laramie, and enter the
service of the American Fur Company as trappers.

It is evident that their new friend was an agent of this fur company, for he guided them to the trading post, which they reached during the latter part of April, 1844.

Of all the fur-trading posts and military forts built between the Mississippi River and the Pacific Coast, and from Canada to Mexico, from the days of the Bents, the Sublettes, Kit Carson, Jim Bridger, and all the other old-time trappers down through the years of the fur trade to the military occupation and the Indian wars, Fort Laramie was the most famous. Located in the heart of the country claimed by the Ogallala and Brule branches of the great Sioux nation, with the Cheyennes, Araphoes, and other nomadic tribes of the great plains only a little farther away, it became the most important point on the Oregon Trail during the great hegira of settlers to the Oregon Country in the latter forties, and the gold rushes of forty-nine and the fifties. Volumes could be written of the old-time trappers, frontiersmen, Indian fighters and military officers who made this post their headquarters during the more than half a century of its existence. It was at this far-flung fur trading post of the Old West that Moses Milner became acquainted with such noted frontiersmen as Jim Bridger, Jim Baker, Jim Beckwourth, and others of lesser fame.

The first post that marked the beginnig of Fort Laramie was built during the summer of 1834 by William L. Sublette, one of the famous Sublette

brothers of the old fur-trading days, and named Fort
William in honor of its founder. Sublette was one
of the partners of the old Rocky Mountain Fur Company, and the newly constructed post on the Laramie
river became its headquarters. However, the next
year all of the property of this company was transferred to Lucien Fontenelle, a representative of the
American Fur Company, a rival organization. After
passing into the hands of its new owners the post was
named Fort John, in honor of John B. Sarpy.

An interesting point in regard to this change of
name is related by Hebard and Brinistool in *The Bozeman Trail*. John Hunton, who first went to Fort
Laramie in 1867 and in 1920 owned the ground where
this historic post stood, informed the authors of the
above-mentioned book that when he first settled
there in 1867 he was told by Antoine Ladeau, an old
half-breed Pawnee trapper, that the Fort John of the
old fur days was another post. The original Fort
William was on the left bank of the Laramie river
about two miles above its confluence with the North
Platte; and according to Ladeau, Fort John was a
separate post nearer the mouth of the Laramie.

The truth of this is established by Joel Palmer's
journal of 1845, which appears in Thwaites' *Early
Western Travels*. Palmer gives the interesting information that in 1845 there were two posts at this
point: "Fort Laramie, situated upon the west side of
Laramie's Fork, two miles from Platte River, belonging to the American Fur Company, and Fort John,

standing a mile below Fort Laramie, and built of the same material (adobe) as the latter, but not so extensive."

In the early forties the American Fur Company selected a site one mile further up the Laramie, where a new post was built. This was named Fort Laramie in honor of Jacques Laramie, a roving French Canadian free trapper who had conducted a fur trading business in that section of Wyoming before 1820. He was later killed by Indians near the site of the fort that bears his name. A description of Fort Laramie in 1845 states that it was about two hundred feet square with adobe walls more than two feet thick and fifteen feet high, surmounted by a palisade. At two of the corners were bastions, or block-houses, so built that they commanded the walls. Brass swivels defended the main gate and the block-houses.

The history of Fort Laramie as a fur-trading post came to an end in 1849, when it was purchased from the American Fur Company by the Federal Government for four thousand dollars, under an act of Congress dated May 19, 1846. This action was taken upon the recommendation of General John C. Fremont, who had first visited the post in 1842, and realized its importance as a military point. In 1890, it was abandoned, the necessity for its occupation as a military post having ceased, and was sold to private parties, John Hunton purchasing most of the buildings. It is interesting to note that between 1846 and 1869 it was located in the territories of Missouri, Nebraska, Idaho, Dakota, and finally Wyoming. During the years of the fur trade and military occupation Fort Laramie was the scene of more Indian councils and treaties than any other point west of the Mississippi.

Fort Laramie, when Moses Milner arrived there in the spring of 1844, was at the height of its glory as a fur post, monopolizing the Indian trade of an area larger than several eastern states. A few days after his arrival our youthful frontiersman joined a party of twenty-five trappers led by Jim Baker, bound for the Yellowstone river and its tributaries to trade with the friendly Indians and act as an escort for the trappers from that region who would soon be on their way back to Fort Laramie with their winter catch of furs.

On reaching the Powder river they discovered a band of hostile Blackfeet camped on the trapping grounds. Seeing that his men were greatly outnumbered, Jim Baker, veteran of many a hard-fought battle between trappers and red warriors, ordered a surprise attack; for he well knew that if the whites were discovered and forced on the defensive their losses would be heavy. Leaving two men with the packs and supplies, Baker led the rest down a small canyon, at the mouth of which the village was located. The Indians were taken completely by surprise, for they did not have the slightest suspicion of danger until the trappers suddenly charged into their

camp. The Blackfeet were routed with a loss of
fourteen killed.

In this, his first Indian battle, young Milner won
old Jim Baker's admiration by shooting two warriors. Later in the day when the trappers were pur-
suing the enemy, an Indian was seen upon the distant
rim of the canyon, apparently out of range of their
rifles, for several men fired at him without result.

"Let me take a rest shot. I believe I can hit him,"
said Milner.

Baker, who was standing nearby, replied, "Let
this red-headed kid take a shot at that Indian."

Lying down and resting his rifle across a boulder,
Mose took aim and fired, and to the amazement of
the trappers the warrior pitched forward down the
canyon wall, landing a short distance from the white
men. The distance was estimated at four hundred
yards; and the Indian was shot in the head. On account of his part in this fight the boy became a great
favorite with the entire party.

Returning to the scene of the first battle, the
trappers found the village deserted, all of the squaws
and children having scattered through the hills like
scared rabbits. Baker gave orders to burn the camp,
and nothing was spared. This battle ended in a complete victory for the whites. They had killed eighteen Indians and destroyed the camp, with a loss of
one trapper wounded.

Although only fifteen years of age young Milner
had killed three warriors; and after the fight was over

Baker made this prediction: "There's a lad who will have a great name on the frontier some day if he keeps on like he did today." It is doubtful if even Jim Baker himself dreamed how that prediction was to be fulfilled in later years.

After a day's rest the trappers continued their journey, visiting several camps of friendly Indians, where they traded for large quantities of furs and a number of horses. Slowly they made they way back through the Yellowstone valley, gathering trappers here and there, until it was a large brigade that returned to Fort Laramie.

After his return to the post young Milner was engaged by the American Fur Company as a hunter. In those days on the old frontier such game as buffalo, elk, deer, and antelope were abundant, and he was very successful. Killing buffalo was his favorite sport; and although only a boy, Mose gained a reputation that was the talk of all mountain men at Fort Laramie. On these hunting trips he would sometimes be away from the fort several days at a time, camping at some village of friendly Sioux; and during the years he was post hunter at Fort Laramie he learned to speak the Sioux language.

After remaining at this post almost three years, young Milner and five other trappers went to Fort Bridger, located on the Black Fork of the Green river in the southwest corner of the present state of Wyoming.

Fort Bridger, another of those famous fur-trad-

ing and military posts of the old west, was erected
in 1843 by James Bridger, one of the most noted
trappers and mountain men the old frontier ever produced. In the beginning it was only a small fort with
a blacksmith shop, built for the accommodation of
emigrants bound for the Oregon country. Its interesting history is second only to that of Fort Laramie.
Mexico then claimed all that region, and Bridger ob-
tained a grant for the land from the Mexican government. Associated with him in the ownership of this
post was Colonel Louis Vasquez, another noted fur
trader of those early days.

The fort was enlarged, and it soon became an
important fur post and point on the California-Ore-
gon trails. It was there that the main trail from the
east forked, one branch going to California and the
other to Fort Hall and Oregon. A stage station on
the overland route was established there in the fifties;
it was also a station for the famous pony express prior
to the Civil War.

The buildings were constructed of logs, with sod
roofs, inclosed by a stockade eight feet high. During
Bridger's *régime* the post was occupied by some fifty
persons, whites, half-breeds, and Indians.

During the Mormon war of 1856, Bridger incurred the enmity of Brigham Young when he acted
as guide for General Albert Sidney Johnston's army
in its march across the plains to Salt Lake City. Upon
the approach of Johnston the Mormons captured
Fort Bridger, confiscated all merchandise and every-

thing else of value, and burned the buildings. Bridger
claimed that his loss was one hundred thousand dollars.

In 1857, Bridger leased the property to the
United States Government for six hundred dollars a
year, which rental was never paid. Thirty years later
the Government paid Bridger's heirs six thousand dollars for the improvements he had made to the property, but nothing was allowed for the land on the
grounds that he did not have a clear title. From June
10, 1858, until October 6, 1890, the date of its abandonment, Fort Bridger was occupied by United States
troops. Recently this historic fort was purchased by
the Historical Landmark Commission of Wyoming,
and will be preserved.

In 1926, there was still living on the Wind River
Indian Reservation, in Wyoming, an old Shoshone
woman, seventy-eight years of age, who was a granddaughter of Sacajawea, the famous woman guide of
Lewis and Clark. This granddaughter's Indian name
was Pow-wo-wok-ka, meaning "fierce eyes"; but
she was known as Barbara Myers. In her youth she
had married a Mexican known as "Long John." They
resided at Fort Bridger until 1872, when they
removed to the Wind River Reservation. During the
Mexican War "Long John" fought in the American
army, for which service his widow received a pension.

When Mose Milner and his five companions arrived at Fort Bridger, he entered the service of Jim

Bridger, the proprietor, who at once took a liking to the boy. Bridger, whose fame has survived the passing of three-quarters of a century, was the most famous of all the trappers produced by the early fur days of the Far West. Even Kit Carson did not surpass him in woodcraft and mountain lore; and no other man of his time knew the Rocky Mountains as well as old Jim Bridger.

Many people were employed about Fort Bridger when young Mose Milner arrived there. He was engaged as livestock herder, his duties being to drive the horses and mules out to the grazing grounds every morning and return them to the corral in the evening. He had to count the animals several times during the day to see that none were missing. For a time he had no trouble; but one afternoon he rushed into the fort and reported that five head of horses had been stolen.

Bridger at once sounded the alarm, and twenty men were soon on the trail of the thieves, young Mose being one of the party. After a chase of several miles, with Jim Bridger in the lead, the thieves, who proved to be a band of ten renegade Indians, were overtaken. At the first sign of pursuit the thieves scattered, and a running fight that lasted until sunset took place. The stolen horses were recovered and six Indians were killed, but the others managed to escape. In this battle Milner's horse was shot from under him; but he used the dead animal as a breastworks and killed the Indian who had fired the shot. One white man was killed, and one badly wounded, but he subsequently recovered.

On returning to the fort, Bridger praised his men for their work, and set out a jug of whisky as a treat; but gave orders that none was to be given to the half-breeds or Indians, a number of whom were employed at various jobs about the post. As the men were passing the whisky around in tin cups, the half-breeds and Indians gathered around, begging for a drink.

Just as Milner reached for a cup of liquor a half-breed suddenly pushed the boy over, seized the cup and greedily gulped the contents. This assault aroused the youth's Kentucky temper and, leaping to his feet, he drew his revolver and killed his assailant. This shooting almost precipitated a battle between the half-breeds and the white men at the fort, but the coolness of Bridger and a few others prevented further bloodshed. However, guards were on duty all night, watching for treachery.

When not loafing around the fort in the dull season these Indians and half-breeds were employed by Bridger as hunters and trappers, and each winter they brought in great quantities of furs. Bridger, therefore, did not want to lose their friendship; and in order to adjust the trouble he held a council at which he told the Indians that the killing was justified; for the dead half-breed had no right to seize the whisky when it was not intended for him. He also told them that, although Milner was only a boy, he was a dangerous one to trifle with. During the following months young Mose won the friendship and respect of all the Indians and half-breeds.

Finally, he left with a party of trappers bound for Fort Laramie, where he arrived in the early spring of 1846. The hardships of that journey were the worst he ever experienced on the plains; but he was a rugged youth and never fell behind the others. During a blizzard that swept the trail for over a day and a night three trappers and all of the pack horses perished in the extreme cold; and after burying their dead companions in the snow the eight survivors fought their way through, finally reaching Fort Laramie more dead than alive.

A LETTER FROM HOME, which the young wanderer received at Fort Laramie, informed him that the entire family intended to emigrate to Warren County, Missouri, and asked him to return at once. Intending to meet his parents in either Kentucky or Missouri, young Mose joined an outfit of mountain men bound for St. Louis with furs. This party left Fort Laramie in April, 1846. Nothing of importance occurred on the journey. The men enjoyed great sport shooting the wild game then abundant in the valley of the North Platte; and Milner kept the outfit well supplied with deer, antelope, and buffalo.

During those hunting trips the lad soon learned to cut out two or three and sometimes four buffaloes from the herd, and drive them close to the camp before killing. This saved much time and labor in going out, sometimes several miles, to bring in the meat. Although young Milner was just past seventeen years of age he looked older, for he stood almost six feet in his moccasins, and his auburn hair which had not been cut for three years, fell around his shoulders. All mountain men of eighty years ago wore long hair.

The outfit reached Fort Leavenworth, Kansas, about June 1, 1846, and the leader decided to remain there a few days to give the men and horses a much-needed rest. War had been declared against Mexico, and Fort Leavenworth was a busy post; for Brigadier General Stephen W. Kearny was mobilizing his famous "Army of the West" at that place for the conquest of New Mexico and California.

With additional troops arriving every day and the war excitement at an intense pitch, it is little wonder that Milner's youthful blood raced at fever heat, and when Doniphan's Missouri Mounted Volunteers arrived early in June, he and two other trappers applied for their wages and were released from further service. They immediately joined the army as packers and teamsters.

On June 30, 1846, General Kearny left Fort Leavenworth with an army of sixteen hundred and fifty-seven men to conquer the Mexican province of New Mexico, a vast territory which included the present states of New Mexico, Arizona, Colorado, and parts of Utah, Wyoming and Texas. It was a long, tiresome march of eight hundred and seventy-five miles across monotonous, barren plains, hot, dreary deserts, and high, rugged mountains to Santa Fe, the ancient capital of the Spaniards and Mexicans in the North. On July 31, the army arrived at Bent's Fort on the Arkansas, five hundred and sixty-four miles from Fort Leavenworth. It is of interest to note

that the two infantry companies had outmarched
the others and reached this point in advance of the
mounted troops.

On August 2, Captain Philip St. George Cooke
was sent in advance, under a flag of truce, with General Kearny's proclamation calling for the surrender
of New Mexico. On the ninth he reached Las Vegas,
and was received by Don Juan de Dios Maes, the al-
calde, who immediately dispatched a messenger to
notify Governor Manuel Armijo at Santa Fe.

It was on August 12 that Captain Cooke and his
little party rode into Santa Fe and boldly presented
to Governor Armijo, in the old Palace of the Governors, General Kearny's demand for the peaceable
surrender of the Mexicans. Armijo agreed to send a
commissioner to meet the advancing Americans, but
he declared that he himself would lead a force of six
thousand men to oppose the little "Army of the
West."

On August 15, when General Kearny entered Las
Vegas without opposition, he was informed that Governor Armijo was gathering a formidable force to
oppose him at Apache Canyon, fifteen miles from
Santa Fe, but when he reached this point on the
eighteenth the enemy had fled. Apache Canyon is a
rugged slash in the mountains that a hundred determined men could have held against the entire "Army
of the West," and in 1862 it was the scene of one of
the battles of the Confederate invasion of New Mexico. The Atchison, Topeka, and Santa Fe railroad
now traverses this rugged gorge.

Without opposition of any kind the Americans pressed on; and at six o'clock in the evening of the eighteenth, after a forced march of twenty-nine miles on that day, the "Army of the West" entered Santa Fe. General Kearny and his staff were received by Lieutenant Governor Donaciano Vigil; and as the sun sank behind the distant Jemez range the Stars and Stripes were raised over the ancient Palace of the Governors, to a salute of thirteen guns from a battery planted on the hills south of the town. Thus the peaceable conquest of New Mexico became an accomplished fact.

With the capital in possession of the invaders all New Mexico subsequently submitted to American rule; but General Kearny received a report that Governor Armijo was organizing an army at Albuquerque, and on September 2 he set out with a small force, accompanied by a large number of Mexican volunteers. When he reached Albuquerque on the fifth he was welcomed by the Mexican officials. From there he continued his march into Valencia County, going as far as Peralta and Tome, returning to Santa Fe on the thirteenth. During Kearny's absence Colonel Alexander W. Doniphan, of the First Regiment, Missouri Mounted Volunteers, had been in command of the army with orders to carry on the construction of Fort Marcy, and this had been almost completed.

The Santa Fe of more than eighty years ago, when the American troops under General Kearny

took possession of the ancient town, was an entirely
different place from that seen by the tourist of today. One writer of that time aptly described it as
a collection of mud huts; and old pictures that have
come down to us from the fifties and sixties show
that at that time the capital of New Mexico and the
second oldest white settlement in North America was
made up of a few sun-baked adobe buildings in the
Santa Fe river bottom, surrounded by naked, scorched
foothills of the snow-capped Sangre de Christo range.

A granite marker placed by the Daughters of the
American Revolution to record the beginning of a
new epoch in New Mexican history stands in the old
plaza, one of America's most historic spots and around
which the fighting men of five nations have marched
during the more than three centuries that have passed
since that day in 1609 when Don Pedro Peralta first
planted the banner of the kings of old Spain over the
parapet walls of the ancient Palace of the Governors.
The inscription informs the curious tourist that: "In
this plaza Gen. S. W. Kearny, U. S. A., proclaimed
the peaceable annexation of New Mexico, Aug. 19,
1846. 'We come as friends to make you a part of the
republic of the United States. In our government all
men are equal. Every man has a right to serve God
according to his heart.' Erected by Sunshine Chapter,
D. A. R. 1901."

On the hill above Santa Fe, where the American
guns could easily destroy this little collection of mud
buildings, General Kearny built Fort Marcy in 1846,

immediately after his occupation of the village; and
to this day the old earthworks, from which the black
muzzles of the cannon held a menace for any Mexicans who might dispute the hated gringos, may still
be seen. Time and the elements have wrought many
changes in the appearance of the original fortification. Rising up as a part of the steep slopes of the
hill, the old embankments may be seen from all parts
of the present city; and a hard climb is necessary to
visit this historic spot.

On August 19, the day following his entrance into
Santa Fe, General Kearny ordered the erection of a
fort on this bluff which is within six hundred yards
of the plaza; and the work was carried out by Lieutenants W. H. Emory, Gilmer, and Peck, of the
Topographical Engineer Corps. It was originally designed for a garrison of two hundred and eighty men,
but when completed would accommodate a thousand.
The walls, built of adobe, were massive, thick, and
strong. The plan was laid out by Lieutenant Gilmer
and L. A. McLean, a volunteer of Reid's company.

The new fort was completed during the closing
days of September. The extreme length of the fortification was two hundred and seventy feet and its
greatest width was one hundred and eighty feet; but
the total dimensions between the exterior walls of
of the moat were four hundred feet long by three
hundred feet wide. One hundred feet from and opposite to the gateway, which faced the east, was a
square blockhouse, ninety-five by eighty-five feet,

with an observation tower at the northeast corner. The elevation of the fort above the plaza ranged from one hundred and fifty-two feet to two hundred and nineteen feet.

A tall flagstaff, erected in the center, must have been unusually high, for it is related that it so aroused the wonder of the natives that old men walked sixty miles to see the wonderful pole towering into the heavens with the strange banner of the gringos floating from its top. The distance walked was probably exaggerated.

Perhaps no fort in the United States was ever built at such a small cost to the government, the work having been done by volunteers from Kearny's army. Each day a certain number of men were detailed for this duty; and each one who worked ten days or more consecutively received eighteen cents per day extra on his month's pay. Always ready to make an extra dollar, young Milner was one of the men who helped build the new fort.

The name Fort Marcy was selected by General Kearny on September 16, 1846, as shown by his official report of that date to the Adjutant General at Washington, in which he says:

"A large number of troops are daily employed under the direction of Lieutenant Gilmer of the Engineers in erecting a fort for the defense and protection of the city, and as this is the capital of the Territory, a new acquisition to the United States, the fort will be an important and permanent one, and I have this day named it Fort Marcy, and now ask for a confirmation of it."

The name was selected in honor of Hon. William L. Marcy, of New York, Secretary of War at that time; and in all its forty-eight years as a military post, this name was never changed. During the early years of American occupation and until just prior to the outbreak of the Civil War, the fortress on the heights was maintained, while the old Palace and other buildings occupied by the Mexicans was also used by the United States military authorities. When Colonel Edwin V. Sumner, of the Second Dragoons, took command of the military department of New Mexico in July, 1851, he made further improvements to Fort Marcy.

The Spanish and Mexican population having accepted the gringos as an established fact and the need for it in this commanding location having passed, the fortification on the hill above the town was abandoned after the Civil War. The military reservation was then extended from the plaza to the old federal building on the north. The barracks and officers' quarters were moved into the city, and this was known as Fort Marcy until the post was permanently dismantled in 1894, after the close of the Indian wars. Some of the old brick buildings that were officers' quarters are now private residences.

Federal troops stationed at Fort Marcy during the Civil War saw active service; and, although it is not generally known, it is a matter of history that Santa

Fe is the only city in the country over which both
the Stars and Stripes of the Union and the Stars and
Bars of the Confederacy flew peaceably at the same
time. When the federal troops retreated to Fort
Marcy after the battles of Pigeon's Ranch and Apache
Canyon early in 1862, the Confederate forces
marched into and occupied a part of the city, and remained while their wounded recovered in the Union
hospital. No conflict took place between the warring
factions during those days; and the best of feeling
seems to have prevailed among the troops. This condition of affairs lasted for nearly two weeks.

It is interesting to note in this connection that
Santa Fe ranks as the second oldest settlement of Eu-
ropeans in North America; Saint Augustine, Florida,
also settled by the adventurous cavaliers of old Spain,
being the first. In 1609 Don Pedro de Peralta came
from Mexico and founded what is now the most historic city in the United States, replacing Don Juan
de Oñate, the colonizer, as governor. In 1598 Oñate
had established the first settlement in New Mexico
at San Gabriel.

Relics of the days of Spanish occupation are on
every hand. The old Palace of the Governors, still
standing on the plaza, was part of the original Indian
pueblo that occupied the site of Santa Fe when the
first *conquistadores* passed that way nearly four hundred years ago, seeking the treasure of the fabled
Seven Cities of Cibola; and during the centuries that
have passed since then the governors of four nations

have ruled the destines of New Mexico from within those walls. Cavaliers sent out long ago by the kings of Spain, Pueblo Indian warriors, soldiers from old Mexico, American troopers, trappers, and frontiersmen and adventurers from the four corners of the world have marched in review before this ancient building during the centuries since Don Pedro de Peralta established his capital there.

On the winding road that leads to Fort Marcy on the hill above, the inquisitive visitor will find, just beyond the Scottish Rite cathedral, the ruins of an old abode building. Not much is left, only a few feet; but it has not changed or weathered any since the author first saw it a quarter of a century ago. This is all that is left of the old Garita where political prisoners were confined and executed during the Spanish and Mexican *régimes*; and it was there that American traders in the early days stopped to pay duty on their merchandise.

Just around the bend from the Garita is the old Spanish cemetery, surrounded by a crumbling adobe wall. This contains the graves of many of Santa Fe's pioneers, men and women who were prominent during the centuries before the coming of the Americans, but are now forgotten. No marker or headstone stands over the spot where they sleep, but at one side are the ruins of the old military chapel built in 1776.

When Kearny left Fort Leavenworth with his "Army of the West" he had intended to continue on

to California and join Fremont. The time had now
arrived to resume this long march; but enough men
must be left in Santa Fe to hold the captured territory. In order to carry out his plans it would be
necessary to divide his force. It was a daring thing
to do, and General Kearny was probably the only officer in the army who would have attempted such a
thing under such circumstances, in the heart of the
enemy country, with only sixteen hundred men, and
over eight hundred miles away from any base. Yet
he divided his force into three columns. Before leaving, however, he established temporary forts at Abi-
quiu and Cebolleta to hold the Navajo and Ute Indians in check, placing Colonel Jackson in command
of the former and Major Gilpin at the latter.

Colonel Sterling Price was expected to arrive
shortly from the United States, with the Second Regiment of Missouri Mounted Volunteers, and the Mormon battalion of four hundred and forty-eight men.
Leaving orders that the Mormons, under command of
Captain Cooke, were to follow him to California,
General Kearny left Santa Fe on September 25, on his
march of over a thousand miles. Colonel Doniphan
was left in command of Santa Fe, with orders to join
General John E. Wool at Chihuahua after Price's
arrival. Captain Weightman's company of artillery
was to accompany the Missourians, while the rest
of the artillery was to remain at Santa Fe with the
battalion of infantry under Captain Angney.

Thomas Fitzpatrick, one of the most noted mountain men and fur traders of his time, was secured to guide Kearny's column across the deserts to California. He had been with General Ashley in the Rocky Mountains as early as 1823, and was later a partner in the old Rocky Mountain Fur Company. He afterwards became a professional guide for overland parties, acting in this capacity for Elijah White on his trip to Oregon in 1842. In 1843 and again in 1845 he was employed by John C. Fremont as a guide for his expeditions to California, and by Colonel Philip St. George Cooke for his dragoons along the Oregon Trail in 1845. Because of a hand crippled by the accidental discharge of a rifle he was first known as "Broken Hand" among the Indians, but this was later changed to "White Head" when his hair turned gray as the result of his experience in a terrific chase by Indians in 1832.

Antoine Robidoux was selected by Kearny as his interpreter, and J. M. Stanley as topographer.

With the Kearny expedition as one of the packers went young Mose Milner. There were many other experienced mountain men in that party, but none were destined to become better known in later years than California Joe.

On September 25, 1846, with five companies of the Second Dragoons, under Major Sumner, General Kearny left Santa Fe on his long march; and on October 6, at a point on the Rio Grande ten miles below Socorro, he met Kit Carson bound for Washington with dispatches from Fremont and the news that

California was in possession of the Americans. Carson, with fifteen men in his party, six of whom were Delaware Indians, had covered the eight hundred miles from Los Angeles in twenty-six days. Sending Fitzpatrick east with the dispatches, Kearny ordered Carson to guide him to California. With this news Kearny felt that he would not need as many troops. Accordingly Major Sumner and three companies of dragoons were sent back to Santa Fe, while the General proceeded with the two remaining companies and two mountain howitzers in charge of Captain Benjamin D. Moore. Much to his disappointment, Mose Milner was sent back with Sumner's troops; but he was to see plenty of action during the next few months.

Following the arrival of the Americans Santa Fe became one of the liveliest frontier towns west of the Missouri; and young Milner met all types of frontiersmen, from the mountain men of his trapping days in Wyoming to army officers. Discipline at the garrison was very strict; but as Milner was a civilian volunteer he was allowed more privileges than the soldiers, being permitted leave of absence for five days at a time without having to report to the boss packer for duty.

Inaction made him restless, and in company with three other packers he started out one morning on a hunting trip, with provisions enough for only one day. Game was scarce, and after riding until nearly evening without shooting anything, Milner proposed that they sleep out and return to Santa Fe the next night. Their horses hobbled and turned loose to graze, Milner entertained his companions with stories of his adventures with Jim Bridger and Jim Baker in Wyoming; and those thrilling tales told by a boy of seventeen made a deep impression upon the other men. They arose early the next morning and resumed their hunt.

About noon they reached a Mexican ranch of several adobe houses. Tired and thirsty, they dismounted at a well where they watered their horses and quenched their thirst. As one of the men was drinking from an old bucket it was suddenly knocked from his hands by a bullet fired by a Mexican sharpshooter, and the man with the bucket was so startled that he almost fell over backwards. Young Mose roared with laughter; and for many a year this was one of California Joe's favorite stories. He always declared that his comrade, who was a pronounced brunette, turned white and that his brown eyes became a beautiful blue.

This shot was the signal for an attack; and instantly bullets began knocking up dust all around the Americans. The poor marksmanship of the enemy was all that saved them from annihilation. One Mexican was seen standing in the doorway of the main house; but the others were under cover, and it was impossible to estimate their number. Realizing that they had run into an ambush, Milner shouted a warning to his companions, but this was scarcely needed;

for in a few seconds all had mounted and were out
of range.

Those fighting men of the old frontier were not
of the breed that runs in a panic before a few bullets,
and as soon as they were at a safe distance they stopped
to form a plan of attack. It was a bold thing to do,
in a hostile country, with no knowledge of the number of Mexicans. But of such stuff were the men of
California Joe's day.

Separating into pairs, Milner and a companion
crept through the sagebrush until they were in a commanding position on one side of the house, while the
others were carefully concealed on the other side. The
enemy evidently believed that the Americans had fled
in a panic, but they little knew the type of men they
had to deal with. In a short time a Mexican walked
from the house to the well for a bucket of water.
Instantly Milner and his companion fired, and the
Mexican fell in his tracks, dead before he hit the
ground.

The story of that battle, in which four Americans
killed twelve of the enemy, reads like the wildest
fiction. The Mexicans rushed from the house to investigate the shots, and as they were standing around
the body of their dead comrade, four more fell before the concealed marksmen, who were among the
best shots on the frontier. The survivors made a wild
scramble for safety. Those Mexicans were brave men,
and in a few seconds three of them appeared at the
door with rifles in their hands eager to avenge their

slain. But they were caught in a trap. Exposed to a deadly cross fire, they soon fell before the guns of the Americans.

With cocked pistols Milner and his companions crept up to investigate. The stillness of death hovered over the ranch. They searched two smaller buildings, and then, just as they started for the larger house four Mexicans dashed out with rifles ready. Three fell as the frontiersmen fired; but the fourth ran for a quarter of a mile before he was overtaken and killed by Milner. After rounding up all the horses they could find in the vicinity, the hunters set out for Santa Fe with twenty-five head; and as they drove them into the garrison the next day they were wildly cheered by the American troops.

The greatest moment in young Milner's life now came. After hearing the story, Colonel Doniphan, the officer in command, sent for the four frontiersmen, and in the presence of the troops he and his staff shook their hands, and congratulated them. Such is war.

Doniphan was attracted to the tall young Kentuckian, with long red hair that reached to his shoulders, and he told him to report to his headquarters. When the Colonel learned that this boy had left home at the age of fourteen and had trapped for the American Fur Company out of Fort Laramie before the war, he was satisfied that he was an experienced mountain man, and immediately appointed him as a guide. And thus the future California Joe, at the age

of seventeen years became a guide for the famous
Doniphan expedition, which made an enviable record
in the Mexican War. While at Santa Fe Milner took
part in the many horse races, shooting matches, and
other forms of sport in which out-door men engage,
and became known as one of the best rifle shots at
Fort Marcy.

On his march to California General Kearny learned
of the threatening attitude of the Navajo Indians,
and he sent a courier back to Santa Fe with instructions for Colonel Doniphan to force them to terms
of peace before starting for Chihuahua. On October
1, Colonel Price arrived with the expected reinforcements, and on the twenty-sixth Doniphan marched
into the Navajo country with four columns. Although no battles were fought, these troops were the
first Americans to explore what is now northeastern
Arizona. Major William Gilpin with two hundred
men marched up the Rio Grande to the Chama; then
across the mountains to the Rio San Juan; and after
proceeding down that valley for some distance he
again crossed the mountains to Red Lake, Arizona,
and the Little Colorado river.

A second detachment went south to Albuquerque
and then west to the Rio Puerco. With another column Captain John W. Reed marched directly
through the center of the Navajo country, while the
remainder of the regiment went further south. These
operations showed the Navajos that, although they
had been able successfully to terrorize the Spaniards

and Mexicans for more than two centuries, the gringo soldiers were a different proposition, and they gladly concluded a treaty of peace at Ojo Oso. When the conquest of the Navajos was completed the various detachments of the First Missourians returned to the Rio Grande, reaching Socorro on December 12. Colonel Doniphan now made preparations to carry out his orders by joining General Wool at Chihuahua.

On December 17, 1846, the Missourians started on the invasion of Mexico, which has come down to us as one of the most remarkable military expeditions in history. With a total force of nine hundred and twenty-four men, Doniphan marched down the Rio Grande, defeated the Mexicans and captured El Paso; then proceeded to the city of Chihuahua, which he captured; and finally marched through seven hundred miles of enemy country to Saltillo. We are not certain as to the column young Milner accompanied into the Navajo country; but it is known that he went as one of the guides into Mexico, where he won official recognition for his ability and endurance. A company of volunteers from Santa Fe which joined the expedition at Doña Ana, gave Doniphan a total force of nine hundred and twenty-four men.

On Christmas day, Captain Ponde de Loan, with five hundred men, made a vain attempt to stop the invaders at El Brazito, on the Rio Grande, thirty miles below Doña Ana. The Mexicans attacked the Americans in their camp. When he saw them coming in a charge, Doniphan ordered his men to hold their fire until the enemy was within easy range; then a terrific volley threw them into disorder and checked the advance. While the Vera Cruz dragoons were rallying to attack Doniphan's left flank, Captain Reed with twenty men suddenly charged and put them to flight. This broke the enemy's resistance, and the Americans marched on El Paso del Norte without further opposition. The Mexican loss in the battle of Brazito was forty-three killed and one hundred and fifty wounded, while the Americans had seven men wounded, and none killed.

On December 27, Doniphan occupied El Paso del Norte, now Ciudad Juarez, Mexico, where he remained in camp for five weeks, waiting for supplies and artillery. On February 1, 1847, a battery of six guns arrived from Santa Fe, and five days later the supply train came in. With a train of three hundred and fifteen wagons the Missourians left El Paso on the eighth on the last lap of their march to Chihuahua, now two hundred miles away across a desert country. That the people of Chihuahua rallied to the defense of their country with both men and money is shown by the following description by Mexican historians of the preparations to repel the invaders:

"Small, indeed, in numbers but perfectly well armed, supplied with provisions of all kinds for a campaign in a desert for months, all paid to the last dollar, and with funds in the chest for the future, the good Chihuahuans looked with pride upon the results of their labors, and in every gun and musket they saw the fruits of their personal exertions. Of all this nothing existed three months before. All was created by them, all was new, all was brilliant, and they are filled with delight in noting the maiden enthusiasm of the troops.

"The enemy, according to reports, was to appear the following day, and that night there was a festival in camp. In every tent, in every friendly group, cheerful toasts were drunk to the liberty of the country, the young men abandoning themselves to the illusive delirium of expected triumph, and thinking more of their expedition to New Mexico to assist their brethren to cast off the American yoke, than of the approaching encounter."

Alas for their expectations of victory on the morrow. On February 25, Doniphan's scouts reported the enemy in force at Encinillas, the country seat of Governor Frias; but as the Missourians approached, the Mexicans fell back to Sacramento Pass, which was well fortified.

According to the plans General Wool should have already been before Chihuahua, he having left San Antonio, Texas, several weeks before; but Doniphan's scouts reported that there was no sign of him. To turn back meant failure and possible disaster for Doniphan's entire command; for the Mexicans would be upon his heels like a pack of hungry wolves. Outnumbered at least two to one, perhaps three to one, by an enemy well armed, with artillery and cavalry, strongly entrenched and confident of success in their

greatly superior numbers, the gallant Doniphan was
not in the least dismayed by the prospect. Wool had
failed him, and Chihuahua must be taken now as a
matter of self-preservation; and Chihuahua was
taken.

The reader must not infer that Doniphan's success was due to either cowardice or lack of skill on
the part of the enemy; to do so would be to detract
from the accomplishments of our own troops. Those
hardy descendants of the gallant *conquistadores* of old
Spain were a brave race of men, and they liked nothing better than a good fight. Wool's failure to reach
Chihuahua on time was because he had had his hands
full helping Taylor at Monterey, and it had been
necessary to hold him at Saltillo to stop the expected
advance of Santa Anna.

Doniphan's success in the face of great odds was
due to several factors, the first and most important
of which was the overconfidence of the Chihuahuans,
born of their greater numbers and better equipment.
Secondly, the Americans were fighting a battle of
desperation; they simply had to win; and finally,
Doniphan was fortunate in beating the enemy in a
race to a ridge, possession of which spelled victory.
If the Mexicans had got there first there would have
been a different story to tell.

The Mexican forces at the battle of Sacramento
Pass were commanded by Generals Frias, the Gov-
ernor, and Conde, Conge, Heredias, and Ugarte.
Some historians claim that they had four thousand

men; but this is greatly exaggerated. Doniphan estimated their number at twenty-nine hundred, while
the Mexicans themselves say two thousand. On February 28, Doniphan's little army arrived before the
Mexican entrenchments at Sacramento Pass. Strategy
was the only weapon that would bring victory; and
in this the Missourian proved his superior military
skill. His quick eye detected a ridge to the enemy's
right that was practically the key to the whole situation, for it commanded their batteries.

Advancing with his entire force, including the
long wagon train, Doniphan marched straight at the
Mexican position as if he intended an attack direct
from the front; but when he was within a mile and
a half of their line he suddenly halted, turned to the
right, and at a quick pace started for the ridge. With
dismay the Mexicans saw their error in overlooking
this valuable position; and then began a race for its
possession between the Missourians and the Mexican
cavalry with four guns.

Doniphan's men won and had time to form before the enemy cavalry came down upon them in a
daring charge. Men less brave than those Mexicans
would have stopped when they lost the race, but they
hoped to sweep over the Missourians by sheer force of
numbers. As they came on in a charge as gallant as
was ever made by an army, Doniphan's artillery
opened fire, and in spite of the support of the Mexican artillery, the cavalry broke, falling back and
throwing the infantry into disorder. Doniphan

quickly followed up this advantage, and by a counter charge was soon in possession of the pass, with the enemy in full retreat.

Doniphan's entire force engaged numbered eight hundred and twenty-four, one hundred men having been left as a guard for the supply train; and he had six guns. He lost a total of nine killed and wounded (some accounts give one killed and eleven wounded); the enemy loss is not definitely known. Some American historians claim the amazing total of eight hundred killed and wounded; but it is doubtful if it exceeded a fourth of that number.

The night of February 28, 1847, was a dark and gloomy one for the Mexicans. They were now plunged into the depths of despair, for the road to Chihuahua was open to the invaders, and everyone who possibly could left the city. On March 1, the Missourians marched into Chihuahua; and Doniphan then learned that General Wool had been compelled to remain at Saltillo to resist the advance of Santa Anna. After a short rest at Chihuahua, Doniphan started to join Wool, and this march of seven hundred miles through a hostile land, the greater part of which was desert, was accomplished by the Missourians in the unprecedented time of forty-five days.

Their term of enlistment expired soon after their arrival at Saltillo; and as they were worn out by the long, forced marches and many hardships they had endured they refused to re-enlist. Few military expeditions in all history may be compared with the

marches made by Kearny and Doniphan, for the latter's men had covered over five thousand miles since
leaving their Missouri homes. Colonel Doniphan, the
commander, lived many years, dying at Richmond,
Missouri, August 8, 1887.

Taking passage on a ship across the Gulf of Mexico, the Missourians arrived at Corpus Christi after
a hard voyage. Fortune favored them, and they soon
secured passage for New Orleans where they arrived
in due time. The gulf city welcomed them as heroes,
and they remained for several weeks, resting and enjoying the liberty from the restraint of army life.
But they were anxious to return to the homes they
had not seen for so long; and so these veterans of
many long, hard marches and battles finally tore
themselves away from the hospitality of New Orleans.
The last stage of the journey was by a river steamer
up the Mississippi to St. Louis, which was finally
reached after many delays and several changes.

It is interesting to note in this connection that the
last survivor of Colonel Doniphan's famous command
was William Fitzhugh Thornton Buckner, who died
at Paris, Missouri, on June 17, 1929, at the age of one
hundred and one years. He was next to the last survivor of the Mexican war, the last being Owen
Thomas Edgar, who died September 3, 1929, at Washington, D. C., aged ninety-eight years.

Young Milner returned to the United States with
Doniphan's men, and as soon as he reached St. Louis
he set out for Warren County in search of his par-

ents, whom he had not seen for over four years. They had probably given him up for dead, for they had received no word from him since he wrote to them from Fort Marcy, saying that he was going to Mexico. Late in January, 1848, the wanderer reached home, and it can well be imagined that his parents and his brother and sister hardly knew him. Only a boy had left them, but a man grown, nearly six feet tall, returned. Jenny, his youngest sister, had died two months before his return. We can well imagine that during the long winter evenings he entertained the family with tales of his wanderings and adventures in the wild land beyond the great plains.

One day while Mose was giving an exhibition of his skill with rifle and pistol, his father said: "Mose, some day you will be known as the best shot in the country if you keep on shooting like that." This prediction became a reality; for in later years California Joe was the best all-around shot in the West.

During the remainder of the winter of 1848, young Mose remained at home, spending his time roaming the forests with his rifle. He kept the family table well supplied with game; but with the coming of spring the old restless spirit returned, and he again set out for the Far West. He went direct to St. Louis, which at that time was the outfitting point for all mountain men. His experience and knowledge of the country about Forts Laramie and Bridger soon won him a place with a party of trappers and traders bound for a year's journey in the Indian country. Although still a boy in years he was looked upon as a veteran, and was selected as guide.

Going up the Platte River, the party stopped at what is now known as Brady's Island, where they built a log cabin to be used as a storehouse and head-quarters. After this was completed two men were left at the camp, while the others divided into three groups to trade with friendly Indian tribes. Their horses were loaded with cheap calico, ribbons, beads, powder, lead, and firearms. Each party went in a different direction, and all agreed not to return until they had disposed of their merchandise. One group headed for the Middle and North Loupe river, and another went to the South Loupe, and the third with Milner journeyed up the Platte.

After several days' travel Milner's party reached the Republican River, and followed that stream until Mose found a village of friendly Sioux. When the Indians learned that he could speak their language he received a warm welcome. He became suspicious, however, of their apparent friendliness when he saw only one gun in the village and learned that five traders the year before had fleeced these same Indians. After promising to return the next morning he hastened back to his comrades with the news; but he warned them that they might have trouble. They agreed that it would be best to induce the Sioux to come to their camp instead of taking their goods to the village; and they decided to have their horses saddled ready for flight in case of an attack.

The next morning just after they had started their fire, one of the trappers who was gathering wood returned to camp with the news that a large party of mounted Indians was coming down the river bank about three-quarters of a mile away. Milner's companions were experienced frontiersmen, and they knew at once that this meant trouble. Running to their horses, they secured their ammunition, and then waited. Yelling like fiends, the Sioux swooped down on them, hoping to stampede their horses. Failing in this they shot a volley of arrows at the trappers, but no harm was done. The whites had selected a position that was ideal for defense, and had tied their horses to some trees below the river bank, which also protected them.

The Sioux charge was met with a deadly fire from the trappers' rifles, and one Indian and two horses were killed before they could get out of range. The two dismounted warriors leaped to their feet and started to run to safety, but the white men were ready with extra guns, and one brave pitched forward with a bullet from Milner's rifle through his brain, while the other went down before the fire of the other two. Withdrawing to a safe distance, the Indians were holding a council among themselves when suddenly a rifle cracked again and another Sioux warrior went to the happy hunting ground. Before the astonished band could realize what had happened another warrior pitched from his horse as the rifle cracked again, and the Indians hastily fled. These shots had been fired by Mose, who had run along the river, using the bank as a shield until he was within rifle range.

Mose then returned to his companions and a council of war was held. The others were in favor of destroying their trade goods, and attempting to escape on their horses; but Milner opposed this plan. He did not like the idea of a running fight from horseback; there was too much danger of being separated and captured. He told his comrades that, as their horses were protected by the river bank and it was impossible for the enemy to surround them, they could hold the Indians off all day and then escape that night, taking their stock of merchandise with them.

Just as this plan was agreed to the Sioux dashed down upon them in another charge; but as they came within rifle range the column split to right and left, and the Indians raced back and forth past the trappers' position, using their horses as shields by riding on the off side and shooting arrows from under their necks. This was a method of fighting used by all the plains tribes. But they could not escape the white men's deadly aim, and before they were out of range two more warriors went to join their comrades.

Milner believed that the Sioux, with seven of their number dead, had had enough fighting, and he proposed that they charge the entire band. Those trappers of old were always ready to take any wild chance, no matter how narrow the margin might be. Leaping upon their horses the three white men recklessly charged the Indians, who fled towards their own village. The white men's horses were fresher and stronger; and in the running fight they succeeded in killing four more of the enemy.

The story of how these three daring trappers held an entire Sioux camp panic-stricken sounds like fiction; yet it is a tale that was told on the frontier for many a year. Those were the days before the Indians were armed with good rifles, and such marksmen as these white men had proved to be was something new to them and struck terror to their hearts. Firing at a distance out of range of bows and arrows, the white men soon had the entire village in a state of excitement and confusion, and the Indians hastily fled.

The trappers now felt that they were safe from further molestation. Returning to their camp, they packed their horses and set out for their permanent headquarters over a hundred miles away. They pushed their horses to the limit of endurance, for they well knew that the Sioux would not forget those dead warriors, and would soon be on the trail seeking revenge. They were greatly handicapped by the slowly moving pack-horses, but by riding the rest of that day and night they reached the safety of their home camp about noon of the next day.

This incident did not deter these old-time frontiersmen, to whom danger was the spice of life; and in a few days they set out in search of a more friendly village, going this time to the South Loupe river, where three of their comrades had gone when the company first separated. Several days later they found a camp of friendly Indians, but could learn nothing of their comrades. Mose and his party remained there for several days, and in a short time disposed of all of their merchandise. With their horses laden down they returned to their headquarters, where they found the three missing men with a large quantity of furs. Everybody was in high spirits over the results of their venture, and while waiting for

the return of the third party they spent their time
hunting. In a few days the others arrived with their
pack-horses loaded down.

The white men had completed their trading in
much less time than theey had expected, but as the
Platte river and its tributaries abounded in beaver
they decided to remain there and trap until winter.
They made many trips and the summer passed
quickly. On one of their expeditions Milner and four
of his comrades went far up into the Dakotas, where
they hunted with several tribes. That was the Far
West in those days, and they were welcomed by most
of the Indians, who had not yet become alarmed at
the encroachments of whites on their hunting
grounds.

While in the land of the Dakotas the trappers met
a large band of wandering Sioux, who were preparing
for the fall buffalo hunt, always the big event of the
year, for it was then that the Indians laid in their
winter supply of meat. The Sioux asked the five
white men to join them, and when they learned that
Milner could speak their language the chief invited
him into his tepee. These Indians had never seen firearms, except possibly a few of the old Hudson's Bay
Company's trade muskets; and when Milner displayed
his long-barreled rifle and two heavy pistols, explaining that he and his four companions could kill enough
buffalo in one day to last the band the entire winter, the chief could not believe him. In order to
prove the superiority of firearms over bows and ar-

rows, Milner told the chief that the white men would accompany the band.

In a few days Indian scouts reported a large herd of buffalo about twenty miles away, and the chief gave orders to move the village some miles nearer the game. As soon as the permanent camp was established, the Sioux hunters with their white companions started on the big hunt, the squaws accompanying them to do the skinning. In later years Milner often said that this was the wildest hunting expedition he ever saw in all his life on the plains. As soon as the buffaloes were sighted the Indians became wild with excitement. The red hunters surrounded the herd, shooting the animals on the outside, and soon started them to milling in such a manner that they could not scatter. This meant a big kill.

The white men kept their promise, and buffalo after buffalo went down before their rifles. The slaughter was kept up by both reds and whites until the terror-stricken animals finally succeeded in breaking away. Then began a wild pursuit, and when the chase was over dead buffalo were scattered along a small valley for over ten miles. Milner afterwards estimated, from the amount of ammunition used, that he killed sixty that day, certainly a large number for one of the old muzzle-loading rifles.

More than enough had been killed to supply the band with meat for the winter. The camp was moved to the scene of the slaughter, and then began the work of skinning and cutting up the meat for drying. In describing the scenes that followed, Milner afterwards told how the Indians split the skulls and heavy leg bones, and ate the brains and marrow raw. Nothing went to waste. The skins were removed and tanned for use in making tepees and clothing; the meat was cut into long strips and dried in the sun; even the entrails were eaten.

Two days after the hunt the trappers bade farewell to their Sioux friends, and set out for their camp on the Platte, which was reached without further incident. Winter was approaching, and as their supplies were running low, they decided to start immediately for civilization. Two days later the furs were packed, and they began the long journey to St. Louis, which they reached November 3, 1848. In those days St. Louis was the fur metropolis of the United States; it was headquarters for all buyers, and naturally all fur brigades headed that way. After selling their furs, Milner and his companions divided the money equally, and then separated for the winter.

A HONEYMOON ACROSS THE PLAINS

IV

AFTER a few weeks spent in St. Louis, Milner paid a visit to his parents in Warren County, intending to remain there only until spring; but the best-laid plans are often upset by the little fellow with the bow and arrow. He remained at home that winter, helping his father and brothers, and spending his spare time hunting with his brother, George. But in the spring just when the western fever had seized him and he was feeling the call again, the Watts family from east Tennessee moved to the land adjoining the Milner farm.

There was nothing unusual in this, as settlers were pouring in from all sections; but in the Watts family were two girls, Nancy Emma and Adeline. Mose helped the father clear the land, split rails, build fences, and plow; but this hardy young mountain man, who had fought Indians and Mexicans as part of the day's work, was not proof against the bow and arrow of Dan Cupid; and he and Nancy Emma, the oldest girl, fell desperately in love. This met with the approval of their parents, in spite of Nancy Emma's extreme youth; for she was only thirteen years and eight months old. Mose did not go West again that spring as he had planned, but remained at home for a year; and on May 8, 1850, his twenty-first birthday, they were married.

The excitement caused by the California gold strike of 1849 was sweeping the country; and young Milner, whose restless spirit would not allow him to remain long in one place, joined a party bound for the New El Dorado, leaving St. Joseph, Missouri, shortly after his marriage. The day after their wedding, Mose Milner, with his girl-bride by his side, left home on a honeymoon across two thousand miles of barren plains and rugged mountains, infested by hostile Indians, to the land of golden dreams on the shores of the far-off Pacific. The parents of both the bride and groom saw that they were well equipped for the long, dangerous journey, which in those days was a matter of several months. Following the custom of all emigrants, this train, on the first day out from St. Joseph, stopped to elect a captain, as military discipline in a rough way was necessary for safety in crossing the plains, and the leader's word was always law. On account of his past experience young Mose Milner was elected to guide the destinies of this train of slow-moving, cumbersome prairie schooners.

The story of that journey, and many incidents in the life of California Joe, were given to Joe E. Milner, one of the authors, by his grandmother, the girl-bride of eighty years ago. This pioneer mother who crossed the plains in a covered wagon in 1850, died at Albany, Oregon, in April, 1915, at the age of seventy-eight years. Contrary to the statements of Buel in his *Heroes of the Plains*, the journey of the wagon train of which Mose Milner was captain was rather uneventful; and the gold seekers arrived near Sutter's Fort, in the Sacramento valley, November 9, 1850, without misadventure. In relating the story to her grandson in later years, this pioneer woman of the fifties stated that nothing of importance or excitement occurred beyond the hardships incident to such a journey in those days. She came from a race of pioneers, and this thirteen-year-old girl-bride of a pioneer enjoyed every moment. This is in direct contradiction to Buel's statement in *Heroes of the Plains* in which he says:

"The first thrilling adventure in which California Joe participated, of which I have any information, may be described as follows: In the summer of 1849 a party of sixty-five hardy adventurers from Kentucky, with California Joe as their leader, attempted an overland journey to California, being impelled by the golden stories of newly discovered wealth along the San Juan. They proceeded without interruption for several weeks, when they reached a canyon near Pueblo. Here a camp was made just before nightfall, and as the party had never been initiated into the perils of Indian treachery, they did not consider the

importance of anticipating and guarding against an
attack from these prairie nomads.

"During the still hours of the night, when the
entire party was sound in slumber, perchance dreaming of vast treasures and the exaggerated blessings
which wealth provides, a band of two hundred vin-
dictive Cheyennes descended, like wolves upon the
fold, from the hillsides and poured into the camp before there was even a suspicion of their proximity.
Lance and arrow, tomahawk and warclub, soon destroyed the night dreams, the golden anticipations,
and out of the party of sixty-five only two escaped,
one of whom was California Joe, but even he was
badly wounded. (Two persons who were well acquainted with Joe during his life assert that his wife
and two little boys were killed at the same time.)

"In the darkness of the night Joe succeeded in
eluding the savages while they were mutilating and
dancing over the bodies of his dead comrades, and
crawling to the Arkansas River, one mile distant, embarked on a log, upon which he floated down to Fort
Lyon, where he was taken out of the water and
cared for."

This story is absolutely ridiculous. In the first
place Indians never attacked during the night; and
in the second place Pueblo and the Arkansas River
were not on the California trail. This was farther
north by way of Fort Laramie. No party of immi-
grants, no matter how green they might have been,
ever started across the plains without an experienced

plainsman as captain, and he would have guarded against such a surprise as is described. And finally, Fort Lyon was not in existence in 1849. This story, like the rest of Buel's version of California Joe's life, is pure fiction. That there is no foundation for it is shown by Mrs. Milner's own statement; and no better proof could be found that she was not killed by Indians in 1849.

The gold-seekers separated as soon as they arrived in California, each following his own inclinations. Leaving his young wife in Sacramento, the gateway to the northern mines, Milner hastened to the gold camps on the American, Yuba, and Feather rivers. Every few months he would return on a visit to his wife, each time bringing considerable gold dust. The amount he accumulated during these mining operations is not known; but his wife afterward stated that it was a considerable sum. At any rate it was enough to encourage him to quit early in 1852.

Reports of the wonderful fertility of the Oregon country had drifted down the coast to California, where the very air was filled with thoughts of gold and nothing of the farming possibilities. These reports attracted Milner, and early in the spring of 1852, he and his young wife set their faces once more on the covered wagon trail. There were no roads, and even the path they followed could hardly be dignified by being called a trail. At Sacramento they joined a party of emigrants; and from northern California through Oregon to the Willamette Valley the country was so rough that their train made scarcely ten miles a day.

On April 16, 1862, the party reached Corvallis, Oregon, and a few days later Milner filed on three hundred and twenty acres, located about two miles from what is now Wren Station, in Benton county. He also purchased three hundred and twenty acres adjoining his homestead, making six hundred and forty acres of the most fertile land in that section. He built a cabin and in a short time had a home established. His wife, who had been ill at Sacramento, rapidly improved in the cooler climate of Oregon. Milner stocked his ranch with the best blooded cattle and horses that could be purchased on the west coast in those days, and he soon had a thriving place, with bright prospects for the future.

But he had spent too many adventurous years as a trapper and mountain man to settle down to the monotonous life of a stock dealer. The frontier was calling him, and he had to go in spite of the entreaties of his wife; but such were the men who made the West safe for the present generation. When she found that she could no longer keep him at home, his wife bade him farewell, and settled down on the farm to wait for his return; but of such stock were the pioneer mothers of the present generation of westerners. They were the real home-builders, and without them the West of today would not exist.

With five men as helpers, Milner started with a pack-train for the northern California mines. The

Rogue River Indians were troublesome at that time, but nothing was seen of them, and the train made the round trip from Corvallis to northern California without incident. This wandering life suited Mose well, and for a time he ran his pack-train, carrying supplies from Oregon to the mines of northern California and southern Oregon. This was a profitable business, and he made considerable money during the next few months.

October 1, 1853, was an important day in the life of Mose Milner, for that was the date of the birth of his first child, Edgar Armstead Milner, the father of one of the authors of this narrative. Mrs. Milner was afterwards the mother of three other children, all sons: George, born February 16, 1855, at Fisher's Landing, Washington; Charles, born February 16, 1857, at Corvallis, Oregon; and Eugene, born March 17, 1859, at Corvallis, Oregon.

Shortly after the birth of his first son, a letter came to Mose from the old home telling of the marriage of his wife's younger sister; and he immediately set out for Missouri to bring the couple to Oregon. As it was at that time impossible to find a wagon train going back to the States, he sailed for San Francisco. From there he went by steamer to Acapulco, on the west coast of Mexico, planning to go overland from that point to Vera Cruz. This was much shorter and not considered as dangerous as the Panama route.

At Acapulco the Mexican officials seized Milner's gold dust, amounting to nearly five thousand dollars, together with that of four or five other Americans, and threw them into prison. At the end of seven days they were released and their gold returned; but Mose found that his had shrunk to one thousand dollars. He tried to recover the balance; but, after finding that he would only lose time, he gave up, and hastened to Vera Cruz, where he caught a boat for New Orleans. From that city he went by boat to St. Louis and in a few days was back at his old home.

Years later, after Milner's death, his widow and her son George, put in a claim against the Mexican government for this lost gold. George Chamberlain, at that time United States senator from Oregon, took special interest in the case, and the law firm of Martin L. Pipes and Sons, of Portland, was retained. After a long search among the records of the Interior Department it was found that Milner had reported his loss to the officials at Washington; but all claims against the Mexican government had been settled in September, 1876, and by an agreement between the two governments no claim prior to that date could be collected. Milner himself did not take his loss seriously, for he once said when relating the incident: "I was robbed by the Mexican government all right, but I got my money's worth shooting greasers by the score in the Mexican war; so the bill is paid."

Shortly after reaching Missouri, Mose, accompanied by his sister-in-law and her husband, went to St. Joseph, where they joined a party of emigrants bound for the Oregon country; and on account of his experience Milner was elected captain and guide of the train. The journey across the plains was almost completed before anything unusual occurred. One day when the emigrants were nearing Fort Laramie, and Milner and several other men were some miles ahead scouting, they discovered a large war party of Brule Sioux. Hastening back to the train Milner gave orders to circle the wagons in the form of a corral and place all stock inside, in order to repel an attack. A shelter for the women and children was hastily made in the center of this inclosure, with bed-clothing, boxes, and everything else available as a barricade. The stock was also placed inside the corral. This left the men free to fight from behind the wagons.

With blood-curdling yells the Indians came down upon the train; but a well-directed volley broke the charge, and the enemy retired out of range, leaving several dead upon the field. The Sioux then adopted the tactics of riding in a circle around the wagons, shooting their arrows, but as they were careful to keep out of rifle range they did no harm. This was only a plan to divert the attention of the white men from Indian sharpshooters who had dismounted and were shooting from the ground, and several of the emigrants' horses were wounded.

Mose Milner was an expert shot, and every time an Indian ventured within range his rifle cracked with deadly effect. In all his Indian fighting he followed the frontiersmen's method of shooting the horse first and then the rider; for, as he said, "the horse is the bigger target, and then in the scramble it is easier to get the Indian." After several hours' fighting the Sioux withdrew with a loss of over fifty killed and wounded. In all their warfare the plains tribes always made a desperate effort to carry their dead and wounded from the field of battle. They believed that if an Indian lost his scalp he could not enter the happy hunting grounds; and many a warrior has paid with his life for his daring in trying to recover the body of a comrade.

During this fight Milner wounded an Indian's horse, and the terrified animal ran straight towards the wagon train in spite of its rider's efforts to turn. Mose's second shot killed the horse, but the instant the Indian struck the ground he leaped to his feet and and ran. The scout's rifle cracked again, and one more Sioux warrior went to join his comrades in the happy hunting grounds. Instantly another Indian sped forward on his horse to recover the body, but as he leaped to the ground Milner fired and he fell dead in his tracks.

After the enemy's retreat Mose rode out with two companions to reconnoiter; and from a high knoll a mile or so from the train they sighted the Indians in council. Directing his comrades to remain in concealment, the scout made a detour of several miles to a small thicket where he tied his horse; and then crawled to a rotten stump within three hundred yards of the enemy. This was a daring feat, for he risked his life every second. He estimated the number of Indians at about three hundred fifty; and he could easily have shot several, but he wanted to get the leader, for he believed his death would end a attack on the wagon train.

The Indians were chanting over their dead, and it was some time before Mose was able to pick out the chief. At last he saw in the crowd a stately looking warrior, at least six feet tall, wearing an eagle-feathered war-bonnet with a double tail that reached to the ground—the unmistakeable badge of a Sioux chief. One hand was raised above his head, swinging a heavy rifle, and he chanted the Brule death song as he danced around the bodies. Taking careful aim, the daring frontiersman fired, and the next instant the chief pitched forward, as a bullet from Mose Milner's rifle crashed through his brain. Instantly the Indians were thrown into confusion; for they believed the emigrants had attacked them. The fact that a lone white man had dared venture so near never entered their minds, and they leaped upon their horses to repel the enemy.

This was Milner's chance. In the confusion that followed he reached his horse, and managed to escape without being seen. From a distance the three white men watched the Sioux as they gathered up their dead warriors and slowly disappeared over the rim of the last swell. Without a leader they were helpless.

Acting under the captain's orders the train remained corraled for three days as a precaution; for they did not know when the Sioux might come down upon them again, seeking revenge for their slain. A careful watch was kept night and day; and when the emigrants resumed their journey the women drove while the men either rode or walked at the sides of the wagons, ready to repel an attack. Nothing further occurred, and when the train finally reached Fort Hall, Idaho, the travelers decided to rest for a few days.

Fort Hall, the most important point on the Oregon Trail west of Fort Laramie, was built as a fur-trading post in the summer of 1834 by Nathaniel J. Wyeth, a merchant from Cambridge, Massachusetts, who had embarked in the northwestern fur trade between 1832 and 1836. With a party of forty men Wyeth erected this post on the upper Snake river, near the mouth of the Portneuf, Idaho. A typical fortress of the early fur days, it was inclosed by a palisade, with a sally-port or double gateway. In 1836, Wyeth sold out to the Hudson's Bay Company; but after the American occupation of the Northwest Fort Hall was abondoned as a fur post, and on recommendation of General John C. Fremont in the latter forties it became one of four military posts established by Congress to protect emigrants along the two thousand and twenty miles of the Oregon Trail. The others were Fort Kearny, Nebraska; Fort Laramie, Wyoming; and Fort Bridger, Wyoming. Fort Hall was twelve hundred and eighty miles west of Independence, Missouri. During the early gold rush days a road branched from there to California. It was abandoned as a fort in 1855; but during the gold rush to Montana in the early sixties it again became an important point for the Argonauts going to and from the northern mines. The site of this historic post of the Old West is on the Oregon Short Line railroad, nine miles north of Pocatello, Idaho.

Leaving Fort Hall several days later, the train reached The Dalles, on the Columbia River. Although the emigrants separated there, this was not the Eldorado of their dreams; but they had reached the wonderful Oregon country, and each one now journeyed to a different section. Young Milner, with his sister-in-law and her husband, went down the river to Fisher's Landing, where he was joined by his wife. This place was just a few miles above Fort Vancouver. One of the officers at the post at that time was young Lieutenant Philip H. Sheridan, fresh from West Point, who, some ten years later, became the noted General Sheridan, of Civil War fame. Lieutenant Sheridan gave Milner the contract for supplying the post with wood, and in this way the two became well acquainted. Years later they were to meet again at Fort Dodge, hundreds of miles away on the Kansas frontier, when the young Lieutenant of Fort Vancouver had become head of the United States Army, and the young Oregon pioneer was General Custer's famous chief of scouts, California Joe.

Lieutenant Sheridan offered to renew the wood contract when it expired, but Milner's restless spirit was calling him away; and, taking his wife, his sister-in-law, and her husband, he returned to his ranch in Benton county. He immediately started his pack-train again, as this was not only to his liking but very profitable.

Milner had brought a Kentucky mare of blooded stock from Missouri, and she soon won a wide reputation as the fastest horse at a quarter of a mile in the Willamette Valley. No matter how good a racer you may have there is always some fellow willing to bet his last dollar on his own horse; and during the next few years Milner's mare brought her owner a handsome sum. Many fast horses were taken to Corvallis to beat her, but they all went down in defeat.

One day in June, 1858, two strangers appeared in Corvallis with a very ordinary looking horse, which no one suspected was a racer. The men attracted little attention, as strangers were always coming and going. Several days later Mose Milner rode into town on his Kentucky mare. In those days the saloons were the loafing places where all men of all classes gathered. One of the strangers engaged Milner in conversation, and gradually bringing the topic around to race horses, boasted that his animal could beat any other in that section at a quarter or half a mile.

Mose and several others present laughed when they saw his horse; and it did not take them long to arrange a match at a quarter of a mile, to take place in five days. One of the conditions insisted upon by the stranger was that both horses should be in town the night before the race so that no "ringers" could be brought in; and as this seemed to insure fair play for both, Mose readily agreed, at the same time covering the stranger's bet of fifteen hundred dollars at even money. A prominent saloon keeper in town was selected as stakeholder.

Nothing in the world has greater charm for outdoor people than a horse race, and on the fifth day settlers for miles around came to town. Mose arrived with his mare the afternoon before. The strangers had plenty of money, and they covered all bets made by the people of the Willamette who backed the Milner mare to a man.

Mose selected as his jockey a young man named Henderson, who had been his partner on several packhorse trips into southern Oregon. He was a good rider and light in weight. Henderson was still living at Corvallis in 1929, at the age of ninety-six years. As the time for the race drew near young Henderson brought the mare from the stable, and, mounting her bareback, started for the race course on the edge of town. Then a strange thing happened. The racer had always been full of life, but gentle and easy to ride. Now her disposition seemed to have changed over night. She was so nervous and excited that Henderson could hardly control her; and it was as much as Mose could do to keep her from running away, although he was an expert rider.

Well knowing that something was wrong, Milner tried to postpone the race; but the owner of the other

horses demanded that the conditions be fulfilled or
he would claim the money. Finally, after considerable argument, Mose instructed Henderson to try and
secure the best position for the start; but the rider
of the stranger's horse was a past master at the game,
and jockeyed well for position. As the starting pistol
cracked both racers leaped forward, the Milner mare
in the lead; but after the first hundred yards she
dashed off the course and became completely unmanageable, compelling Henderson, who was riding bareback, to dismount. When the stranger's horse dashed
over the finish line, an easy winner, Mose was furious;
for he suspected that he had been a victim of confidence men, and after a consultation with friends he
instructed the stakeholder to hold all bets until the
Kentucky mare had been examined. When the owner
of the winning horse came in to collect his money,
Mose stepped up and said: "Stranger, that race was
crooked in some way, and you know it. You will
never get one dollar from that stake-holder and
neither will your friend."

A heated argument followed and threats were
flung back and forth. All men went armed in those
days and many a dispute was settled by the law of
the six-shooter as the court of last resort. Realizing
that it was impossible to collect as long as Mose lived,
the stranger made a sudden attempt to draw his revolver; but the next instant he fell dead, shot by
the scout in self-defense. The settlers were aroused
by the attempt on Milner's life; and they gave the

friends of the dead man just one hour to leave town; but before the time arrived every gambler had disappeared. The stake-holder paid all debts to Milner and his friends when an examination of the Kentucky mare showed that she had been doped.

Ｎᴇᴡꜱ ᴏꜰ rich gold strikes in eastern Washington and northern Idaho reached Oregon early in the summer of 1859, and on June 3, Mose Milner left The Dalles with a pack train bound for the new fields; but at Walla Walla he sold his entire outfit for a good price, reserving only his Kentucky mare, and then set out for the Salmon River diggings. Several miles from Grangeville, Idaho, he filed on a claim located on the main trail; and in the fall of 1859 he built the first log cabin on the site of a camp which he named Mount Idaho. The next spring he constructed a toll road three miles long, which shortened the distance to the mines by several miles. This proved a profitable venture, for he made a charge of one dollar each for all persons or horses that traveled the cut-off. He also built a large addition to his cabin, and then opened a tavern, serving meals to travelers at one dollar each; but the wanderer who was penniless and hungry never left his door without food. His generosity extended even further, and years later Joe E. Milner met many men who had been grubstaked by his grandfather at Mount Idaho. Those pioneers never forgot his kindness, and it brought returns in later times.

All classes of humanity passed over the gold trails in the sixties. One day in the early fall of 1860, a half-breed riding a broken-down buckskin pony, stopped at Mount Idaho, and told Milner that he had had a successful summer in the Salmon River diggings, and was on his way to Lewiston for the winter. The stranger's horse was placed in the log stable beside the Kentucky mare. The next morning the half-breed went out to feed his horse before brakfast, saying that he would pay his bill when he returned. This was a custom of the country, and Mose thought nothing of it; but a few minutes later Earnest Allen, an employe, came running to the cabin with the news that the half-breed had just ridden away on the Kentucky mare.

Seizing his rifle, Milner instructed Allen to remain at the house until his return, and then started in pursuit, He knew the country like a book, and instead of following the main road he took a short cut across the mountains, striking the trail several miles from Mount Idaho late that afternoon. A close inspection for tracks satisfied him that the thief had not passed that way, and he sat down on a boulder to await his coming.

Finally, the sound of an approaching horse was heard, and Milner hastily concealed himself at the side of the trail. In a few minutes the half-breed appeared on the stolen mare; and taking a careful rest, Milner sent a bullet crashing through his brain. Quickly catching the horse, Milner tied her to some brush and then returned to the victim. On a piece of paper he wrote the following: "Warning to horse thieves, Mose Milner, Mt. Idaho." Leaving the body on the spot, he returned to his cabin, which he reached about midnight; and thereafter Mose Milner was reckoned a dangerous man to trifle with.

From this incident the reader must not gain the impression that Mose was a killer. In those early days before courts had been organized the law of the six-shooter ruled, and each man was his own enforcement officer. Men taking the law into their own hands meted out swift justice; and horse stealing was the unforgivable crime, punishable by death. It was the code of the Old West to shoot first and argue afterwards. This tradition of pioneer times is best illustrated by the words of an old-timer to Joe E. Milner when he said: "You could shoot all the men you wanted to, but it was never safe to steal a man's horse."

It was at Mount Idaho in 1861 that Mose Milner had a fierce fight with a mountain lion, and not in New Mexico, as claimed by Buel in relating this incident in *Heroes of The Plains*. The true story of that battle was told many times to Joe E. Milner by his grandmother, his father and uncles; for it was one of the traditions of the family.

Early one morning Mose started out to hunt deer,

but had only gone a short distance when it began to rain. Returning to the cabin he secured a heavy overcoat that reached almost to his ankles, and, accompanied by a small dog belonging to Allen, he set out again. Some two hours later he killed a deer, and after dressing it started back with the carcass slung over his back. A few minutes later the dog started to chase a cub cougar. Mose quickly captured the little cat, and was carrying it by the back of the neck when the mother suddenly sprang from the limb of a tree, where she had been concealed by the thick foliage, and landed on his back, knocking him down in spite of his two hundred pounds weight. His rifle flew in one direction and the cub in another; but Mose did not have time to secure his gun, for the old cougar was making things interesting. Scratching and biting, the maddened lion soon tore his heavy overcoat to ribbons; but the garment undoubtedly saved his life, for it acted as a shield until he succeeded in drawing his hunting knife. The big cat had fastened her teeth in his shoulder, and as he was forced to strike backwards to reach her his blows were ineffectual and only increased her fury. Milner was a powerful man, and with several desperate backhanded lunges he finally drove the blade in to the hilt several times. The animal fell desperately wounded, still full of fight, but before she could recover the scout drew his six-shooter and ended the battle with a bullet through her brain.

Milner had been fearfully lacerated by the ani-

mal's claws, and its teeth had inflicted painful wounds
on his neck and shoulders. After a slow, torturous
journey of several hours he succeeded in reaching his
cabin, where he fainted from loss of blood. Two days
later Allen took the wounded man to Lewiston, where
he was put in the care of two doctors; and his wife
came from Corvallis to nurse him. He was confined
in bed for three weeks, and remained in town all
winter, recuperating from his wounds. When spring
came he still felt the effects of his terrible battle, so
he sold his toll road and claim at Mount Idaho.

The later history of Mount Idaho, which is interesting in connection with the life of California Joe,
is told in the following story taken from the *Morning
Oregonian*, of Portland, Oregon, October 7, 1923:

"Lewiston, Idaho, Oct. 7.—Associated Press dispatches from Washington, D. C., a few days ago told
of the discontinuance of the postoffice at Mount Idaho, because the government found itself unable to
induce any person to qualify for the position as postmaster. The mail hereafter will be distributed
through the Grangeville, Idaho, postoffice.

"Mount Idaho has suffered the irony of fate. It
was at one time the county seat of Idaho County,
and was thought destined for future greatness. Today, however, the town is but a memory of the importance it once occupied in the history of Idaho.
Mount Idaho was established as a station in 1861.
Mose Milner was the real father of the town, for he
built its first dwelling, a log cabin. This log cabin,

with an addition or two, served the town for many years as a hotel. Because of its favorable location, the little hamlet became an important and popular resting place for those traveling to and from the mines, and for many years is population was numerous and floating. The postoffice at Mount Idaho was among the first established in the state. Its establishment took place early in the history of the town. The first postmaster at Mount Idaho, a man named Brown, was also the village blacksmith, and the proprietor of a general merchandise store. In 1876, as a result of the addition of the Elk City region and Camas Prairie to Idaho County, Mount Idaho became the county seat. At this time it had a population of about one hundred.

"Mount Idaho occupied a prominent position in the history of the Nez Perce Indian war. It was to this place that the terrified settlers flocked on June 14, 1877, and remained until Chief Joseph's hostile warriors had left the state. It was at Mount Idaho also that the settlers built the famous stone fort, within the walls of which they expected to defend themselves to the last. At one time nearly the whole population of Camas Prairie, about two hundred and fifty persons, were assembled in and around this defense. It was in the form of a circle, about one hundred and fifty feet in diameter, with a wall about five feet high. While the population of Mount Idaho has dwindled away in recent years, its history will always cause it to occupy a prominent position among the old settlements of Idaho, and a memory to the famous frontiersman, Mose Milner."

By the spring of 1862, Milner had about regained his strength; but he carried to his grave the deep scars he received in that terrible battle with the cougar.

News of the discovery of gold in large quantities came drifting down across the mountains from Montana; and in the summer of 1862, Milner set out for the new diggings with a party of five other hardy adventurers from Lewiston. Their destination was the famous Alder Gulch, at Virginia City, where they arrived in September after a hard journey.

Virginia City at that time was one of the wildest of the roaring camps of the old Montana gold fields. There was no law or order; and in a short time the bandits became so bold that the honest miners founded the organization is known in history as the Montana Vigilantes. They created their own courts and tried each prisoner as soon as arrested; and when a man was sentenced to be hung the order of the Vigilante court was executed forthwith. There were no appeals. If a man was ordered to leave camp, he did so at once, without further argument, for death was the penalty of delay. As there was no law or organized government in Montana at that time those pioneer miners made their own laws. It is interesting to note in this connection that few lawyers were permitted to plead before the miners' courts. As a rule a man was appointed as prosecutor, and another to defend the prisoner. The Vigilante movement spread through all the Montana mining camps, and some thirty bandits were hung, including the notorious Henry Plummer, sheriff of Bannock, and leader of the most desperate gang of criminals that ever infested any section.

At the time Milner arrived in Virginia City one of the Vigilantes was a big Irishman. A bully and a coward, he was quarrelsome when intoxicated, but was always careful to pick on a man not his equal in strength. As a result he was generally disliked in the camp. At this time Mose was engaged in supplying a small camp near Virginia City with fresh venison and elk, and coming in one day with a deer over his shoulder, he met this man on the trail. Milner's dog was running ahead, and as it passed the Irishman gave it a kick that sent it howling back to its master. "If you want to start a good fight, kick a man's dog," is an old proverb, and in this case it brought results. The Irishman was ahead, going in the same direction, and Mose could not catch up. But his anger was thoroughly aroused. As soon as he reached camp he disposed of the deer, and then went to Harry Pearson's saloon, where he found his man. Walking up to the big box stove, Mose sat down to watch the Irishman, and was talking to some friends when the bully kicked the dog again.

Like a flash Milner leaped to his feet, and running up to the Irishman, delivered his ultimatum: "You've been runnin' things in this camp to suit yourself, an' people around here are gettin' tired of it. You've got 'em all afraid of yo'. I've been waitin' for a chance to kill yo', an' now I've got one. If you're not armed you'd better get your gun, for I'm goin' to kill yo' before mornin'. I'm not afraid of yo' or all your vigilance committee."

Just then Pearson, the proprietor of the saloon, shouted: "Mose, if you kill him I'll give you two gallons of the best whiskey in the house."

Without a word the Irishman left with several friends, going to his cabin; and in a few seconds Mose went out, but returned in a short time with a shotgun.

"Are you going to his cabin?" asked one of his friends.

"Yes," was the reply.

"Well, I'll go along with you."

Upon entering the gulch they saw that a big fire blazing in the fireplace of the Irishman's cabin lighted up the interior, and Milner yelled: "Come out o' there. I'm goin' to shoot."

Instantly all the men rushed out with the exception of the Irishman, who slammed the door shut. Just as Milner opened it a little to locate his enemy a shotgun roared from the interior, the buckshot tearing a big hole in the door frame close to his head, and wounding the man who had accompanied him in the throat. Flinging the door open, Mose leaped in and with one shot ended the bully's career.

Taking his wounded friend, Milner returned to

Pearson's saloon, and as he walked in the proprietor asked, "Well, Mose, did you kill him?"

"Yes, I killed him all right," was the reply.

"Here's your whiskey," Pearson said, as he handed out a two-gallon jug.

"Harry, I won't charge you but one gallon, an' it's worth it to rid the gulch of such a bully an' coward," Mose told Pearson; and turning to the crowd he said, "I suppose his friends will be lookin' for me now."

"If they do they will find us all here right back of you," was the reply from the miners.

Expecting trouble, the crowd remained with Milner all night; but nothing occurred, and the next morning they learned that the Irishman's friends were really glad he was dead.

However, the Vigilance committee at Virginia City tried the case at a meeting that night, and came within one vote of finding Mose guilty. Some felt that the honor and dignity of the organization must be upheld. This action aroused Milner's fighting blood, and, riding over to Virginia City, he told the Vigilantes in no uncertain language his opinion of their conduct. When he asked why they had not gone to his own camp to hold their meeting there was no reply; and he then declared that some of them would have been killed. No further action was taken in the case. This incident is related in the history of Montana, just as given here. During the hectic days that followed there were several killings in Alder Gulch.

Milner spent the winter at Virginia City, hunting and taking life easy, but in the spring of 1864 he set out alone on a prospecting trip. He was compelled to walk and lead his pack mule, for his beloved Kentucky mare had been killed by the long, cold winter, and he was without a mount. Two weeks later he made a rich discovery on a small creek fifteen miles from Virginia City, and staked out two claims, which he immediately recorded. The miners' laws of that time allowed the discoverer of a new location one extra claim by right of discovery.

After erecting a small cabin, Mose started to wash gold. The location proved very rich, and in a short time he had taken out over ten thousand dollars worth of dust. His provisions were running low by that time, and after posting a notice of discovery and ownership, he went to Virginia City for a fresh supply. He spent three days with his friend, Harry Pearson, and then started back with two loaded pack mules.

In the early days following the discovery of gold at Alder Gulch, Montana was infested with claim-jumpers, who never hesitated at murder to gain their ends. The law of the six-shooter ruled. Claim-jumping was one of the crimes punishable by death; but in spite of the efforts of the Vigilantes the men engaged in this nefarious occupation did a flourishing business; and when the man whose claim was seized showed an inclination to resent the matter, the dispute was settled on the spot by force of firearms.

When Mose came within sight of his cabin he saw by the smoke curling from the chimney that he had visitors, and his suspicions were aroused when he saw three men panning out gravel in the creek. Three rifles were leaning against a tree, and he immediately concluded that his claims had been jumped.

The strangers did not see him until he ordered them in a loud voice to leave. Then the trio jumped up, and started towards him, but he immediately covered them with his six-shooters, and said: "The first man who comes another foot toward me is goin' to get shot."

The leader, seeing that Mose was between them and their rifles, stopped and said: "This is a deserted claim. We have been here two days, and it belongs to us and not to you."

"You're a —— liar. Didn't you read my notice in the cabin? Those claims belong to me an' I've got 'em recorded," roared Mose, now thoroughly enraged.

"All right, we'll leave if this is your claim; but we want our rifles and things we have in the cabin," the leader replied, but it was plainly evident that he only wanted to get the guns.

Mose was not to be caught in a trap of this kind, for he knew that if he gave them their weapons they would immediately turn upon him. His answer was: "Yo' can't have those rifles, an' no more talk about it. Get off my claims in one minute."

Sullenly the trio turned, but stopped after they had gone a few feet. Mose could not see whether they were armed with revolvers or not, but after they had exchanged a few whispered words the leader suddenly turned and rushed at Milner. The latter fired instantly, killing him in his tracks. Well knowing the desperate character of claim jumpers and not daring to take any chance with the other two, he shot again, and another fell, while the third fled down the gulch with Mose in pursuit. But he had only gone a short distance when he found himself bottled up in a pocket from which he could not escape, and as he turned on Milner the latter shot him to death.

Returning to the cabin, Mose found positive evidence among the effects of the three that they were claim-jumpers and members of the band that in recent months had committed most of the robberies and murders in that section. The next day he reported the affair to the Vigilantes at Virginia City. The news created great excitement; but the committee held no meeting, for Mose's reputation was such that his story was believed. Friends of the dead man talked of revenge, but made no attempt to carry out their threats. After the excitement died down Mose returned to his claims.

It was at this period of his life that Milner received the nickname of "California Joe." A few miles out of Virginia City he met four men on their way to town, and as they halted on the trail to exchange greetings, one asked his name. Thinking they might be friends of the dead claim-jumpers, Mose replied, "My name is Joe."

"What part of the country are you from?" asked another.

"California, where yo' find real gold," Mose replied.

"So your name is Joe, and you're from California, are you? Well, we'll just call you 'California Joe.' "

After leaving the northern gold fields, Mose always replied when asked his name, "Just call me 'California Joe,' the name they gave me up in Montana in '64." The Old West was quick to take up names of this kind, and from the day he met the four strangers until his death thirteen years later he was known as "California Joe"; and as such we will hereafter refer to him.

The four strangers made a favorable impression on Joe, and he invited them to file on the claims adjoining his. Two agreed, but the others said they would come in a few days. After reaching camp his new friends helped him bury the dead claim-jumpers; and for many years afterwards the place was known as Dead Man's Gulch. A few days later they were joined by the other two; and California Joe and his new friends worked their claims until early summer, when they were forced to discontinue as the creek dried up, shutting off their water supply. Returning to Virginia City, Joe and his new friends went immediately to Pearson's saloon, and the frontiersman announced to his friend: "Harry, I have a new name now. The boys here call me 'California Joe.' How do you like it?" Pearson and the other miners evidently liked it, for Mose Milner was ever afterwards known as "California Joe."

THE RESCUE OF MAGGIE
REYNOLDS
VI

Few incidents in the history of the Old West have been as badly misrepresented as California Joe's rescue of little Maggie Reynolds from the Cheyennes. This incident was the subject of a poem entitled *California Joe*, written by Captain Jack Crawford, the poet scout, who exercised poetic license by creating a fictitious story not borne out by facts; but that is a poet's privilege. However, Buel took it for granted that this was all based on fact.

The truth of the rescue of Maggie Reynolds is given here for the first time in print. That this is the correct story there can be no doubt, for it has been handed down in the Milner family, from California Joe himself, who related it to his sons, to Joe E. Milner, who heard it from his father.

After remaining in Virginia City about two weeks, Joe secured an outfit and set out alone on a trapping and hunting expedition along the Yellowstone. During the summer he met several roving bands of Cheyennes; and as he had learned to speak

their language during the years he had spent at Forts
Laramie and Bridger, he spent much of his time with
them, often accompanying their braves on hunting
excursions as far as the Missouri River. One day
while walking through a Cheyenne camp he saw a little white girl standing in the opening of a tepee; but
when he stopped to speak she was immediately seized
by a squaw and jerked out of sight. Wondering who
the child might be, Joe made inquiry among the Indians, but they refused to talk.

A few days later he returned to a cabin he had
built on the Yellowstone; but he could not banish
thoughts of this little white girl, held as a prisoner
in an Indian village. As winter was approaching, he
decided to go to Fort Laramie, which he had not seen
since he had passed through there with the second emigrant train he had guided to the Oregon country
years before. The days when he had trapped at this
post for the American Fur Company came back to
him, and he longed to see it again. And so with Fort
Laramie as his destination he left his cabin on the
Yellowstone. In that wild country in those days
white settlers were almost unknown, but to his
amazement he found a large cabin some seventy-five
miles south of his starting point. Several children
were playing around the doorway as he rode up, and
a white man came out to greet him.

The stranger invited the trapper into his cabin,
explaining that a few months before he had settled
there with his family. Milner never knew his host's

first name, for he was always addressed by his family as "Pap" Reynolds, and as such we will refer to him. An instant later California Joe gazed in astonishment at Mrs. Reynolds as she came forward to greet him with extended hand, for she was the very image of the little white prisoner he had seen in the Cheyenne camp. Her face was matured and older, but there was no mistaking the resemblance.

Turning to her husband, Joe said: "Mr. Reynolds, there's a little white girl held prisoner in a Cheyenne village up on the Missouri river that looks like your wife. Can it be that she belongs to yo'?"

"My God, man," cried Mrs. Reynolds, "that's my daughter Maggie who disappeared over three months ago when those Indians were here. They were supposedly friendly, but I knew they had stolen her."

Joe related the circumstances of his meeting with the child, and when he volunteered to rescue her, Reynolds wanted to accompany him, but the trapper refused permission. The father insisted that his oldest son, Charles, should go along; but Joe explained that the success of such a venture depended solely upon his cunning and knowledge of the country, and he must not be hampered with anyone. He then directed the family to be ready to leave immediately upon his return, for he knew that the Indians would be hot on his trail. Early the next morning the trapper set out on his mission. Mrs. Reynolds had told him that the child was eleven years of age, very bright, and could be depended upon to carry out any instructions he might give her.

Several days later he came within sight of the village, and concealed himself while he watched the camp and made plans for the rescue. Luck favored him, for the next morning he saw something unusual was on foot. The horses were driven in close to the village, and other preparations made for an expedition of some kind. At first he could not determine its nature, and for a time he was afraid they were going to move, in which case the rescue would have been much more difficult. All of the able-bodied men prepared to leave, and Joe concluded that they were making ready for the fall buffalo hunt. This would aid him, unless the village followed the trail of the herd; for the hunters would be gone several days, perhaps a week or more.

The next morning Joe was awake before sunrise, carefully watching every move in the village; for he knew that if the camp was not moved most of the squaws would follow the hunters to do the skinning and pack the meat. This would leave the village in charge of only the old men with a few squaws and children, and would offer a favorable opportunity for his attempt. As he watched, the hunters and squaws mounted and the cavalcade filed away to the buffalo herds.

When the last riders had disappeared from view, Joe concealed his heavy rifle and entered the village, armed with two six-shooters. Taking advantage of the hearty welcome he received from his Cheyenne friends, he made a tour of the entire camp, and in this way put in most of the day, going from one tepee to another. When he learned that the hunters would not return until they had secured their winter's supply of meat, he was delighted, for he knew that this would require several days. In order to allay any suspicion that might possibly arise, he informed the Indians that he would remain until the return of the hunters.

Cautiously he looked for Maggie Reynolds, but it was late in the afternoon before he finally located her in a tepee with two Indian children. In order to allay any suspicion that he was interested in the child he remarked: "That white girl's no good; too much trouble. Where'd yo' get her?"

Then he walked away and sat down to talk to some old men and squaws. California Joe always liked children, and in a short time a group of young Indians gathered around. This solved a difficult problem, for he had been planning how he might talk to Maggie Reynolds without detection. This gave him the opportunity, and he began playing with the children, chasing them and then hiding in the tepees when they chased him. It was great sport for the youngsters; and at the end of a half-hour Joe concealed himself in the tepee in which the white girl was held prisoner.

Several children were with her, but they could not understand English; and without turning his head or looking at her, the scout quickly told little Maggie his plans for her rescue. She started to cry; but he ordered her to stop at once; and then, in answer to his questions, she informed him that she slept in that same tepee with a couple of old men and squaws, who were very kind to her. Joe instructed her to crawl out under the edge of the lodge that night after everyone had fallen asleep, and he would watch for her. He then ran out of the tepee so as not to create suspicion, and resumed his game with the Indian children.

Joe sat up until late that night, talking to the men so that they would fall asleep quickly when they retired. Fortune favored him, for he was given a tepee within a short distance of that in which Maggie Reynolds slept, and he could easily watch from the interior without detection. Seating himself on a pile of buffalo robes, he waited patiently for two hours, and then saw the girl crawl carefully out. In an instant he was at her side, and cautiously they stole out of the village to the spot where he had concealed his rifle. The dogs barked a little, and he dared not attempt to secure a horse for fear of raising too much of a disturbance. With the child upon his back, California Joe traveled all that night and until noon the next day, when he stopped to give her a much needed rest. Several hours later they resumed their journey, and after two days of hard traveling arrived safely at the Reynolds cabin.

The family was eating the noon meal when the

tall, bearded trapper, looking like an apparition, appeared in the doorway with the lost child upon his shoulders. To the grief-stricken parents he was an angel dressed in buckskin. For his part, California Joe felt more than repaid by the scene he witnessed in that little cabin on the frontier. Weeping, the mother clasped her child to her breast, and the father, strong man that he was, broke down and cried.

After the greeting was over Joe took Reynolds outside, and informed him that they must leave at once; for he knew word had been sent to the hunters as soon as the child was missed, and doubtless a party of warriors had long before this discovered his trail. Reynolds had not been idle during Joe's absence, and he had everything in readiness for immediate flight. In a short time they set out for the Powder River country, where Joe hoped to find some trappers; and several days dater they discovered a party of eight white men building a cabin on that stream, where they expected to spend the winter trapping.

They now felt safe, and after resting a few days continued on to Fort Laramie, where Reynolds remained with his family during the winter.

The Reynolds' dropped out of sight after they left the fort the next spring, and nothing more is known of them. Mr. Franklin W. Hall, of Houlton, Maine, informed the authors recently that Charley Reynolds, the oldest son and the boy who wanted to accompany California Joe when he went back to the Indian village to rescue his sister, was the same Char-

ley Reynolds who, as chief of scouts of General George
A. Custer's ill-fated expedition, was killed June 25,
1876, while fighting with Major Reno's command at
the battle of the Little Bighorn, River, Montana.
There is some dispute over the identity of Custer's
chief of scouts. E. A. Brininstool, in *A Trooper With
Custer,* claims to have located relatives of Charley
Reynolds, and gives several letters received from
them. Mr. Hall, mentioned above, was a personal
friend of California Joe and fought Indians with
him in the Black Hills; and he also knew Charley Reynolds. Therefore, we must consider him an authority
on the identity of General Custer's famous scout. In
a way Mrs. Elizabeth B. Custer, widow of the general, corroborates Mr. Hall in her book, *Boots and
Saddles,* when she states that Charley Reynolds' identity was not known. It is well to bear in mind that
Mrs. Custer was personally acquainted with him.

We will refer once more to J. W. Buel's *Heroes of
The Plains,* in which that author accepts as truth the
story of Maggie Reynolds' rescue told in Captain
Jack Crawford's poem. We quote the following
from Buel:

"California Joe's courtship and marriage as told
by himself, and repeated in sweet, pathetic story by
one of nature's noblemen, Captain Jack Crawford,
is unquestionably one of the most sympathetic and
lovingly sorrowful recitals that was ever created by
imagination or found in any of the peculiar phases
of human life. Its reproduction here will thrill the

hearts of every lover of the most noble instincts of human nature, and perhaps bring tears to the eyes of many, moved by that fellow feeling which establishes a universal kinship among mankind. It has been asserted that California Joe married the little girl he had rescued, six years afterwards; but it is possible the name of the girl, Maggie, being the same as that of his wife, gave rise to this belief. The circumstances as here related, concerning the rescue of Reynolds' daughter, are undoubtedly true; but that he married this same girl afterwards is scarcely worthy of belief."

In that last sentence Buel redeems himself. Joe E. Milner, the oldest grandson of California Joe, states positively that his grandfather was only married once; but Buel is again in error when he says her name was Maggie; for, as stated in a previous chapter, it was Nancy Emma Watts.

Captain Jack Crawford, one of the noted army scouts and Indian fighters of his day, was a personal friend of California Joe. Crawford died in New York in 1922 at the age of seventy-six years. His fame as a poet of the pioneer West gained him the title of the "Poet Scout." His production entitled *California Joe* follows:

Well, mates, I don't like stories,
    Nor am I going to act
A part around this campfire
    That ain't a truthful fact.
So fill your pipes and listen;
    I'll tell you—let me see,
I think it was in fifty,
    From that till sixty-three.

You've all heard tell of Bridger?
    I used to run with Jim,
And many a hard day's scouting
    I've done 'long side of him.
Well, once near old Fort Reno
    A trapper used to dwell;
We called him old Pap Reynolds—
    The scouts all knew him well.

One night, the spring of fifty,
    We camped on Powder River;
We killed a calf of buffalo,
    And cooked a slice of liver;
While eating quite contented,
    We heard three shots or four,
Put out the fire and listened,
    Then heard a dozen more.

We knew that old man Reynolds
    Had moved his traps up here,
So picking up our rifles,
    And fixing on our gear,
We mounted quick as lightnin'—
    To save was our desire,
Too late; the painted heathens
    Had set the house on fire.

We tied our horses quickly,
   And waded up the stream,
While close beside the water
   I heard a muffled scream.
And there among the bushes
   A little girl did lie;
I picked her up and whispered,
   "I'll save you or I'll die."

Lord, what a ride! Old Bridger,
   He covered my retreat,
Sometimes the child would whisper,
   In voice so low and sweet,
"Poor papa! God will take him
   To mama up above;
There's no one left to love me,
   There's no one left to love."

The little one was thirteen
   And I was twenty-two;
Said I, "I'll be your father,
   And love you just as true."
She nestled to my bosom,
   Her hazel eyes so bright,
Looked up and made me happy
   Though close pursued that night.

A month had passed and Maggie
   (We called her Hazel-Eye),
In truth was going to leave me,
   Was going to say "Good-bye."
Her uncle, mad Jack Reynolds,
   Reported long since dead,
Had come to claim my angel,
   His brother's child, he said.

What could I say?   We parted.
    Mad Jack was growing old.
I handed him a bank note,
    And all I had in gold.
They rode away at sunrise,
    I went a mile or two,
And parting said, "We'll meet again
    May God watch over you."

Beside a laughing, dancing brook
    A little cabin stood,
As, weary with a long day's scout,
    I spied it in the wood.
A pretty valley stretched beyond,
    The mountains towered above,
While near the willow bank I heard
    The cooing of a dove.

'Twas one grand panorama,
    The brook was plainly seen
Like a long thread of silver
    In a cloth of lovely green.
The laughter of the waters,
    The cooing of the dove
Was like some painted picture,
    Some well-told tale of love.

While drinking in the grandeur,
    And resting in my saddle,
I heard a gentle ripple,
    Like the dipping of a paddle.
I turned towards the eddy—
    A strange sight met my view;
A maiden with her rifle
    In a little bark canoe.

She stood up in the center,
    Her rifle to her eye;
I thought, (just for a second)
    My time had come to die.
I doffed my hat and told her
    (If it was all the same)
To drop her little shooter,
    For I was not her game.

She dropped the deadly weapon,
    And leaped from her canoe;
Said she, "I beg your pardon,
    I thought you were a Sioux;
Your long hair and your buckskin
    Looked warrior-like and rough;
My bead was spoiled by sunshine,
    Or I'd killed you, sure enough.'

"Perhaps it had been better
    You dropped me then," said I,
"For surely such an angel
    Would bear me to the sky."
She blushed and dropped her eyelids,
    Her cheeks were crimson red,
One half-shy glance she gave me,
    And then hung down her head.

I took her little hand in mine—
    She wondered what I meant,
And yet she drew it not away.
    But rather seemed content.
We sat upon the mossy bank,
    Her eyes began to fill,
The brook was rippling at our feet,
    The dove was cooing still.

I smoothed the golden tresses,
    Her eyes looked up in mine.
She seemed in doubt, then whispered,
    " 'Tis such a long, long time
Strong arms were thrown around me—
    'I'll save you or I'll die.' "
I clasped her to my bosom,
    My long-lost Hazel Eye.

The rapture of that moment
    Was almost heaven to me;
I kissed her mid her tear drops,
    Her innocence and glee;
Her heart near mine was beating,
    While sobbingly she said,
"My dear, my brave preserver,
    They told me you were dead.

"But, oh! those parting words, Joe,
    Have never left my mind,
You said, 'We'll meet again, Mag,'
    Then rode off like the wind;
And oh! how I have prayed, Joe,
    For you, who saved my life,
That God would send an angel,
    To guard you through all strife.

"And he who claimed me from you,
    My uncle good and true,
Now sick in yonder cabin,
    Has talked so much of you.
'If Joe were living, darling,'
    He said to me last night,
'He would care for Maggie,
    When God puts out my light.' "

We found the old man sleeping.
"Hush, Maggie, let him rest."
The sun was slowly sinking
  In the far-off glowing west;
And tho' we talked in whispers,
  He opened wide his eyes,
"Dream—a dream," he murmured,
  "Alas, a dream of lies."

She drifted like a shadow
To where the old man lay,
"You had a dream, dear Uncle,
  Another dream today?"
"Oh, yes, I saw an angel,
  As pure as mountain snow,
And near her, at my bedside,
  Stood California Joe."

"I'm sure I'm not an angel,
  Dear uncle, that you know,
These arms are brown, my hand too—
  My face is not like snow;
Now listen while I tell you,
  For I have news to cheer,
And Hazel Eye is happy,
  For Joe is truly here."

And when a few days after,
  The old man said to me,
"Joe, boy, she ar' a angel,
  An' good as angels be;
For three long months she's hunted,
  An' trapped an' nus'd me, too;
God bless ye, boy; I believe it—
  She's safe along wi' you."

The sun was slowly sinking,
    When Mag, (my wife) and I
Came riding through the valley,
    Her tear drops in her eye.
"One year ago today, Joe—
    I see the mossy grave—
We laid him 'neath the daisies
    My uncle, good and brave."

And comrades, every springtime
    Was sure to find me there—
A something in that valley
    Was always fresh and fair;
Our lives were newly kindled
    While sitting by the stream,
Where two hearts were united
    In love's sweet, happy dream.

Franklin W. Hall has informed the authors that
Jim Bridger covered California Joe's retreat with
Maggie Reynolds. Crawford also mentions Bridger
in his poem; but the Milners have no record of his
taking any part in this adventure. The version we
have given is the one that has been handed down
from California Joe to his sons. However, as Mr.
Hall was personally acquainted with Joe during the
Black Hills gold rush, we must accept his statement
as correct; for he speaks with the authority of a man
who heard the scout himself relate the story.

S HORTLY AFTER reaching Fort Laramie with the Reynolds family California Joe went with six trappers to Fort Bridger, which at that time was occupied by United States troops, having been leased by the government, as related in a previous chapter. While hunting near the fort one day, Joe and his comrades met five Mormons in a covered wagon on their way to Salt Lake City. As soon as he learned that they were members of Brigham Young's clan, Joe asked: "Are yo' of the same tribe that slaughtered the helpless men, women, and children at the Mountain Meadow Massacre a few years ago?"

This bold inquiry was resented by the Mormons, and a heated argument followed. Joe, thoroughly aroused to anger, finally shouted: "Get out o' that wagon, yo' assassins, and we'll fight it out right down here on the ground."

The Mormons refused to accept the challenge, and after making an insulting remark started to drive away; but Joe seized the bridle of one of the lead horses. Resenting this action, the leader drew his revolver and fired, the bullet just grazing the crown of Joe's head. He ducked in front of the horse for protection, at the same time drawing his pistol and returning the fire with fatal effect. The driver fell to the ground, and before the startled man at his side could recover from his surprise another bullet from the trapper's deadly six-shooter inflicted a mortal wound.

Turing to his comrades Joe shouted: "Come on, boys, an' avenge the Mountain Meadow Massacre."

The three remaining Mormons begged so hard for their lives that they were allowed to depart with their dead in the wagon. This affair created much excitement among the Latter Day Saints and California Joe's life was threatened. The news traveled over the frontier, and the trapper was heralded as the first man to avenge the Mountain Meadow Massacre, in Washington county, Utah, September 16, 1857.

This sanguinary affair, one of the foulest crimes ever committed on the western frontier, was for many years a blot against the people of Utah. A caravan of emigrants on their way to California was surrounded, and after a fight of two days, one hundred and twenty men, women, and children were massacred. It was reported at the time that this atrocity was committed by Indians, but it later developed that they had been led by Mormons under John D. Lee. After the government started an investigation in the early seventies and his part in the affair became known, Lee fled to the Grand Canyon,

in Arizona; but on November 8, 1874, while visiting
one of his wives at Panguitch, Utah, he was captured
by William Stokes, a deputy United States marshal.
After a lengthy trial at Beaver City, Utah, during
September, 1876, he was found guilty of murder in
the first degree; and on March 23, 1877, was taken
to Mountain Meadows and executed before a firing
squad, according to Utah law.

General Carlton, who visited Mountain Meadows
two years after the massacre and buried the bleached
bones of the victims which had been gnawed and
scattered by wild animals, erected a rude monument
on which this inscription appeared: "Here 120 men,
women and children were massacred in cold blood
early in September in 1857. They were from
Arkansas."

On a cedar cross erected on the spot these words
were carved: "Vengeance is mine, I will repay, saith
the Lord."

The cross and monument were destroyed, but
were rebuilt by United States soldiers. The cross was
again torn away. This second monument, which was
still standing as late as 1875, consisted of a pile of
stones twenty feet long by seven feet high.

Efforts made by federal authorities to implicate
the Mormon church in this affair failed; for it was
shown at Lee's trial that the massacre was the work of
men acting without authority from the church leaders. Brigham Young had issued orders that the wagon
train was to be allowed to proceed through Utah.

The historian of the Mormon church kindly furnished the authors with an interesting description of Mountain Meadows as the place appears today. This historic spot is located about thirty miles northwest of St. George, and twelve miles due west of the little town of Pine Valley. In early times it was a beautiful place, in a high valley on the rim of the Great Basin, and a noted camping place on the old Spanish Trail from Santa Fe, New Mexico, to California. But today Mountain Meadows is a barren, desolate spot. At the point where the emigrants camped was a large spring, which made an oasis of the meadows; but the road was cut deeper and deeper by the increasing travel until a channel was formed, and down this the melting snows and heavy summer rains ran. As this channel became deeper with the passing years the spring was finally drained, and no water now appears on the surface at this point. The water from the drained spring flows through the channel, which in some places is twenty feet deep. As a result of this drainage the meadows have disappeared, and the land is now covered with sagebrush. The soil is very productive, and where water can be secured for irrigation ranches exist. Some years ago the government withdrew from entry forty acres surrounding the site of the massacre.

The only burial the victims were ever given was by General Carlton in 1859; and many of their bones have long since been washed away by the heavy rains. By a strange twist of fate the only monument of any description now at Mountain Meadows is a pile of rock that marks the spot where John D. Lee paid the price of blood lust.

Shortly after the killing of the two Mormons, California Joe left Fort Bridger; but whether this affair had anything to do with it or not we are unable to say. The feeling held against him by the Latter Day Saints was very bitter; and it was reported that the Danites, or Destroying Angels, had received orders for his death. However, as danger was always welcomed by California Joe, it is more than probable that his wandering disposition carried him to other fields in search of new adventures, and not fear of Mormon retribution. We next find him at Fort Lyon, Colorado, where he was employed by Major E. W. Wynkoop, the commandant, as post scout and Indian interpreter. This was very much to his liking, for he was frequently sent on long journeys alone to the Cheyennes and Arapahoes, in an effort to induce these tribes to cease their wandering life and settle down at the fort.

Public feeling among the people of Colorado at that time was very bitter against the Indians. It was the old story. The riff-raff that infested the frontier, especially the mining camps, regarded Indians as legitimate game, to be killed wherever found. To them "the only good Indian was a dead Indian." Naturally the tribes resented this attitude and war followed. It is a significant historical fact that the first white men were peaceably received by the aborigines; and none of the so-called Indian wars occurred until the red warriors retaliated for outrages commited upon them by whites. We do not wish to tear the halo of romantic worship from the heads of any of the old-time frontiersmen; but it is well to remember that many of the early pioneers of the Far West were men who had left their homes in the East with the sheriff only about two laps behind them.

The state of public feeling in Colorado in 1864 had reached such a pitch that one of these so-called Indian wars was in progress. It is true that the Cheyennes and Arapahoes had committed depredations; they had raided emigrant trains and scattered ranches, and had captured a few white prisoners; but this was only in retaliation for outrages by the whites. What would we do today if a foreign people came into our land to dispossess us of our homes, kill our fathers and mothers, and outrage our women? No crime committed by Indians in North America ever equalled the treachery, the cruel, savage ferocity, or the blood lust of the whites at the massacre of the Cheyennes and Arapahoes at Sand Creek, Colorado, November 27, 1864. That the Colorado volunteers went there for the express purpose of murdering these Indians there is not the slightest doubt. Although Colonel Chivington did not have the discipline of a regular army officer over his men, there is no doubt but that they carried out the orders of their superiors.

An old pioneer in Montana, who was of the volunteers that marched from Denver, informed one of the

authors many years ago that the troops went to Sand
Creek with the expressed intention of killing those
Indians; and he distinctly heard Colonel Chivington
reply, "Nits make lice, boys," when he was asked
what should be done with the children.

The people of Colorado have for years tried to
excuse this terrible affair, but it will remain forever
a blot on the history of their state. No excuse could
be found at the time for the Sand Creek barbarities;
and none has been found after the passing of nearly
seventy years. An unfortunate chain of events made
this massacre possible. In June, 1864, Governor
Evans of Colorado sent a circular to the plains tribes
inviting the friendly Cheyennes and Arapahoes to go
to Fort Lyon where they would be safe, as the government intended to wage war against the hostiles.

Through California Joe's efforts the Cheyennes
and Arapahoes were induced to go to Fort Lyon for
a peace conference; but after they arrived Major
Wynkoop informed the chiefs of both tribes that he
was not authorized to conclude a treaty with them
until the terms were ratified by Governor Evans, who,
unfortunately, was the superintendent of Indian affairs for Colorado Territory. However, Major Wynkoop pledged his word that the Indians who remained
near the fort would receive military protection until
he received further instructions.

The people of Colorado wanted blood, and nothing short of a massacre would satisfy them. To them
the only good Indian was a dead Indian. The aborig-

ine must be wiped out so that nothing would stand
in the way of seizing his valuable lands; and, yielding
to the popular clamor for blood, Governor Evans,
who had undergone a change of heart, informed
Major Wynkoop that it would be unwise to treat
with the tribes on any terms until they had been fully
punished for past depredations. He was further informed that a regiment of volunteers had been
organized for the purpose of carrying out this work.
After that had been accomplished there would be
plenty of time to talk of peace.

Major Wynkoop had pledged protection to the
Indians while peace negotiations were in progress,
and he considered his word his bond. Immediately
upon receiving this message from Governor Evans,
he sent California Joe to the Cheyenne and Arapahoe
villages to induce them to move to a location near
Fort Lyon, where they would be under the eyes of
his soldiers, never dreaming that white men would
attack a peaceable village. On account of his friendly
attitude toward the Indians, Major Wynkoop was
succeeded in the command of Fort Lyon by Major
Anthony, who continued to issue rations for a time
to the Cheyennes and Arapahoes camped near the
post; but later informed them that he could no longer
feed them, and advised that they had better go where
they could hunt for a living. He then selected a location on Sand Creek, about forty miles from Fort
Lyon. They obeyed, and he returned some of the

arms that had been taken from them by Major Wynkoop, but not all.

Early in November, 1864, the volunteers, composed of the First Colorado Cavalry, commanded by
Colonel J. M. Chivington, and a battalion of the
Third Cavalry left Denver, and marched direct to
Fort Lyon. That Major Anthony, commandant of
the post, took a prominent part in the slaughter is
shown by his own testimony and that of others,
which are matters of record in the report of the
special committee appointed by Congress to conduct
an investigation of the Sand Creek Massacre. Major
Anthony's testimony shows that when he took command of Fort Lyon the Indians were camped nearby.
By his own admission their friendship for the whites
was so great that they not only surrendered their arms
but they frequently gave him information of raids
being planned by the hostiles. And yet he stated that
it was fear and not principle that prevented him from
killing them when he had the band completely in his
power.

When Colonel Chivington reached Fort Lyon,
Major Anthony joined him with men and artillery;
and at daybreak of November 27, 1864, the doomed
Cheyennes and Arapahoes found their camp surrounded by white soldiers, ready for action. Evidently thinking there must be some mistake, Chief
White Antelope, who had always been the steadfast
friend of the white race, ran towards the soldiers
waving his arms frantically and shouting, "Stop,

stop." Before he had gone far he saw that there was
no mistake; the soldiers had come to kill; and, fold-
ing his arms, he stood facing them like a hero of old
until he fell, shot through and through.

Floating over the lodge of Black Kettle, head chief
of the Cheyennes, was a United States flag with a
small white flag tied beneath as a token that he was
friendly. It is little wonder that this noted chief afterwards went on the war path and became the
scourge of the frontier until he was killed by General
Custer's Seventh Cavalry at the battle of the Washita
four years later. It is easy to understand that men
who had suffered at the hands of hostile Indians could
become so inflamed that they would kill unarmed
warriors and even women and children in the heat of
passion; but the barbarities committed that day by
white men surpassed any outrage of the Indians in
all their long years of warfare. To this day the people of Colorado still grope for excuses for the Sand
Creek Massacre; but no justification for the atrocities
of that terrible day are possible, for the testimony
taken before the congressional committee gives too
many of the revolting details. The following from
Major Wynkoop's own testimony tells the story
clearly and briefly:

"Women and children were killed and scalped,
children shot at their mothers' breasts, and all the
bodies mutilated in the most horrible manner. The
dead bodies of females profaned in such a manner that
the recital is sickening. Colonel J. M. Chivington

all the time inciting his troops to their diabolical outrages."

Robert Bent's testimony is particularly revolting:

"I saw one squaw, whose leg had been broken,
lying on the bank. A soldier came up to her with a
drawn sabre. She raised her arm to protect herself;
he struck, breaking her arm. She rolled over and
raised her other arm; he struck, breaking that, and
then left her without killing her. I saw one squaw
cut open, with an unborn child lying by her side."

The following pathetic incident related by Major
Anthony himself seems beyond belief:

"There was one little child, probably three years
old, just big enough to walk through the sand. The
Indians had gone ahead, and this little fellow was behind, following after them. The little fellow was
perfectly naked, traveling through the sand. I saw
one man get off his horse at a distance of about seventy-five yards and draw up his rifle and fire. He
missed the child. Another man came up and said,
'Let me try the son of a b——. I can hit him.' He
got off his horse, kneeled down, and fired at the little
child, but he missed him. A third man came up, and
made a similar remark and fired, and the little fellow
dropped."

With the troops that accompanied Colonel Chivington from Fort Lyon was California Joe, who afterwards told that in all his experience on the plains
he never saw a more savage or wild band of men than
those at Sand Creek that day. He stated that the

cruelties and mutilations practiced by Chivington's men were beyond belief. Every man tried to take a scalp of either a buck or a squaw, and no mercy was shown. The exact number killed will never be known, the various reports ranging from seventy to six hundred. Little resistance was possible; but fortunately the Indians had a few arms that had been returned to them by Major Anthony, and only this saved the entire band from annihilation.

Governor Hunt, one of the first settlers of Colorado, testified before the congressional committee that Black Kettle and White Antelope had been the friends of the whites ever since he had been in the country, and he knew of no acts of hostility committed by them or with their consent. Another witness, whose name is not given, told the committee that three days later he was at the scene of the massacre, and saw the following take place:

"I saw a man dismount from his horse and cut the ear from the body of an Indian, and the scalp from the head of another. I saw a number of children killed; they had bullet holes in them; one child had been cut with some sharp instrument across its side. I saw another that both ears had been cut from . . . I saw several of the Third Regiment cut off fingers to get rings off them. I saw Major Sayre scalp a dead Indian. The scalp had a long tail of silver hanging to it."

The "victorious" troops marched back to Denver, and on December 22, paraded through the streets, exhibiting the scalps and other trophies of the "battle." *The Rocky Mountain News* of December 22, in describing this parade of Colonel Chivington's men "before their admiring fellow citizens," said: "All acquitted themselves well. Colorado soldiers have again covered themselves with glory." When the scalps were exhibited from the stage of a theatre that night the audience applauded rapturously. But the white people paid dearly for this "great victory." Immediately the plains tribes went on the warpath. Black Kettle, the former champion of the white man, became his most bitter enemy, and during the next four years his warriors ravaged the settlements of Colorado and Kansas.

Helen Hunt Jackson in *A Century of Dishonor*, describes the Sand Creek affair in great detail, and quotes many passages from the testimony taken before the congressional committee. That she had the courage of her convictions is shown by the fact that when this book was published Mrs. Jackson was a resident of Colorado Springs, Colorado.

In his official report of January 15, 1865, Major Wynkoop, again in command at Fort Lyon, said:

"In conclusion, allow me to say that, from the time I held the consultation with Indian chiefs on the headwaters of Smoky Hill up to the date of this massacre by Colonel Chivington, not one single depredation had been committed by the Cheyenne and Arapahoe Indians. The settlers of the Arkansas valley had returned to their ranches, from which they

had fled; had taken in their crops, and had been resting in perfect security under assurance from myself
that they would be in no danger for the present.
Since this last horrible murder by Colonel Chivington
the country presents a scene of desolation. All communication is cut off with the States, except by sending large bodies of troops, and already over a hundred
whites have fallen victims to the fearful vengeance
of these betrayed Indians."

The report of the Indian Peace Commission for
1868 gives the astonishing information that the war
that followed as a result of the Sand Creek Massacre
cost the government $30,000,000 and carried con-
flagration and death into the border settlements. During the spring of 1865 no less than eight thousand
troops were withdrawn from the effective forces engaged in the Rebellion to meet this Indian war, which
did not end until the death of Black Kettle at the
battle of the Washita in 1868. As General Custer's
chief of scouts during that historic winter campaign,
California Joe took part in this engagement, a detailed account of which will be found in a subsequent
chapter.

CALIFORNIA JOE remained
at Fort Lyon during the winter; but in the spring of
1865 he went to Fort Union, New Mexico, where he
met the famous scout and Indian fighter, Kit Carson
As Joe rode into this post on his favorite mule and
dismounted in front of the sutler's store, Carson, who
was standing nearby, turned to another man and
asked: "Who is that six-foot giant with his hair
hanging down his back, getting off that mule?"

Joe heard the question, and turning to the scout
with a smile, he said: "Well, my friend, I don't know
who you are; but I came down here from Fort Lyon
to see Kit Carson and help him kill Indians."

Carson immediately made himself known, and at
the end of a long talk engaged Joe as a civilian scout
for an expedition he was leading from Fort Union
to establish an army post at either Cedar Bluffs or
Cold Spring on the Cimarron route of the Santa Fe
Trail. The two frontiersmen became warm friends
during the few months that California Joe served under Carson; and the former often said afterwards that

he never knew a better Indian fighter, or a braver man.

The only battle in which California Joe took part under Carson was the fight at Adobe Walls, in the Texas Panhandle. During the Civil War the plains tribes were very active against Federal troops on the border, and after his successful conquest of the Navajos in Arizona, Colonel Carson was ordered to lead an expedition against the Kiowas and Comanches. These tribes, together with a number of Arapahoes, were known to have established a winter camp on the Canadian River, in what is now Hutchinson County, Texas, about two hundred miles from Fort Bascom, New Mexico, and Carson decided to strike them at that point.

Scouts reported between four and five thousand adults in the camps in the vicinity of Bent's old trading post, known as Adobe Walls, then in ruins. Fort Bascom was selected as the starting point, and on November 10, 1864, Carson arrived there to take command of what is known in history as the Kiowa-Comanche expedition. With a force of fourteen officers, three hundred and twenty-one enlisted men, and seventy-five Ute and Jicarilla Apache Indian scouts from the Maxwell agency, Kit Carson set out on what proved to be the only Indian expedition in which he was defeated. His command was composed of companies from the New Mexico and California Volunteers.

Leaving Fort Bascom on November 10, the army

marched along the Canadian by easy stages until it reached Arroyo de la Mula, thirty miles from Adobe Walls, on the twenty-fourth, and went into camp. Carson sent two Indian scouts to locate the enemy, and shortly after sundown they returned with information that they had discovered a fresh trail in the Canadian Valley. This led Carson to believe that there was a camp of Kiowas and Comanches in the vicinity.

The wagons were left in charge of Colonel Abreu, and with the cavalry and infantry, a force of thirteen officers, two hundred and forty-six men, and Lieutenant Pettis' twelve-pound howitzers, Carson marched about fifteen miles that night. After he had found the trail located by the Indian spies he traveled until midnight, and then halted, while he sent his scouts ahead under California Joe. Two hours before daybreak they returned with the news of a large village in the vicinity of the old Adobe Walls fort.

Immediately Carson gave the command to march, and the entire column moved forward. When an enemy picket was heard calling in Spanish on the opposite side of the river just before dawn, Carson sent Major McCleave with one company across to capture any hostiles he could find before they could alarm the village, and with the main column he advanced at a rapid pace. At the first alarm his Indian scouts had stripped and prepared for battle. Just at daylight shots were heard, and three Indians were seen racing for the village. Carson ordered the cavalry under Lieutenant Heath to charge, while he remained to push the battery with all speed.

When the howitzer company finally arrived within sight of the village, the tepees of white tanned buffalo hides at first deceived the inexperienced soldiers who thought they were Sibley army tents, but Carson soon explained. The colonel found upon his arrival with the battery that the cavalry had driven the enemy from the village, which contained about one hundred and fifty lodges; but McCleave had been stopped in his pursuit by a number of warriors who made a stand in the river bottom. The troopers had dismounted and were deployed as skirmishers, while their horses were held under guard within the ruined walls of the old adobe fort. Bringing the two howitzers up at a gallop they were quickly put into action and the bursting shells soon drove the hostiles from the field.

Believing that the enemy had been defeated, Carson gave orders to unsaddle and eat breakfast, intending to destroy the village later; but as his men were in the act of obeying he discovered a large force of Indians advancing from another village of at least three hundred and fifty lodges, about three miles away. The tired troopers climbed back into their saddles again, and were surrounded almost immediately by at least one thousand well-mounted warriors. Repeatedly the enemy charged with bravery, but were repulsed with great loss. The fighting Kiowas were led by Little Mountain, Stumbling Bear,

and the notorious Satanta. All day long the battle
raged fiercely. Reinforcements of Comanches, Apaches, and Arapahoes arrived from other villages
during the afternoon, and the little command of
white troopers were soon fighting for their lives
against fully three thousand warriors, the flower of
the fighting tribes of the old Southwest. Only their
two howitzers saved the white men from being completely overwhelmed, and they were forced to take
refuge within the old adobe fort.

California Joe killed several horses and Indians
at long range. Early in the battle his mule was shot
from under him, and he fought the remainder of the
day on foot.

Carson's position was now a hazardous one. If
his supply train, guarded by only seventy-five men,
should be cut off and captured the main column
would be in a bad way. Late in the afternoon he
gave orders to mount, and started an advance on the
village from which the enemy had been driven at
daybreak. Stubbornly the Indians contested every
foot of the way, setting fire to the grass in his rear.
When his rear guard was driven in by the flames,
Carson countered by firing the grass in front, and
took a position on a knoll where the grass was short.
Under cover of the flames and smoke the Indians
charged the white lines, but were repulsed by the howitzers.

Just before sunset the troops reached the village,
which was full of Indians trying desperately to save

their property. A couple of shells from the howitzers drove them out, and while half of the command held the enemy in check, the others fired the lodges. The entire camp was soon a mass of flames, but before the work of destruction began every man secured a fine buffalo robe as a souvenir of the battle. Numerous articles of white women's and children's wearing apparel were found. Darkness had fallen by the time the destruction was completed, and Carson proceeded to extricate himself from his perilous position, for he well knew that with the coming of dawn the attack would be renewed if he remained in the vicinity.

The wounded who were not able to mount their horses were loaded upon the gun carriages and ammunition carts, and the column set out through the night in search of the supply train. Besides suffering fatigue and hardship on that march their position was perilous in the extreme. They were not in fighting condition, and at any moment the red warriors might sweep down upon them under cover of the darkness. For three hours they plodded wearily up the valley; and then off to the right several camfires gleamed dimly through the night. Cautiously they approached. It was either the enemy or the supply train; and finally their hearts leaped with joy when they heard the challenge of a sentinel. The men were almost exhausted after having spent thirty-six hours in marching and fighting with only a few mouthfuls of hardtack and salt pork and bacon eaten raw.

The next day was spent resting in camp. Carson

kept close watch, expecting the Indians to renew the battle; but only a few warriors were seen on the distant hills. Early on the morning of the twenty-seventh the column broke camp and started on the return, although the officers wished to attack the large Comanche village seen in the distance on the day of the battle. The return to Fort Bascom was made by easy marches on account of the wounded.

Carson's losses in this campaign were two soldiers killed and ten wounded, and one Indian scout killed and five wounded. He placed the enemy loss at sixty killed and wounded. However, three years later, two Mexicans living in Algodones, New Mexico, who had been trading with the Comanches and Kiowas and were in the Comanche village during the battle, reported that the Indians lost nearly one hundred killed and between one hundred and one hundred and fifty wounded.

The little known battle of Adobe Walls was perhaps the greatest engagement with Indians that ever took place west of the Mississippi river. Opposed to Carson's command of approximately three hundred men were three thousand of the best warriors of the Kiowa, Comanche, Apache and Arapahoe tribes, all well armed and supplied with plenty of ammunition. That the little column of white soldiers was not massacred to a man is little short of miraculous; and not long before his death in 1868, Carson told George Bent that all that saved him was the old Adobe Walls fort. To this may be added the wholesome respect the Indians entertained for the two howitzers, and Carson's excellent generalship. It is interesting to note in this connection that Buckskin Charley, the Ute chief who accompanied Carson's Indian scouts, was still living on the Southern Ute Indian reservation, in Colorado, a few years ago.

Some account of the history of the old adobe fort that played such an important part in this battle will be of interest. In the early thirties a band of traders and trappers sent out by Colonel William Bent, from Bent's Fort on the Arkansas River, in Colorado, built this as a trading post. Jim Murray, one of the noted trappers of his time, was in command of the little force; but it is curious to relate that three other members, destined to become famous in Western history, were Kit Carson, Lucien B. Maxwell, and Uncle John Smith. For three years the post prospered, and then one night a raiding band of Apaches stole every horse. This compelled the trappers to abandon the place and travel to Bent's Fort on foot; and the place was never again occupied. The ruins of the adobe fort trading post were familiar to every plainsman, soldier, and buffalo hunters who passed that way during the next thirty-five years; and the ruined walls were still standing on Bent Creek as late as 1883 when William Dixon homesteaded the land upon which it stood, but all traces of them have now disappeared.

In the spring of 1874, a company of buffalo hunters from Dodge City, Kansas, established a station at this point during their invasion of the Texas Panhandle, and erected three buildings a short distance from the original fort. This was the scene of another terrific encounter between red men and white, the fame of which has overshadowed Carson's battle. At dawn on June 27, 1874, the buffalo hunters to the number of only twenty-eight were attacked by over seven hundred Cheyenne, Kiowa, and Comanche Indians, led by Chiefs Quanah Parker, Big Bow, Lone Wolf, Minimic, Red Moon, Gray Beard, Stone Calf, and White Shield. By another heroic defense this red horde of destruction was beaten back time after time with a loss of only three white men. This engagement has come down in the history of the Old Southwest as the famous battle of Adobe Walls, while Carson's has been almost forgotten.

A few years later the famous Turkey Track cow outfit established its home ranch at the site of the battle. This, one of the largest ranches in the Texas Panhandle, finally passed into the possession of W. T. Coble, of Amarillo, Texas, who still runs it as a cattle ranch. In 1924 ten acres of ground surrounding the site of the battle of 1874 were deeded by Mr. Coble to the Panhandle Historical Society, and on June 27, of that year, a granite monument was unveiled to the memory of the twenty-eight buffalo hunters who fought at Adobe Walls. But no monument stands to the heroism of Kit Carson and his men who battled a much larger force at the same place.

WHILE fighting with Kit Carson, California Joe became acquainted with a prospector and Indian fighter named George Lewis; and after the battle of Adobe Walls they formed a partnership to hunt for gold in Colorado. During the rest of that winter, however, they remained in New Mexico, scouting with Carson part of the time, and it was well into the summer before they were ready to start on their prospecting trip. As Lewis had no money, Joe paid for the outfit. With a spring wagon and four horses, two extra to be used in case of emergency, they left Santa Fe, July 8, 1865. Nothing occurred for several days; but one night a terrific storm came up, and they hastily moved their bed under the wagon for shelter. Just before daylight they were awakened by a commotion among the horses, which had been hobbled out to graze. Suspicious that something was wrong, both men hastily secured their rifles and went to investigate. They arrived just in time to see three men unhobbling the animals, and when the prospectors opened fire the

thieves ran to their own horses, mounted and made
their escape, taking two of Joe's animals that they
had unhobbled. Both had been driven hard the day
before, and were not in condition to travel fast.

Joe and his companion hastily unhobbled the other
two, and, taking only time to put bridles on, they
started in pursuit. The trail of the robbers was
easily followed over the wet ground, and after a few
miles they saw them in the distance; but their own
horses were winded by the hard gait and they were
forced to stop for a short time. As soon as possible
they resumed the pursuit, and reached a small canyon
in time to see the thieves going down the side. Instantly the prospectors opened fire, but on account
of the long range their bullets fell short. However,
the fugitives abandoned the stolen horses, and made
a wild dash across the canyon to a trail that wound
along the opposite side to the rim above. Joe and
Lewis were closer by that time, and after dismount-
ing, opened fire. Joe hit the man in the head, and as
he fell to the trail the riderless horse dashed on to the
top. The second man leaped from his horse, placed
his wounded comrade on his own saddle, and then
mounted behind; but another shot from Joe's rifle
killed him, and as he fell to the ground, the first man
wounded toppled over dead. In the meantime a well
directed shot from Lewis knocked the third outlaw
from his horse.

Crossing the canyon, Joe and Lewis examined the
dead men, and found some letters in their pockets

which gave their names; but these names are not known today. Joe never mentioned them to his wife, nor did he leave any written record of them. In a pocket of the third man was a small prayer book, probably a gift from some mother who vainly waited and watched for many a year for her wandering boy's return; but nothing was found to identify him. California Joe afterward sent this prayer book to his wife at Corvallis, Oregon; and it is now in possession of one of the authors, having been given to him by his grandmother a short time before her death. Yellow with age and gnawed by the teeth of time, it is an interesting relic of days long gone. The back and first seven pages are missing, and so is the title page and the name of the publisher, but the title of *Key to Heaven* and the contents show that it is of the Catholic faith. It contained one hundred and twelve pages, and was originally about an inch and a quarter thick by three and one-quarter inches wide and five and one-quarter inches high.

After recovering their horses, California Joe and Lewis returned to camp, and resumed their journey to Colorado, where they spent the summer prospecting. With a number of other prospectors they remained in the mountains that winter; and as it was impossible to mine by their primitive methods during the intense cold weather, they spent their time hunting. In this way they kept the camp supplied with fresh elk and venison. Lewis was a mountain man with a long experience as a hunter and Indian fighter,

and he was the only man California Joe ever had as a
partner for any length of time. Both were of a restless disposition, and in the spring of 1866 they set out
for New Mexico. Arriving at Santa Fe without incident, they spent some time there enjoying life in the
ancient Spanish capital after their long months in
the wilderness. Finally, tired of an inactive life in
town, they formed a partnership with three other
miners for safety against roving Indians, and set out
on a prospecting tour in what was then known as
the Black Range, in northern New Mexico.

They were warned not to go into that section, as
it was infested with hostile Apaches and several prospectors had been killed there. But they were an adventurous band, and danger was the spice of life to
them. The warning received before leaving Santa
Fe proved well founded, for shortly after they established a camp a few miles from the hamlet of El Vado,
they were attacked by a roving war party. In the
fierce battle that followed Lewis and one other man
were killed, and the others barely escaped with their
lives. In relating the story of the fight, California
Joe told how his suspicions of danger were first
aroused by the nervous actions of the horses grazing
some distance from the camp. Turing to his comrades, he said: "There's something wrong with those
horses; I believe Indians are around, and we're in a
fine fix, with our horses unsaddled and turned loose a
quarter of a mile away."

Picking up his rifle, he started to investigate, but

had only gone a short distance when he caught sight of several Apaches hiding among the rocks. The Indians fired several shots at the white man as soon as they found they had been discovered; but they were shooting at long range and no damage was done. Joe ran back to the camp where he found his comrades with rifles ready for action. Immediately the scout took charge, and after directing the men to take all their ammunition, ordered them to run for some boulders on the flat below, and keep the Indians from capturing their horses. This was accomplished without loss, although bullets kicked up little spurts of dust all around them; and from the shelter of the rocks the miners fought all afternoon. It was a sharp-shooting contest, with the odds in favor of the white men, for they were better shots at long range. Every time a puff of smoke revealed the location of an Indian, a miner's rifle cracked and frequently scored a hit. The number of Apaches killed was never known for they carried their dead away.

California Joe afterwards said that these Apaches were the most cunning warriors he ever encountered in all his years of Indian fighting. They seldom showed themselves. With sagebrush tied to their heads to conceal their movements they would crawl cautiously through the brush and from rock to rock, always getting a little nearer the white men. Then a shot would ring out and a puff of smoke spurt from what appeared to be a harmless clump of sage. Several times two or three Indians attempted to reach the

horses, but were always driven back by the deadly
rifles of the white men. Late in the afternoon George
Lewis was shot through the throat, and died half an
hour later.

When night came with its welcome relief from
the hot sun, the fighting ceased, and the prospectors
prepared to escape from their perilous position; for
they knew that the Apaches would return in larger
numbers at break of day. Gathering their ammunition and what food they could carry in their saddle
bags, they tied sacks around their horses' hoofs to
muffle sound, and silently stole out of camp. Hoping
to throw the enemy off the trail for a few hours they
headed in a direction opposite to that which they had
followed the previous day. All night long they rode,
never stopping to rest until the light of approaching
day appeared in the east. Then Joe climbed to the
top of a high peak to look for signs of pursuit. Presently he discovered a large party of horsemen which
his trained eye told him, even at that great distance,
were Indians, and he hastened to his three comrades
with the warning. Escape was useless, for their horses
were worn by the long night ride; and so they made
such hasty preparations as were possible to defend
their position.

Concealing themselves, they lay in ambush until
the Apaches appeared, and then poured a deadly fire
into their ranks. For a moment all was confusion in
the Indian ranks; but those warriors were too old at
the game of wilderness warfare to be thrown into

much of a panic. Quickly recovering from the surprise of the attack, they scrambled for shelter behind
the rocks; and then it was the old game of sniping
back and forth. All day long the battle raged
fiercely; for the Apaches were determined to avenge
their dead. California Joe detailed one of his comrades to load rifles for him, and he kept two guns hot.
In telling the story afterwards he remarked: "I've
always wondered what those Apaches thought of the
fast shooting I gave them that day; for every time I
shot either an Indian or a horse was hit."

That the Apaches did not close in on them was
largely due to Joe's marksmanship at long range.
Fortunately the prospectors were able to keep their
horses under the protection of their rifles, where the
enemy could not reach them, although several attempts were made to start a stampede. When
darkness closed in the Apaches withdrew, for Indians
never fight at night, and the besieged men had their
first opportunity to secure a little food and water.
They were all seasoned frontiersmen, and they knew
that their only chance of escape was under cover of
the night. Quietly they mounted their horses, and
with California Joe in the lead, managed to get
past the Indian sentinels without detection. Several
hours later they found water for their horses, and
after giving them a short rest resumed their flight.
All night long they rode through the darkness, hiding
their trail as much as possible; and late the next day
they reached Santa Fe, practically exhausted.

SCOUTING ON THE KANSAS BORDER

X

AFTER a few weeks of inaction at Santa Fe, California Joe joined a government supply train bound for the army posts in Kansas. This outfit was under a guard of cavalry of sufficient strength to protect it from roving war parties, and after an uneventful journey it reached Fort Riley, Kansas, in the fall of 1866. General Hancock established Fort Harker shortly after Joe's arrival in Kansas, and he engaged the frontiersman as scout for the Fifteenth Infantry. From that date until 1871, Joe served as civilian scout for troops operating against hostile Indians in Kansas, Indian Territory, and Texas. He remained at Fort Harker until the next spring when he joined General Alfred Sully at Fort Dodge.

It was at Newton, Kansas, then a trail-end cowtown, that California Joe first met James B. Hickok, famous on the Old Frontier as "Wild Bill." When Joe arrived in Newton with a company of soldiers and a supply train, the town was infested with gamblers and border crooks of all kinds and variety.

These human vultures made their living by fleecing
and robbing soldiers, and cowboys just up the trail
from Texas; and few men who drank and gambled
left town with any money. The saloon was the common meeting place in those days, and every plainsman went there as soon as he arrived in town. Drinking and gambling were the principal forms of amusement, and immediately after his arrival Joe followed
the usual custom.

When he awoke the next day with a clear head
he discovered that he had been robbed of several hundred dollars. Going to the saloon where he had played
the previous night he learned from the bartender that
he had lost his money in a crooked poker game. Immediately he went out and gathered several of his
soldier friends. As they returned to the saloon and
entered by a rear door they saw the gambler who had
been running the game standing at the bar; but when
Joe started in his direction he ran out the front door
and down the street, with the scout in pursuit shouting for him to stop. When he threatened to shoot,
the gambler only increased his speed towards his own
camp where he had friends. Realizing that it was
impossible to catch him, Joe drew his six-shooter, and
as he fired five shots in rapid succession the gambler
fell dead. As men poured from every saloon to find
out what had occurred, the scout immediately realized that his victim might have friends who would
take up the fight, and he quickly reloaded. His
fighting blood was up, and, turning on the advancing

crowd with a six-shooter in each hand, he shouted:
"If any of yo' fellows are friends of that dead thief,
just step up an' we'll shoot it out."

Not a man moved as Joe faced them. It was a
wild crowd, ready for anything from a shooting to a
lynching; but no one cared to tempt this enraged
man who could handle his six-shooters with such
deadly accuracy. As he stood there watching every
move of the men before him, Joe saw a tall, good-
looking man with hair that fell below his shoulders,
laughing as if the scene amused him greatly. This increased the scout's anger, and he cried out: "Yo' big
long-hair, if yo' want to laugh at me step out here
and we'll shoot it out."

This challenge only seemed to amuse the stranger
a little more, for he laughed harder than ever as he
turned and walked away with some friends. The
man was Wild Bill Hickok. Both plainsmen had
heard of each other, but they had never met before.

The killing of a man in the trail-end towns in
those days was a matter of only passing interest. When
the excitement over the shooting had quieted down,
Joe returned to the saloon, and while engaged in a
game of cards with some soldier friends a stranger
informed him that Wild Bill would like to see him
in his camp on the edge of town.

"Was that tall long-hair I invited to fight, Wild
Bill?" asked Joe, as he looked up for a second.

"Yes," replied the stranger.

"You tell Wild Bill to go to hell; I'm playing

cards now," was the message the scout ordered delivered.

A couple of hours later Wild Bill entered the saloon, and, walking up to Joe, who was standing at
the bar, invited him to have a drink. Nothing averse
to this friendly overture, the latter accepted, and after a couple of rounds they sat down together. This
was the beginning of a warm friendship that lasted
until Wild Bill's murder in Deadwood, South Dakota,
August 2, 1876. In fact, Hickok was one of the few
plainsmen with whom California Joe ever formed an
intimate and lasting friendship; and during the remainder of Joe's stay in Newton he was constantly
in his new friend's company. Both were six feet two
inches in height, with long, flowing hair that hung
below their shoulders, and belts that held two Colt's
six-shooters; they made a striking and picturesque
appearance together, even in the day when striking
men were the rule in all frontier towns.

Wild Bill invited California Joe to join him and
Charles Utter, famous in western history as "Colorado Charley," in the freighting business; but Joe
declined as he desired to continue as a scout at the
forts on the Kansas frontier, a life of danger that
appealed to him. Wild Bill himself did not remain
long in partnership with Colorado Charley. The life
of an army scout called him, and he soon joined General Penrose as chief of scouts in the campaign against
the Cheyennes, Kiowas, and Arapahoes.

After leaving Newton, California Joe was with

General Sully in several skirmishes with the Kiowas. After one of these engagements he was sent from Fort Dodge with dispatches to Fort Harker, where he again met Wild Bill, and made the acquaintance of the famous plainsman, "Buffalo Bill" Cody, who was serving with General Carr as chief of scouts. Returning to Fort Dodge, Joe again joined the Third Infantry as chief of scouts under General Sully. On August 10, 1868, this command engaged in two desperate battles with Indians on the Cimarron River. In an attack on the advance guard the enemy was repulsed with a loss of two killed, and without casualty to the troops; but in a fight with the rear guard one soldier and ten Indians were killed and twelve were badly wounded.

Two days later the hostiles attempted to stampede the stock by dashing into Sully's camp, but were beaten off after a hot fight. Later in the day a large force attacked the main column, and were repulsed after a battle of several hours. Two soldiers were killed and three wounded; while twelve Indians were reported killed and fifteen wounded. On August 13, General Sully's command was again attacked, but the enemy was routed with a loss of ten killed and twelve wounded. The troops lost one killed and four wounded. California Joe took part in these engagements, and was highly praised by General Sully for bravery under fire.

General Hazen was in need of an experienced scout at Fort Zarah, and after the return of Sully's expedition Joe was transferred to his command. The old records of the Military Division of the Missouri show that scarcely a day passed during August and September that some fight did not take place between troops and Indians on the Kansas frontier. Such was the state of affairs that every supply train had to travel with a strong escort; and on October 2, California Joe went as guide and scout with a detachment sent to guard a train approaching Fort Zarah. Shortly after the departure of these troops one hundred mounted Indians boldly attacked the fort, but were driven off.

The escort with California Joe reached the wagon train without incident; but a short time later the scout, who was well in advance looking for danger, discovered the war party that had just been repulsed at Fort Zarah. Hastening back to the train, he gave orders to corral immediately, but in the excitement the inexperienced drivers were unable to carry out this command before the enemy swooped down upon them. Circling around the train at a fast pace, the red warriors concealed themselves by riding on the off-side of their horses as they fired under their necks. This was the old style of attack; but while the teamsters were green the soldiers were experienced in plains warfare, and saved the train from falling into the hands of the enemy. During the fighting sixteen head of mules belonging to four teams were driven off, and the teamster guarding them was killed.

Following his usual custom in battle, California

Joe killed several warriors at long range, and shot a number of horses. Following several futile attempts to capture the train, the Indians finally withdrew, and attacked a ranch eight miles from the fort, driving off one hundred and sixty head of stock. After the attack was repulsed the train proceeded to Fort Zarah unmolested; and Joe gave General Hazen a report of the fight. Fort Zarah was kept in almost a constant state of seige during the next few weeks. On October 10 eight horses and mules were run off from the herd; and on the 23rd two men who had ventured too far from the protection of the post were killed and scalped. Two Indians were killed in this affair, but the remainder of the band escaped before troops could overtake them.

IN AN EFFORT to break the power of the Southwestern tribes and end the Indian war then ravaging Kansas, Colorado, and Texas, General Sheridan, commander of the department, planned a winter campaign against the hostiles. In the fall the tribes had always retreated to their villages in remote sections, where they were safe from the troops until spring. Fighting Indians when the ground was covered with snow was something unheard of; but Sheridan was determined to make the hostiles feel the power of the government, and in the fall of 1868 he decided to carry the war into the enemy's country in the dead of winter.

It is not easy today to understand the terror that gripped the settlers of the Southwest during that bloody year of 1868. The condition of affairs is best described from the government reports, which show that raids and murder through New Mexico, Colorado, Texas, and Kansas were of frequent occurrence. Matters reached a head early in August when the Cheyennes, Arapahoes, and Sioux swept through the settlements on the Saline River, Kansas, north of Fort

Harker; and scarcely a day passed thereafter that did not see some raid or fight with troops.

S. T. Walkley, acting Indian agent, and P. Mc-Cusker, United States interpreter, reported that in January, 1868, twenty-five persons were killed, nine scalped, and fourteen children captured in northern Texas; but these children were afterwards frozen to death while held in captivity. In February seven more adults were killed in this same locality, fifty horses and mules were stolen, and five children were captured. Two of the latter were surrendered to General Leavenworth and the three remaining were taken to Kansas. One person was killed and three children belonging to a Mr. McElroy were captured; and in July four persons were killed on the Brazos River, in Texas. In nearly all cases horrible barbarities were perpetrated upon the victims.

The government reports state that so boldly had this system of murder and robbery been carried on that in six years no less than eight hundred persons had been murdered, the hostiles escaping from the troops by traveling at night when their trail could not be followed, thus gaining enough time and distance to render pursuit fruitless in most cases. This wholesale marauding was carried on during the season when there was plenty of grass for the Indian ponies; and when winter came on the savages would hide away in remote and isolated places, to live upon their plunder, glory in the scalps taken, and in the debasement of the unfortunate women whom they held prisoners. Many years of these depredations, with perfect immunity to themselves and families, had made the Indians bold.

In planning his winter campaign, General Sheridan directed General Getty, commanding the District of New Mexico, to send out a column from Fort Bascom, New Mexico, under command of Brevet-Lieutenant-Colonel A. W. Evans, of the Third Cavalry. Another under General E. A. Carr, left Fort Lyon, Colorado, while the main expedition, consisting of eleven troops of the Seventh Cavalry, commanded by General George A. Custer, was to go from Fort Dodge. The Nineteenth Kansas Volunteer Cavalry was organized by the people of that state to aid Custer; and several companies of the Third and Fifth Infantry were added to the expedition. General Hazen, in command of Fort Zarah, ordered California Joe to report to Fort Dodge, giving him a warm letter of recommendation to General Sully, and when Custer read this he immediately engaged him as his chief of scouts, with Jack Corbin, another noted plainsman of the period, as his partner.

Established in September, 1864, by General Grenville M. Dodge, in command of a regiment of "Galvanized Yankees" enlisted as Wisconsin Volunteers, Fort Dodge was the farthest outpost of civilization between the Missouri River and New Mexico; and from that time until the close of the Indian wars in 1878 it was the most important army post on the southwestern frontier. Located in the very heart of a hostile land, it was the center of many Indian battles during the next few years. This historic outpost of the Old West was the scene of several important Indian councils; and during the wars a number of famous army officers, among them Hancock, Sheridan, Custer, and Miles, were located here. The first fort was a primitive affair, consisting of dugouts in the river bank surrounded by a stockade.

These were replaced by substantial stone buildings in 1867, all of which are still standing. The old headquarters where Sheridan, Custer, and Miles organized their expeditions is now the home of the superintendent of the Fort Dodge Soldiers' Home, which was established at the old post in 1882 by the State of Kansas when the fort was abandoned by the federal government. Along the old military streets, lined with giant cottonwoods, where the troopers of long ago marched, the Indian fighters of a past generation peacefully stroll in the sunset of life as they await "Taps." All along these same streets such famous plainsmen and scouts as California Joe, Jack Corbin, Wild Bill Hickok, Apache Bill, and a host of others were familiar figures in other days.

When the Nineteenth Kansas Cavalry failed to reach Fort Dodge by November 12, General Sheridan decided not to wait, and on that date the expedition, consisting of eleven troops of the Seventh Cavalry with several companies of the Third and Fifth Infantry, all under command of General Custer, set out for Indian Territory, where it established

Camp Supply, one hundred miles south of Fort
Dodge, as a base of operations. General Sheridan accompanied the column to this point, from which he
directed all operations.

The plan of campaign was to allow the small
column from Fort Bascom to march to the Canadian
River and establish a depot at Monument Creek,
where it was to remain as long as it could be supplied,
or at least until some time in January. This force of
five hundred and sixty-three men, commanded by
Lieutenant-Colonel Evans, consisted of six troops of
cavalry, two companies of infantry, and four mountain howitzers. General Carr with seven troops of
the Fifth Cavalry from Fort Lyon, was to unite with
Captain Penrose's force then in the field, consisting
of one troop of the Seventh and four of the Tenth
Cavalry, and after establishing a depot on the headwaters of the North Canadian, this command was to
operate south towards the Antelope Hills and the
headwaters of the Red River. These columns were
really intended as beaters-in to drive the hostiles towards the main force under Custer, who expected to
strike the Indians on the headwaters of the Washita,
or farther south on the branches of the Red River.
Camp Supply, established as the base of operations
for this expedition, was maintained as a military post
for many years afterwards.

Early in the morning of November 23, 1868,
General Custer left Camp Supply with his famous
Seventh Cavalry on what proved to be one of the

most important campaigns against the hostiles during all the years of Indian warfare in the Southwest. It was a typical winter campaign. A blizzard was raging, with snow a foot deep when the troops left camp; and as "boots and saddles" rang out through the storm, the troopers faced a dreary prospect. So dense was the falling snow that it was not safe for anyone to wander out of sight of the marching column. All view of the surrounding country was cut off, and with no landmaks visible, the Osage guides were compelled to lay their course by instinct. But to the familiar tune of that old marching song, "The Girl I Left Behind Me," the men of the Seventh Cavalry set out in search of the foe.

Custer with compass in hand led the column, and late in the afternoon the first camp was made on Wolf Creek. During the second day they were not hampered by falling snow, for the weather had cleared; but it was bitter cold. Shortly after leaving Camp Supply the trail of a large war party was found, showing that the hostiles were active in spite of the storm. It was learned afterwards that this band had killed the mail carriers between Forts Dodge and Larned, an old hunter near Fort Dodge, and two couriers sent back by General Sheridan with letters.

The expedition reached the Canadian River on the twenty-fifth, and after a conference with Little Beaver and Hard Rope, of the Osages, and California Joe and the white scouts, Custer decided to send a strong force up the valley the next morning to look

for Indian signs. Major Joel H. Elliott was selected
for this important task; and after his departure early
next day, Custer faced the task of getting his troops
across the river.

After a long search California Joe found a safe
ford; but three hours of hard work were required to
get the entire command, including the wagons, across.
Just as Custer was about to give the order to continue the march, a solitary horseman was seen coming from the direction taken by Major Elliott. This
proved to be Jack Corbin, the scout who had accompanied the latter, and he brought news of the discovery of the trail of a large war party about twelve
miles up the river. Elliott had crossed the Canadian
and was in pursuit. Corbin was sent back to Elliott
with orders to follow the trail, while Custer started
with his command in a direction that would overtake
Elliott about dark. The latter was instructed to wait
for the main column. Captain Louis McLane Hamilton, a grandson of Alexander Hamilton, was detailed
to remain with the wagon train; but upon his own request and after he had secured another officer who
was willing to take his place with the wagons, he was
permitted to accompany the column.

All day long the command pushed through the
snow without stopping for rest or refreshments until
the trail was discovered late in the day; and then a
few troopers and scouts were selected to overtake
Elliott. Hour after hour the main column struggled
on, and it was not until long after darkness had fallen

that the command was given to stop for refreshments and rest. The force had been traveling without pause since four o'clock in the morning, and the order was most welcome. At ten o'clock the pursuit was resumed. They were now nearing hostile territory, and two scouts were kept well in advance to guard against a surprise attack. Next came the remainder of the Osage guides and white scouts under California Joe. Silently the troops moved forward. No word was uttered by any man, and the order was given that no matches were to be struck, not even to light a pipe.

At last one of the Osage guides in front stopped and told Custer that he smelled fire. The officers could detect nothing, and they believed that the Indian was afraid, but Custer gave the order to advance more cautiously than ever. Half a mile further they discovered the embers of a fire and the Indian triumphantly announced that he was right. Custer called for volunteers to investigate, and all of the Osages and a few of the white scouts were soon on their way. The Osages returned in a short time with the report that this fire had evidently been kindled by boys from the hostile camp who were herding the horses.

Cautiously the march was resumed, every soldier tense with the excitement of coming battle, Custer in advance with two Osages. When they reached the crest of a hill the barking of a dog betrayed the presence of Indians in the valley below. Hastening back to the column, Custer divided his command of eight

hundred mounted men into four divisions, and made
his plan of battle. It was still four hours before daylight, and the time was spent in surrounding the village. The night was bitterly cold, but no fires could
be lighted, and the men were not even permitted to
stamp their feet to keep warm. The village was in
heavy timber, and the Osage scouts doubted the ability
of the white men to make a successful attack. Disaster loomed as a certainty to them.

While making the rounds of his troops to see that
everything was in readiness for the attack at dawn,
Custer asked California Joe if he thought the hostiles
would fight, and the frontiersman predicted a desperate engagement. Among the scouts under Joe was
the noted Romero, from Fort Dodge, a Mexican who
had spent much of his life among the Indians.

At the first signs of day Custer gathered his men;
and while they were standing ready for the battle
signal, the troopers suddenly saw beyond the crest
of the hill that separated them from the village what
appeared to be a signal rocket shoot up, apparently
from the hostile camp. Slowly and majestically it
rose higher and higher, seeming to increase in size,
while its colors rapidly changed. Custer stated afterwards that in less perilous times they would have regarded it as a beautiful phenomenon; but to their
excited imaginations it appeared as a signal from
either Elliott or Thompson, and they fully believed
that the Indians had discovered them.

The order to advance was quickly given, and the

column moved forward to Custer's greatest Indian victory. The early morning air was bitterly cold, but the men were ordered to remove their overcoats and haversacks so that nothing would hamper their movements. According to the plan of battle Custer's column was to attack at daybreak without waiting to find out if the others were in position. It was their business to be ready. The movements of the horses over the crusted snow made considerable noise; but if the hostiles heard they evidently believed it was their own ponies. The white tepees scattered in irregular order among the trees came into view. The faint columns of smoke ascending from the openings at the top told of the feeble fires kept up during the night as a protection against the intense cold.

Custer led the advance. Immediately behind him was the band, each man with his instrument ready to begin playing at the signal; but just as the general was about to give the long-awaited order a rifle shot rang out sharp and clear from the far side of the village. Quickly turning in his saddle he gave the command to charge. Instantly the band burst into music, and the rollicking notes of *Garry Owen*, the battle tune of the famous Seventh Cavalry, were answered by cheers from the men of the other detachments who were in their places, waiting.

The hostiles were taken compleely by surprise as the white soldiers swept through their village like a hurricane, their carbines and revolvers viciously spitting death on all sides. But the warriors of Black

Kettle's band came from old fighting stock, and
quickly recovering, they seized their rifles and bows
and arrows, and rallied against the invaders. From
behind trees and the river bank, which was nearly
waist high, they made a determined resistance, fighting with desperation and courage. A few minutes
after their first charge the whites were in possession
of the village; but the victory was not yet won, for
the enemy was pouring in a well-directed fire. Major
Benteen's horse was shot through the neck by a four-
teen-year-old boy whom that officer was compelled
to kill to save his own life. After reaching the center
of the village the troops disposed of these scattered
bands, and then moved down the valley; but Custer
soon found it impracticable to dislodge with mounted
men the Indians who had taken cover behind trees
and rocks, and his troopers were ordered to fight on
foot, taking advantage of any shelter possible. Slowly
the enemy was driven from this cover to the river
bank.

When the fighting was at its highest pitch a
trooper saw a squaw kill a white boy with a knife, and
he immediately shot her. This child was Willie Blynn,
who had been captured with his mother, Mrs. Clara
Blynn, in Kansas a few weeks prior to the battle of
the Washita. The soldier was T. P. Lyon, of the
Seventh Cavalry, who is still living in Los Angeles.
The body of Mrs. Blynn was found after Custer's
men captured the village.

Seventeen warriors were found intrenched in a

deep depression in the ground, where they were protected from the fire of the troops except when they raised their heads. All efforts to dislodge them failed with heavy losses to the whites, and they were only silenced by sharpshooters who picked them off as they raised their heads to shoot at the white invaders. This method of fighting was employed against Indians in similar positions; and the bodies of thirty-eight warriors were found after the battle in a deep ravine near the edge of the village. Many of the squaws and children remained inside of the lodges; and after the capture of the village Romero, the Mexican, assembled them, with the assurance that they would suffer no harm.

Alarmed by the fighting, many of the Indian horses had rushed into the village, as was their habit in times of danger, and had been captured. When the battle was at its height California Joe discovered a herd of ponies nearby, and asked for some men to help him bring them in. Custer could not spare a single man at the time, but gave Joe permission to capture them himself if possible. Half an hour later the scout, aided by two squaws whom he had pressed into service, dashed in with three hundred horses.

Some of the early authors, especially J. W. Buel and writers of dime novels of that period, gave Buffalo Bill and Wild Bill the credit of being the principal scouts for Custer on this expedition. As an example of these misleading statements we quote the following from Buel's *Heroes of the Plains*:

"Buffalo Bill and Wild Bill did almost the work of a regiment; braver men never went into action, both fighting as though they were invulnerable. In the fury and rout which followed the first charge, Wild Bill gave chase to Black Kettle, head chief of the Cheyennes, engaged and overtook the fleeing red warrior, stabbing him to death. But the accomplishment of this heroic action would have cost him his own life, had not Buffalo Bill ridden with impetuous daring into the very midst of fully fifty Indians, who had surrounded Wild Bill, intent on either his capture or his death.

"The two daring and intrepid scouts plunged furiously into the midst of the Indians, each with a revolver in either hand, and literally carved their way through the surging mass of redskins, leaving a furrow of dead Indians in their wake. Such fighting, such riding and such marvelous intrepidity combined, were doubtless never equalled.

"If no other exploit than this were credited to the valor of the two Bills, their names would deserve inscription on Fame's enduring monument."

This would be interesting if true; but unfortunately for the glory of these noted plainsmen they were miles away at the time, and neither ever claimed to have been in the fight. On the day of the battle of the Washita, Buffalo Bill was with General Carr's command in Colorado, searching for General Penrose, who had been snowed in with his troops on the Canadian River; and Wild Bill was with the latter.

About the middle of the morning while the fighting was still going on in the village, Custer discovered a band of a hundred Indians in full war regalia intently watching the scene from a nearby hill; and through Romero he learned from a captive squaw that a number of Cheyenne winter villages, almost as large as Black Kettle's camp, were located in the valley, the nearest being only two miles away. She also informed him that many Kiowas, Arapahoes, Comanches, and Apaches were camped along the river. This information warned Custer that he was in a perilous position. At any moment an overwhelming force might sweep down upon his little band, in which case the "Custer massacre" might have occurred eight years earlier. By that time the firing had almost ceased; and, leaving as few men as possible to take care of the scattered warriors who were still fighting, the commander gathered his troops and prepared to repulse an attack which he felt might be made at any moment.

A temporary hospital had been established in the center of the village to care for the wounded; for Custer's casualties had been heavy. Captain Hamilton had been killed early in the fight, and Colonel Barnitz was apparently dying from a wound near the heart. Nothing had been seen of Major Elliott since he rode into the village with his men at daylight that morning. Two other officers had been wounded, and the casualties among the enlisted men had been severe.

Just when their ammunition was running low and the prospect was rather dark, Major Bell, the quartermaster, with a small escort succeeded in eluding the Indians, and dashed into the village with a fresh supply from the train. Almost as soon as he arrived the Indians attacked from all directions, and the fighting was soon raging so fiercely that it was impossible to attack the other villages.

In addition to being burdened with sixty prisoners and his own wounded, Custer had eight hundred and seventy-five captured ponies. These were so wild that it would have been very hard to drive them, and could they have done so successfully this wealth of animals would have been so tempting that the Indians would have followed the retreating troops night and day. There was only one thing to do, and Custer did it with his usual promptness. The village was burned and the horses were all killed to keep them from falling into the hands of the enemy again. The troops had found in Black Kettle's camp eleven hundred and twenty-three buffalo robes which were all burned with the exception of those taken by the soldiers as a protection against the zero weather. The captured property destroyed before starting on the retreat included over five hundred pounds of powder and lead, four thousand arrows and arrow heads, seven hundred pounds of tobacco and dried buffalo meat, and a number of rifles, pistols, bows, saddles, and lariats.

Just as the column was ready to start the retreat,

an old squaw who was Black Kettle's sister asked permission to speak to the great chief of the whites; and time was taken to hear what she might say. She told Custer that her brother had been killed in the very first charge; for it was he who had discovered the advancing enemy, and leaping from his lodge had fired the first shot that had been the signal for Custer to order the charge. Then Black Kettle summoned his warriors with a piercing war whoop, but almost the next instant he fell, riddled by the opening volley of the whites. The squaw also informed the commander that Little Rock, the second chief, and other prominent warriors had been killed in the subsequent fighting. It is interesting to note here that Black Kettle had once been the friend of the whites; but the Sand Creek massacre had turned him into a bitter enemy.

After she had completed her recital the squaw selected a girl of about seventeen, and placing her hand in Custer's the old woman proceeded with a strange ceremony. Not knowing its significance the general stood quietly, for he did not wish to offend his captives; but finally he asked Romero to explain the meaning, and to his astonishment he was informed that he had just been married to the young squaw. Then the white chief with many thanks and expressions of appreciation for the honor declined to accept his new wife.

After driving off the Indians in the last attack, parties were sent out to look for dead and wounded, but no trace could be found of Major Elliott and nineteen enlisted men. One of the scouts finally reported that shortly after the battle started he had seen this officer with several men in pursuit of some warriors who had escaped through the lines. Parties were sent in the direction indicated, but after searching the country for two miles no trace of the missing men was found.

Only an hour of daylight remained, and the Indians were again gathering in force around the command. Custer gave the order to march, and the column moved forward, with colors flying and band playing, in the direction of the other camps down the valley. At a loss to understand this move the enemy silently watched from a nearby hill; but when they saw the troops headed for their villages they were aroused to action. The warriors could not fire upon the column without endangering the lives of the captives, so they hurried down the valley to defend their homes now threatened with destruction.

Custer pushed in this direction until his troops reached the first of the villages deserted after the attack on Black Kettle's camp; and then he executed a strategic movement designed to deceive the enemy. As soon as the darkness sufficed to cover its movements, the column faced about and returned over the way it had come; and about ten o'clock the battle ground was reached again. Continuing, the command marched until two o'clock in the morning when a halt was made until daylight, Colonel West's squadron being sent on to reinforce the guard with the train.

One of the teamsters with the supply train was a man known on the frontier as "Holdout" Johnson. Years later Joe E. Milner spent a winter with him; and as soon as he learned that his companion was a grandson of California Joe, Johnson related many unpublished incidents of the Washita campaign and the Jenny expedition in which he also served as a teamster. Johnson was a young man when he went out with Custer in 1868; and although he was twenty years the junior of California Joe the two became firm friends. Nothing is known of Johnson's life prior to the fall of 1868 when he joined the Washita expedition at Fort Dodge. During the winter he spent with the grandson of his old comrade he would talk by the hour of his experiences on the frontier and the men he had known; but he never mentioned his early life except when intoxicated, when he would say: "I'm A. J. King of Texas." Mr. Milner last saw him at Ely, Nevada, in 1910, broken in health and feeble beyond his years, but with the spirit of the old days still alive in him.

Several incidents of the Washita campaign related by Johnson are worth recording. He drove the lead wagon; and when ammunition was rushed to the troops his team was doubled up, and with six horses he drove to the limit of their endurance under the escort led by Major Bell when that officer dashed through the Indian lines to Custer's men with a fresh supply.

After this slight diversion we return to Custer's command, which had gone into camp at two o'clock in the morning to rest; but the march was resumed at dawn, and continued until two o'clock the next afternoon. During the day the column was harassed by several Indian scouts shooting at long range whenever the opportunity presented itself. Johnson told how one venturesome warrior would ride rapidly towards the troops, shielding himself by clinging to his pony's side, and retreating after firing at close range.

Finally an officer called to California Joe and asked: "Joe, can't you hit that fellow over there? He's having too good a time, shooting at us and doing all kinds of fancy riding."

"Well, he's a long ways off; but I'll try an' get the pony first and him next," replied the scout.

Bringing out two sacks of corn from a wagon, Joe placed them on the ground and then laid down, using them as a rest for his rifle. Waiting until the warrior came within range again, Joe took careful aim and fired. His bullet struck the horse in the shoulder, and as the animal fell its rider pitched to the ground. Leaping to his feet the Indian ran to his horse and attempted to secure the bridle which he evidently prized, for it turned out that it was decorated with the scalps of white victims. He might have escaped if he had not stopped to save this possession so dear to his heart. As he was struggling with his horse California Joe's rifle cracked again, and the warrior pitched forward with a bullet in his hip.

The scout was preparing to shoot again when the officer said: "Joe, that Indian is still alive. If we had him we might make him tell us something of Black Kettle's band."

"I'll go out an' bring him in," Joe replied without a moment's hesitation.

Accompanied by one of the soldiers who volunteered, the scout ran to the wounded Indian, and seizing him by his long hair, dragged him across the snow to the column, while the trooper secured the prized bridle. A crowd of officers and men gathered around the prisoner, but he refused to talk. As California Joe looked curiously at the bridle in his comrades hand he saw something that attracted his attention, and when he examined it he discovered the long, golden scalp lock of a white woman.

In a rage he turned to the prisoner and shouted: "So you've been scalpin' white women, have yo'? Well, I'll just give yo' some o' your own medicine."

Seizing the Indian by the hair, Joe drew his hunting knife, cut off a piece of his scalp, and then handed the knife to the soldiers gathered around, some of whom secured similar souvenirs. When they had completely scalped their victim Joe finished the work by killing him. A scalp for a scalp was the unwritten code of the old frontier.

One of the officers who witnessed California Joe's

long-range shooting on this occasion measured the distance and found that it was six hundred and thirty-five yards. When Custer's attention was called to it he declared that it was one of the longest shots he ever heard of under similar circumstances.

The command halted for a much needed rest in the afternoon of the day following the battle, and Custer wrote a detailed report to General Sheridan waiting at Camp Supply. Carrying this dispatch was a perilous mission, for the bearer must travel through a country infested by Indian scouts. After careful thought, the general decided that California Joe could accomplish this better than any other man in the command.

The prospect of so dangerous a journey did not disturb the scout in the least. Informed that he was at liberty to select as many men as he wished for an escort, Joe replied that he would consult his partner; and when he returned a short time later he told the commander that they had decided that it would be safer to go alone. He explained that two could hide their trail and conceal themselves better than a larger number, and they were willing to take the chance. Few men, even on the frontier of that time when brave men were the rule and not the exception, would have cared to attempt such a journey through a country covered with snow and infested with hostile Indians, without a large escort. After darkness had fallen California Joe and his partner, Jack Corbin, set out on their mission, apparently feeling no more anxiety than they would over an ordinary journey by rail or steamboat.

The dress of the two scouts as described by General Custer is well worth recording. California Joe was attired in a large cavalry overcoat with a cape, and belted around his waist beneath the coat, were a Colt's revolver and hunting knife. He also carried a long breech-loading Springfield rifle. Corbin was similarly attired except that he carried two revolvers and a Sharps carbine. Joe was mounted upon his favorite mule, while Corbin rode a fine gray horse. As Custer shook hands with them Joe's parting words were: "Well, I hope an' trust yo' won't have any scrimmage while I'm gone, because I'd hate mightily now to miss anything of the sort, seein' I've stuck to yo' this far."

The two scouts made their way without incident to Camp Supply, where they delivered the report. After a short rest they were sent back by General Sheridan with dispatches for Custer. Custer's troops reached Wolf Creek by easy marches. The scouts met them near Camp Supply, and delivered the dispatch which was general field orders No. 6, containing the thanks of General Sheridan to Custer and all of the men in his command for their heroism during the hard campaign and the battle of the Washita.

On December 1, when the expedition reached Camp Supply, it must have made an imposing spectacle as it marched in with the Osage guides in the lead, chanting their war-songs, firing their guns and

uttering shrill war-whoops. Next came the white
scouts, with California Joe mounted on his mule, his
ever-present pipe going like a blast furnace. Behind
them were the Indian prisoners. Then came the
troops led by the band playing *Garry Owen,* Custer's
favorite battle tune. In this order the Seventh Cavalry, destined to win everlasting fame under Custer's
leadership in later years on the Little Big Horn,
marched in review before General Sheridan after its
first great Indian victory.

Captain Hamilton's body was borne back on the
retreat from the battlefield, and buried with military
honors at Camp Supply. Colonel Barnitz, who was
seriously wounded, recovered after several weeks.
The Indian losses at the battle of the Washita were
one hundred and three warriors killed; but the number of wounded was never known.

XII

O_N D_{ECEMBER} 7, o n e week after its arrival at Camp Supply, the Seventh Cavalry was again in the saddle, headed for the scene of its recent victory in an effort to learn the fate of Major Elliott and the nineteen men who had disappeared on the morning of the battle. This time General Sheridan accompanied the command, which was reinforced by the Nineteenth Kansas Volunteer Cavalry, commanded by Colonel Samuel J. Crawford, who had resigned as Governor of Kansas to lead this regiment against the hostiles. It had arrived at Camp Supply too late to accompany Custer on the first expedition; but it was with him throughout the subsequent campaign which ended in the capture on Elk Creek of Medicine Arrow's village of the Dog Soldier band of Cheyennes.

California Joe went with the second expedition as scout; and as the column which was now a formidable force marched away, he turned to General Custer and remarked: "I'd just like to see the streaked countenances o' Satanta, Medicine Arrow, Lone Wolf, an' a few others o' them, when they ketch the

fust glimpse o' this outfit. They'll think we're
comin' to spend an evenin' with 'em sure, an' have
brought our knittin' with us. One look'll satisfy 'em
—thar'll be some o' the durndest kickin' over these
plains that ever war hearn tell uv. It's goin' to come
as nigh killin' uv 'em, to start 'em out this time o'
year as if we had an out an' out scrimmage with 'em.
The way I looks at it they have just this preference;
them as don't like bein' shot to death can take their
chances at freezin'."

Nothing of interest occurred during the march,
and early in the day of December 10, the expedition
reached the Washita, where it camped a few miles
below the spot where Black Kettle's village had stood.
With one hundred men under command of Captain
Yates and several from the Kansas regiment, Generals
Sheridan and Custer hastened to the battle ground.
Evidence of the fight was on every hand. Scattered
about they found the frozen bodies of many Indians
killed in the fight; but Black Kettle, Little Rock and
several other head men had been removed by their
people. It was evident that the hasty flight of the hos-
tles from the other villages had prevented the removal of all of the dead from the Washita battle
ground. Some Indian dogs were found in the vicinity, and the soldiers captured several puppies, which
were taken back as mascots. These dogs and their
descendants were kept by the Seventh Cavalry for
several years.

After an examination of the village the search for

Major Elliott was started. No better description of the discovery of the mutilated bodies of the missing men can be found than that in General Custer's official report to General Sheridan, and from this we quote the following:

"After marching a distance of two miles in the direction in which Major Elliott and his little party were last seen, we suddenly came upon the stark, stiff, naked, and horribly mutilated bodies of our dead comrades. No words were needed to tell how desperate had been the struggle before they were finally overpowered. At a short distance from where the bodies lay, could be seen the carcasses of some of the horses of the party, which had probably been killed early in the fight. Seeing the hopelessness of breaking through the line which surrounded them, and which undoubtedly numbered more than one hundred to one, Elliott dismounted his men, tied their horses together, and prepared to sell their lives as dearly as possible. It may not be improper to add that in describing, as far as possible, the details of Elliott's fight, I rely not only upon the critical and personal examination of the ground and attendant circumstances, but am sustained by the statements of Indian chiefs and warriors who witnessed and participated in the fight, and who have since been forced to enter our lines and surrender themselves, under circumstances which will be made to appear in other portions of this report.

"The bodies of Elliott and his little band, with

but a single exception, were found lying within a circle not exceeding twenty yards in diameter. We found them exactly as they fell, except that their barbarous foes had stripped and mutilated the bodies in the most savage manner.

"All of the bodies were carried to camp. The latter was reached after dark. It being the intention to resume the march before daylight the following day, a grave was hastily prepared on a little knoll near our camp, and, with the exception of that of Major Elliott, whose remains were carried with us for interment at Fort Arbuckle, the bodies of the entire party, under the dim light of a few torches held by sorrowing comrades, were consigned to one common resting place. No funeral note sounded to measure their passage to the grave. No volley was fired to tell us a comrade was receiving the last sad rites of burial, that the fresh earth had closed over some of our truest and most daring soldiers.

"Before interment, I caused a complete examination of each body to be made by Dr. Lippincott, chief medical officer of the expedition, with direction to report on the character and number of wounds received by each, as well as to mutilations to which they had been subjected. The following extracts are taken from Dr. Lippincott's report:

"Major Joel H. Elliott, two bullet holes in the head, one in left cheek, right hand cut off, left foot almost cut off . . . deep gash in right groin, deep gashes in calves of both legs, little finger of left hand cut off, and throat cut.

"Sergeant Major Walter Kennedy, bullet hole in right temple, head partly cut off, seventeen bullet holes in back and two in legs.

"Corporal Harry Mercer, Troop E, bullet hole in right axilla, one in region of heart, three in back, eight arrow wounds in back, right ear cut off, head scalped, and skull fractured, deep gashes in both legs, and throat cut.

"Private Thomas Christer. Troop E, bullet hole in head, right foot cut off, bullet hole in abdomen and throat cut.

"Corporal William Carrick, Troop H, bullet hole in right parietal bone, both feet cut off, throat cut, left arm broken.

"Private Eugene Clover, Troop H, head cut off, arrow wound in right side, both legs terribly mutilated.

"Private William Milligan, Troop H, bullet hole in left side of head, deep gashes in right leg . . . left arm deeply gashed, head scalped, and throat cut.

"Corporal James F. Williams, Troop I, bullet hole in back; head and both arms cut off; many and deep gashes in back . . .

"Private Thomas Dooney, Troop I, arrow hole in region of stomach, thorax cut open, head cut off, and right shoulder cut by tomahawk.

"Farrier Thomas Fitzpatrick, Troop M, bullet hole in left parietal bone, head scalped, arm broken . . . throat cut.

"Private John Myres, Troop M, several bullet holes in head, scalped, nineteen bullet holes in body . . . throat cut.

"Private Cal. Sharpe, Troop M, two bullet holes in right side, throat cut, one bullet hole in left side of head, arrow hole in left side . . . left arm broken.

"Unknown, head cut off, body partially destroyed by wolves.

"Unknown, head and right hand cut off . . . three bullet and nine arrow holes in back.

"Unknown, scalped, skull fractured, six bullet and thirteen arrow holes in back, and three bullet holes in chest.

"In addition to the wounds and barbarities reported by Dr. Lippincott, I saw a portion of the stock of a Lancaster rifle protruding from the side of one of the men; the stock had been broken off near the barrel, and the butt of it, probably twelve inches in length, had been driven into the man's side a distance of eight inches. The forest along the banks of the Washita, from the battle ground a distance of twelve miles, was found to have been one continuous Indian village. Black Kettle's band of Cheyennes was above; then came the other hostile tribes camped in the following order: Arapahoes under Little Raven; Kiowas under Satanta and Lone Wolf; the remaining bands of Cheyennes, Comanches, and Apaches. Nothing could exceed the disorder and haste with which these tribes had fled from their camping ground. They had abandoned thousands of lodge poles, some of which were still standing, as when last used. Immense numbers of camp kettles, cooking utensils, coffee mills, axes, and several hundred buffalo robes were found in the abandoned camps adjacent to Black Kettle's village, but which had not been visited before by our troops. By actual examination it was computed that over six hundred lodges had been standing along the Washita during the battle, and within five miles of the battle ground, and it was from these villages, and others still lower down the stream, that the immense number of warriors came who, after our rout and destruction of Black Kettle and his band, surrounded my command and fought until defeated by the Seventh Cavalry about 3. P. M. on the 27th ult. . . . In the deserted camp, lately occupied by Satanta with the Kiowas, my men discovered the bodies of a young white woman and child, the former apparently about twenty-three years of age, the latter probably eighteen months old. They were evidently mother and child, and had not been long in captivity, as the woman still retained several articles of her wardrobe about her person—among other things a pair of cloth gaiters, but little worn, everything indicating that she had been but recently captured, and upon our attacking and routing Black Kettle's camp her captors, fearing she might be recaptured by us and her testimony used against them, had deliberately murdered her and her child in cold blood. The woman had received a shot in the forehead, her scalp had been removed, and her skull horribly crushed. The child also bore numerous marks of violence."

Mrs. Fred Walton, a niece of Major Elliott, is still living near Lyons, Kansas; and an interesting article on the battle of the Washita and her uncle's death appeared in *The Daily Globe*, of Dodge City, Kansas, on March 6, 1930. This was partly reprinted from an interview given by her to the *Lyons News*, and partly taken from a story in the *Oklahoma Magazine* in 1908. Mrs. Walton makes the statement that her mother always accused General Custer with deliberately bringing about Major Elliott's death.

Major Elliott was a native of Centerville, Indiana, and at the outbreak of the Civil War was a student at Earlham College. Like thousands of other adventurous young men in sixty-one he answered his

country's call to the colors by enlisting as a private
in an Indiana cavalry regiment; and before the end
of the rebellion had risen to the rank of captain. Soldier life appealed to him, and during the readjustment
of the army, following Lee's surrender, he received a
commission in the regulars; but his family claimed
that he was never popular with the West Point officers, of whom Custer was one, because of the fact
that he had risen from the volunteer service.

Sarah Elizabeth Elliott, his younger sister, married
M. J. Barr and settled in Kansas after the war. She
was the mother of Mrs. Fred Walton, who says that
Mrs. Barr always charged Custer with abandoning
Elliott to his fate when, many soldiers having heard
the firing of his squad not a quarter of a mile away,
the general made to effort to send him aid. This is an
unwarranted injustice to the memory of a brave man.
No matter what Custer's personal feelings may have
been he was too much of a soldier to abandon a comrade at such a time. The records show that Elliott
and his men were found two miles from the village
instead of a quarter of a mile away, and Custer had
no knowledge whatever of the Major's predicament;
for he had his own hands full with the fighting in the
village. The reports of the battle all show that the
Seventh Cavalry was menaced by an overwhelming
force of Indians, and it is doubtful if Custer could
have reached Elliott, even had he known of his plight.
It is a matter of history that Custer only extricated

himself from a very serious position by his superior
military tactics.

Mrs. Walton relates an interesting sequel that occurred years later when her parents were building a
new house in Sterling, Kansas. One of the workmen
was a half-breed who, as a small boy, had been with
the Indians at the battle of the Washita. He well remembered the massacre of Elliott's men, and he told
the Barr family how the Indians had stripped the
bodies of jewelry and other valuables, even cutting
off fingers to secure rings. He said that two watches
had been taken from Major Elliott's body. This story
recalled an old tradition in the family, that he had
purchased a watch for Mrs. Barr, his little sister, but
had never lived to present it.

CUSTER'S RESCUE OF MRS.
MORGAN AND MISS WHITE
XIII

THE NEXT MORNING the expedition started on the trail of the retreating Indians, which led down the Washita towards Fort Cobb; but it was later discovered that the Arapahoes and Cheyennes had left the valley, going towards the Red River. Custer followed the Kiowas for seven days through an almost impassable country where from two to three hundred men were constantly at work building a road and bridges for the supply train. On the morning of the 17th the Osage scouts, who were always well in advance, galloped back with the news that a party of hostiles were approaching under a flag of truce. With the Osages was a white scout from Fort Cobb, carrying a dispatch from General W. B. Hazen, directing Custer to get in touch with Satanta and other Kiowa chiefs, whom Hazen declared were friendly.

This scout had been accompanied by another man, but had been captured by Satanta, who was then with the Indians bearing the flag of truce. Custer advanced to meet them; and his first act was to

compel the release of this prisoner. Then he ordered
the chiefs to go with him to Fort Cobb with their
villages, meanwhile commanding them to remain
with the troops. A messenger was sent back with
instructions for the villages to follow; but it turned
out afterwards that this Indian carried orders from
the chiefs of their tribe to hasten to the headwaters
of the Red River. The next day application was
made to Custer for permission to send back another
messenger; and this was continued until at least half
of the Indians with the expedition had departed. Custer then divined their scheme, and decided to hold
some of the leaders as hostages; but two were as good
as twenty for this purpose, and he allowed the others
to slip quietly away until only Satanta and Lone Wolf
were left. These two chiefs were taken to Fort Cobb
where they were held prisoners until their followers
should surrender. Satanta and Lone Wolf made many
promises, and the former's son, who was a constant
visitor at the fort, carried messages to the Kiowas but
they failed to come in. Spring was near at hand, and
at last General Sheridan issued an order that unless
the hostiles came in by sundown of the next day the
two chiefs would be hung. This had the desired effect and before the time limit had expired the villages
of both were at the fort.

While Custer had been busy fighting Indians in
Indian Territory, Lieutenant Colonel A. W. Evans
had been operating against the hostiles in western
Texas. From Fort Bascom he marched to the Cana-

dian, and established a depot at Monument Creek, after which he struck off south to the headwaters of the Red River. Striking a trail of Comanches, he followed it until he came up with the enemy on December 25; and in the battle that followed twenty-five Indians were killed, a large number wounded, and their village captured and burned. He then moved to a point twelve miles west of Fort Cobb. Meanwhile General Carr's operations along the Canadian west of the Antelope Hills forced the various bands of Arapahoes and Cheyennes into the eastern edge of the Staked Plains, which was barren of game. This forced a majority of the hostiles under Little Robe, Little Raven, and Yellow Bear to surrender.

During the negotiations General Custer performed one of the bravest feats of his career. Selecting forty men, two officers and a medical officer, and accompanied by Little Robe and Yellow Bear, with California Joe as chief scout, he started in search of the Arapahoes and Cheyennes. It was a daring thing to do, for the hostiles could easily have annihilated his little band. At the end of several days of hard marching a village of Arapahoes was discovered on the left branch of Mulberry Creek, and after a conference the chiefs agreed to return to the Agency, a promise that was kept.

Custer had sent back to Fort Cobb for supplies, and while waiting for them Little Robe started in search of his Cheyennes. The Arapahoes left for the Agency, and Custer had to wait three days before

Colonel Cook arrived under the guidance of California Joe, with the much needed supplies. Before reaching Custer, Cook's party met the returning Arapahoes, and believed that they intended to massacre them. Acting on the advice of California Joe, the little band of whites decided to sell their lives as dearly as possible. Cook remained awake all night, but the prospect of a fight did not trouble Joe in the least, for he slept soundly. As Cook and Joe stood watching the advancing Indians the next morning, the scout asked: "What do yo' think about it now, Colonel?"

"Well, Joe, we must do the best we can. There's no use in running," was the reply.

"You're right," replied the scout. "An Injun'll beat a white man runnin' every time, so I spect our best holt is fitin'; but, Lord a-mercy, look at 'em. Thar ain't enuff uv us to go half round."

When the peaceable intentions of the Arapahoes were discovered the relief of the white men can well be imagined. After the arrival of Colonel Cook with the supplies Custer set out in search of the Cheyennes; but when he crossed the Red River and found no trace of them he decided to turn back, as his animals were nearly famished. Neva, a Blackfoot who had served under General Fremont, was sent with two young Arapahoes in an effort to locate the tribe. Daniel Brewster, a young man who had joined Custer at Fort Dodge, and whose sister, Mrs. Anna Belle Morgan, was believed to be held prisoner by this band,

was given permission to accompany them. Before
Custer reached Fort Cobb, he was overtaken by Neva,
who informed him that they had discovered the trail
of the Cheyenne village about two weeks old; and as
it led straight west into the Staked Plains, the Blackfoot saw the folly of attempting to overtake the
fugitives. He and Brewster returned, but the two
Arapahoes decided to continue in search of the Cheyennes. Brewster had fallen behind, but reached the
camp a few hours after Neva.

The march back to Fort Cobb was resumed, and
the next day a strange incident occurred. A horse
strayed during the night; and when a trooper who
was sent after it failed to return, a searching party
went out to look for him, but no trace of the missing man was found, and the command had to go on
without him. As time passed and nothing was heard
of him, he was given up for dead. Then one day
months later, after the expedition had returned to
Kansas, the missing trooper walked into General Custer's headquarters at Fort Hays, hundreds of miles
from the spot where he had disappeared in northwestern Texas. He explained that after leaving camp
he became bewildered, and was unable to find his way
back. Finally he turned south, and after two months
of solitary wandering reached a military post on the
Red River. From there he returned to his regiment
by crossing the Gulf of Mexico on a ship from Gal-
veston to New Orleans, and then up the Mississippi

and Missouri rivers to the nearest railroad point to Fort Hays.

After the return to camp, which was now located at the present site of Fort Sill, General Sheridan decided to send Custer with the Seventh Regulars and the Nineteenth Kansas Cavalry, a total force of about fifteen hundred men, after the Cheyennes. Colonel Crawford, commander of the volunteers, had returned to Kansas on February 12, 1869, to hasten the pay of his men, and Lieutenant Colonel Horace L. Moore succeeded to the command of the regiment. California Joe accompanied the little army as chief of scouts.

This was one of the most memorable expeditions in the history of Indian warfare in the Southwest. Information in the hands of the military authorities led to the belief that the Cheyennes held two white women prisoners, and every effort was made to secure their release alive. These women were Mrs. Anna Belle Morgan, the sister of David Brewster already mentioned, and Miss Sara C. White, both of whom had been captured the year before on the Kansas frontier. Mrs. Morgan had been torn from her husband while a bride of only a month. No trace of either had ever been found, but it was believed that they were held by this band of Cheyennes.

On March 5, the trail of the fleeing hostiles was discovered leading straight into the bad lands on the borders of the Staked Plains; and then began one of the most remarkable pursuits in all the history of Indian warfare, an exploit recounted around frontier campfires for years to come. For days Custer and his men pushed through a barren land where no white man had ever been before. Their food became so low that the officers divided their scanty supply with the privates, General Custer turning his own personal store over to his men with the remark that he could go without food as long as any of them. With such a commander there was no thought of turning back. A dashing, picturesque fighter, who gloried in all the pomp and triumph of war, a swashbuckler, some called him, Custer never asked his men to do that which he would not do himself; and every soldier who ever served under him was always ready to follow his leader to the death, as many of them did a few years later.

With Custer in the lead, the troopers of the Seventh Cavalry, veterans of many a hard Indian campaign, and the no less gallant Kansas farmer boys, doggedly held to the trail with starvation staring them in the face, as it led them into an unknown, barren land where an Indian could scarcely find enough to eat. It was not a battle they were seeking; they could get that nearer home and without so many hardships; but they were resolved upon the release of the two white women.

Hungry, determined, gaunt to the point of emaciation, they were finally rewarded on March 15, when the Osage scouts discovered Medicine Arrow's village of the Dog Soldier band of the Cheyennes concealed among the bleak sand hills on Elk Creek, a tributary of the North Fork of the Red River. No time was wasted; and the hostile camp, containing two hundred lodges and about a thousand Indians, was soon surrounded; but not before the two white women had been carried into the hills.

Always on the aggressive, Custer boldly entered the village and demanded the captives. It was a daring thing to do; for at the first hostile movement the troopers on the surrounding hills, keyed to the highest pitch, would have swept the camp with a deadly fire, even though their general were in the path of their bullets. When Custer learned that the two women had been spirited away at the first alarm, he promptly seized Medicine Arrow, Big Head, and Dull Knife and without a word rushed them to his own camp. Then he informed their followers that the chiefs would be held as hostages until the prisoners were brought in.

When the troopers found that the white women were not in the camp they were furious, and only their commander's restraining hand prevented a massacre. As time passed and the prisoners did not appear the men became more and more impatient. But Custer knew how to deal with Indians. He waited for three days, and then informed the chiefs in the presence of a delegation from their village that their lives would be forfeited unless the white women were delivered to him by four o'clock the next afternoon. He promised to hang the chiefs from the limb of a

nearby tree at that hour unless they complied with
his terms. There followed a tense period of waiting.
Custer was not certain that the band had not already
murdered the captives; and that the chiefs might be
temporizing in order to gain time while making plans
for escape. If the white women failed to appear on
time and Custer should put his threat into execution
Indian sympathizers in the East would undoubtedly
succeed in having an inquiry made; yet he was determined to hang the chiefs at four the next afternoon unless the white women were delivered.

The chiefs hastily sent a message to their people
and the usual stoicism of the red man vanished as the
declining sun slowly but surely cast the long shadows
of three nooses around their necks. When three
o'clock passed and no sign of the captives was seen,
the chiefs sent for Custer, and one tried to obtain permission to enter the village and hasten the release of
the white women. But Custer was firm, and renewed his promise promptly to hang all three at
exactly four o'clock.

As the sun was slowly sinking towards the distant
hills, a group of mounted figures suddenly appeared
against the sky line two or three miles to the west.
The distance was too great to make out the character
of the riders; but the eyes of the chiefs suddenly
brightened with renewed hope. Their people had not
failed them; for as Custer examined the approaching
group through his field glasses he made out two white
girls mounted on one horse. Brewster begged for

permission to meet them, but Custer refused to allow him to leave camp. The commander explained afterwards that he was afraid that when the young man saw the forlorn condition of his sister he might attempt revenge on some of the Indians.

As the prisoners were Kansas women, Custer deemed it only fitting that they should be received by Kansas soldiers; and so he detailed Lieutenant Colonel Horace L. Moore and Majors William C. Jones and Richard Jenkins, of the Nineteenth Cavalry, to receive them.

That deliverance was one of the most dramatic incidents in all our Indian history. The women were brought nearer, and after they had dismounted their Indian captors rode away. On the hill above was General Custer, who, his enemies have said, would rather charge an Indian village, killing men, women, and children, than accept its peaceable surrender; yet in this case he had stayed his warlike hand for the sake of the lives of two white women, and by that act he forever endeared himself to the people of Kansas. Gathered around the General were his officers and the enlisted men of the Seventh and Nineteenth Cavalries waiting for the captives.

The bleak sand hills were bathed in the rays of the setting sun, and the winding desert stream below turned a brilliant red under the reflected light. As the three officers detailed to receive the two girls advanced to meet them, the silence was suddenly broken by a heartrending cry as young Brewster, who could restrain himself no longer, bounded away to greet his sister. As he dashed past the Kansas officers and clasped the taller of the two girls in his arms, tears coursed down the cheeks of the hardened Indian fighters on the hill above. It was a moment that no man there ever forgot. This act told Custer and the waiting men that their hardships had not been in vain; that the two white women advancing to their lines were Mrs. Morgan and Miss White.

Silently the soldiers awaited their approach. As the captives reached a brook that flowed just beyond the spot where the officers were standing, Custer stepped forward, and with outstretched hand, bade them a hearty welcome. This was the signal for the others, and the next moment officers and men were struggling about them, each eager to grasp them by the hand.

The horror of their captivity had written its story in deep lines of suffering upon their faces. Mrs. Morgan was only twenty-five years of age at that time, and Miss White was just nineteen, but they looked like women of sixty. Both seemed dazed, as if it were hard to comprehend that they were again safe among friends. They were attired in the Indian clothing, which was in no way like the picturesque costume of buckskin and beads generally attributed to squaws. The entire dress of each was made of flour sacks with the printed brand of the mills still visible. Both wore leggings and moccasins, and their hair hung in two long braids down their backs. Before releasing them their captors had added various rude ornaments worn by squaws, such as brass wire bracelets and rings, and strings of colored beads.

"Sister, do take those hateful things off," cried young Brewster, after the greetings were over.

Fortunately Custer had a white woman cook with the expedition. The two women were turned over to her, and in a short time they appeared clad in civilized garments. The story of their year of captivity was one of suffering and abuse. They had been the property of one chief after another, and as each one tired of them he sold them to one of his fellows. During the day they had been compelled to carry heavy burdens; and when the men were not around, the squaws, inflamed by jealousy, beat them with clubs.

After the deliverance of the captives the officers of the Nineteenth Kansas told Custer that they felt that he had made a mistake when he refused to attack the Cheyenne village as soon as it was sighted, and they had felt a little bitter; but they were now frank in saying that the rescue of these two women was more to them than any victory they could have won, if the captives had paid the price with their lives.

James S. Morgan was waiting at Fort Dodge to greet his wife when the expedition arrived there, and Custer relates that the reunion was a most happy one. The Seventh Cavalry had been ordered to Fort Hays, and both women were taken there while arrangements were made to send them to such of their relatives as had survived the Indian raids. As the

Morgans had lost everything, the soldiers made up a
collection of several hundred dollars to be divided
among the two women. Both survived their terrible
experience many years; but Mrs. Morgan eventually
lost her mind as a result of her captivity, and died
in an asylum at Topeka, Kansas, on June 11, 1902.
Miss White married H. C. Brooks, and was still living
a few years ago with her son near Concordia, Kansas.

Survivors of that historic expedition are now
very few. On Memorial Day, 1930, Robert Ralston,
a member of Company D, Nineteenth Kansas Cavalry, was still living at the age of eighty-six years at
the Fort Dodge Soldiers' Home; and his wife, whom
he married sixty years ago, resided there with him.
David L. Spotts, of Company L, Nineteenth Kansas,
lives in Los Angeles; and there are a few others scattered here and there, but the authors have been unable
to learn their names.

Some idea of the condition of affairs which
brought about this winter campaign of 1868 and
1869 may be gained from the government records,
which show that from March 2, 1868, to February
9, 1869, there were officially reported in the Department of the Missouri three hundred and fifty-three
officers, soldiers, and citizens killed, wounded, and
captured by the hostile tribes. The Indian losses during this period were officially reported at three
hundred and nineteen killed, two hundred and eighty-
nine wounded, and fifty-three captured. The number of hostiles who surrendered as a result of the
campaign was about twelve thousand.

After the close of the campaign California Joe accompanied the Seventh Cavalry back to Fort Dodge. It was during this expedition that he first met Captain David L. Payne, afterwards famous on the plains as the "Cimarron Scout." At that time Payne was captain of Company H, of the Nineteenth Kansas Cavalry; and as he was a veteran frontiersman a strong friendship developed between them. It was evidently from this acquaintance that Captain Payne secured the information which he furnished Buel.

California Joe accompanied General Custer to Fort Hays on the Kansas Pacific railroad, and there for the first time in his life saw a train. The plainsman immediately decided to take a trip to Fort Leavenworth, about four hundred miles east; and a few days after he left an officer of the Seventh met in front of the leading hotel in Leavenworth, but what a different California Joe. The changes wrought by a barber and the proprietor of a men's furnishing store were so great that the officer scarcely recognized

Custer's chief of scouts of the previous winter. He was always a commanding figure under any circumstances; but now he attracted considerable attention. The long, curly locks and heavy beard had been neatly trimmed, while the latest style in men's clothing, direct from the East, had replaced the rough garb of the frontier. Joe did not make these changes because he preferred the clothing of civilization; but he wished to create a sensation, and he certainly succeeded. The next day he boarded a train for Fort Hays, well satisfied with the first glimpse of civilization he had had in years.

After his return to Fort Hays, Joe made the acquaintance of that famous scout and plainsman, John B. Omohundro, known over the West as "Texas Jack." He has been dead for nearly half a century and many other "Texas Jacks" have come and gone; but the name of this noted plainsman who was the partner of Buffalo Bill and Wild Bill, still survives throughout the land. He is described as a pleasant man who made friends easily, a man with a smile and a joke for all, but very dangerous when his anger was aroused. During the days California Joe spent at Fort Hays he and Texas Jack became warm friends.

It was while California Joe was at Fort Hays during this period that his old friend Wild Bill Hickok was the peace officer at Hays City, located a short distance away. No character in all western history has been given such a sanguinary reputation. Many of the stories told are pure fiction or are greatly exaggerated; but the fact remains that he was one of the most noted man-killers of the Old West. Much of his reputation was made while marshal of Hays City and Abilene, two of the wildest trail-end towns on the Kansas frontier. The day California Joe went to Hays City to visit his friend he carried his usual equipment of two six-shooters and Bowie knife. Posted along the main street were several signs notifying all men that they must disarm as soon as they entered town, but Joe paid no attention to the notice.

While walking along the street he came face to face with Wild Bill and after a hearty handshake the marshal said: "Joe, you'll have to put your guns away as long as you're in town. I do not allow any weapons carried by anyone if I know it."

Always ready with an answer the scout replied: "Well, Bill, those are good orders to me, but what do you do if you don't know it?"

Well knowing the temperament of his friend, Wild Bill explained that it was the law of the town which he must uphold, and that if they appeared together while Joe was still armed it would create a bad impression, although Bill well knew that Joe would not cause any trouble. Without another word the scout entered a nearby saloon, unbuckled his belt and handed it over to the bartender. Then turning to his friend he said laughingly: "Bill, this is the first time I ever had to surrender without firing a shot; an' I've killed at least a hundred Indians in my lifetime."

California Joe remained in Hays City for several days as Wild Bill's guest. They were constantly together, exchanging stories of the late Indian campaign, in which both had served as scouts, but Joe had seen the most action.

On February 12, 1870, the day Wild Bill killed three soldiers in Paddy Welch's saloon in Hays City, California Joe was at the fort. When the news of the fight was brought in the greatest excitement prevailed, and General Sheridan issued orders for Wild Bill's arrest, dead or alive. After the shooting the marshal knew that his days as an officer at Hays City were over. A friend concealed him from Sheridan's troopers, and when he had recovered from his own wounds so that he could travel, he made his escape from that section. Joe heard the story of this fight from several eye-witnesses. The soldiers were intoxicated, and he always declared that Wild Bill saved his own life only by his superior marksmanship.

When the spring of 1870 came with little prospect of Indian fighting, Joe decided to seek other scenes, and on May 3, he again mounted his mule, and headed toward the setting sun. In Colorado he met a miner named George Wilson, with whom he formed a partnership for a prospecting trip; and they remained together for three years. After hunting gold for two years with some success they heard of a new strike at Pioche, Nevada, and decided to go to the new camp. In Salt Lake City they invested their gold in twelve hundred head of cattle, and with the

aid of several cowboys whom they hired for the trip,
started on the long drive across the desert to Nevada.
When they reached a valuable water-right forty
miles from Pioche, they decided to establish a cattle
ranch; for with the open range for grazing and a
ready market in the new mining camps springing up
in eastern Nevada, the venture promised handsome
profits.

In June, 1873, Mrs. Milner with her second son,
George, came from Corvallis, Oregon, to visit her
husband whom she had not seen for several years; and
when they arrived on the fifth they found Joe waiting to greet them. Pioche was then a wide-open,
roaring camp, where shootings were so frequent that
"a man for breakfast" was the common expression.
The wild life of the camp and the hot Nevada country held little appeal for Mrs. Milner, who had spent
so many years in the mild climate of Oregon, and on
July 10 she left for San Francisco, her husband promising to join her there in the fall.

At that time there were from five to six thousand
people in the country around Pioche, and on July 4,
a big celebration was held at that place. Typical of
the Old West, this was the forerunner of the rodeos
and frontier day exhibitions of the present time. One
of the main events was a shooting match with both
rifle and revolver, open to anyone with a fifty dollar
entrance fee. In addition to the purse the winner
was to receive the title of the best all-around shot in
the West.

Mrs. Milner and her son witnessed this contest; and in later years she told the story many times. Ten men had entered; and it was decided that the order in which they would shoot should be decided by the number each would draw from a hat. California Joe, the first to draw, pulled out number ten, which placed him the last on the list. The targets were made of cloth, tacked on a frame, and set up at distances of one hundred and five hundred yards for rifle shooting; and from fifty to one hundred and fifty yards for a six-shooter. Each man was allowed a certain number of shots at each range, with any caliber or make of rifle or revolver. A record was kept of every shot fired.

Standing beside his wife and child, California Joe watched the other nine. There were some good shots entered that day, but their scores never seemed to worry Joe, for a smile constantly played over his face. When his turn came, he stepped up to the line with a big fifty caliber Sharps rifle, which he had purchased in Denver. His first shot at one hundred yards off-hand was almost dead center, and when he repeated this three times a roar went up from the crowd; but when he hit the bull's-eye twice out of three times at five hundred yards off-hand, the people almost went mad. Then, handing his rifle to his son, he drew his forty-four Colt's six-shooters and gave a rare exhibition of his marvelous skill with these weapons. Such shooting had never been seen before in all the West; and California Joe was declared the champion.

That night he proceeded to celebrate his victory in true frontier style by shooting out all the street lights.

Following his wife's departure for San Francisco, Joe sold his interest in the cattle ranch to his partner and prepared to join her in California; but as he was about to leave Pioche he was employed as a guide for a party of sixty miners who were anxious to go to northern New Mexico, where a new strike had been made. Nothing of importance occurred on the trip, and when Joe had completed his agreement he went to Denver, and then direct to San Francisco. His roving disposition and love of the frontier would never permit Joe to remain long in one place, and after spending several months in California with his wife he again turned his face to the gold camps, while Mrs. Milner returned to their home in Oregon. But this could scarcely be called California Joe's home, for in fifteen years he had spent little time there. His home was wherever night overtook him.

This time he went to a gold camp called Woolsey's Flats, in the Sierra Nevada Mountains of California; and while there he wrote his famous letter to General Custer. As he did not know his old commander's address, Joe directed it in care of the War Department, at Washington, D. C., and from there it was forwarded to General Custer, stationed at Fort Mc-Keen, afterwards known as Fort Abraham Lincoln, in Dakota Territory. This letter, which is typical of the man, follows as he wrote it, without corrections:

Sierra Nevada Mountains, California,
March 16, 1874.

Dear General after my respects to you and Lady i thought
that i tell you that i am still on top of land yit i have been in
the rocky mountains the most of the time sence last I seen you
but i got on the railroad and started west and the first thing I
knew I landed in san Francisco so I could not go any further
except goin by water and salt water at that so i turned back and
headed for the mountains once more resolved never to go rail-
roading no more i drifted up with the tide to sacramento city
and i landed my boat so i took up through town they say thar is
20 thousand people living that but it looks to me like to be 100
thousand counting chinaman and all i cant describe my wolfish
feeling but i think i look just like i did when we was chasing
Buffalo on the cimarone so i struck up through town and i come
to a large fine building crowded with people so i bulged in to
see what was going on and when i got in to the counsil house i
took a look around at the crowd and i seen the most of them
had bald heads so i thought to myself i struck it now that they
are indian peace commissioners so i look to see if i would know
any of them but not one so after while the smartess lookin one
got up and said gentlemen i introduce a bill to have speckle
mountain trout and fish eggs imported to california to be put in
the american Bear and yuba rivers—those rivers is so muddy that
a tadpole could not live in them caused by mining—did any
body ever hear of speckle trout living in muddy water and the
next thing was the game law and that was very near as bad as
the Fish for they aint no game in the country as big as a mawk-
ing bird i heard some fellow behind me ask how long is the
legislature been in session then i dropt on myself it wuzent
indian commissioners after all so i slid out took across chinatown
and they smelt like a kiowa camp in August with plenty of
buffalo meat around—it was gettin late so no place to go not
got a red cent so i happen to think of an old friend back of
town that i knowed 25 years ago so i lit out and sure enough he
was thar just as i left him 25 years ago baching so i got a few
seads i am goin to plant in a few days give my respects to the
7th calvery and except the same yoursly

CALIFORNIA JOE.

When Joe told Custer in this letter that he did not have a red cent he probably intended it as one of his jokes; for Mrs. Milner afterward stated that her husband left San Francisco for Woolsey's Flats with twenty-five hundred dollars in gold dust.

During all the years of California Joe's wanderings he wrote to his wife at Corvallis, Oregon, whenever he had the opportunity; and these letters, which are still preserved by the family, throw much light on his wanderings and adventures. Life at Woolsey's Flats was a little tame after his years of Indian fighting, and he longed for the plains again. Leaving California about the middle of April, the next heard from him was a letter written to his wife from Cheyenne, Wyoming, on May 3, 1874, in which he stated that he was going soon to Laramie, where he expected to engage in the freighting business.

As he needed a helper, Joe made an agreement with one Charles Anderson, whom he met at Cheyenne, by which the latter was to receive one-third of the profits in exchange for his work. Anderson had a partner called "Vic" (his real name was never known); and he requested permission to take him along. Joe did not like the man's appearance; but he agreed to let him accompany them, working for his board.

Joe purchased a six-horse team and large wagon at Cheyenne, and with his companions made two successful freighting trips with government supplies to Fort Carlin. They were in camp a short distance

from Laramie, preparing for a third journey, when
Vic proposed a trip to town for a good time. Anderson volunteered to keep camp. Never for a moment
suspecting that anything was wrong, Joe readily con-
sented; but it developed later that this was part of a
plan by his partners to steal the outfit. Vic was to
get Joe intoxicated and keep him in town until Anderson could sell the horses and wagon. Later that
afternoon while they were making a round of the
saloons, a friend informed Joe that he had heard two
strangers say that they had just bought a six-horse
team and freight wagon from a man named Anderson.

This aroused the scout's suspicions, and, leaving
Vic in a saloon engaged in drinking, he started in
search of Anderson. When he arrived in sight of the
camp Joe saw him sitting on a box in front of the
tent. Anderson's conscience evidently troubled him,
for as soon as he saw Joe he seized a Winchester and
fired five shots at him. The scout was astonished at
his partner's attempt to murder him in cold blood,
but, instant in his course of action, he drew his six-
shooter and rushed for the tent while Anderson was
reloading. The latter started to run, but a shot from
Joe's revolver struck him in the shoulder, knocking
him down.

As he lay in the dust with California Joe towering
over him, Anderson burst into tears and confessed.
The scout hastily returned to Laramie with his partner, and secured medical attention for the latter's

wound, paying for it out of his own pocket. Then he started in search of Vic, but that worthy had disappeared. Joe found the men who had purchased his outfit from Anderson, and after explaining the situation, returned their money; but later he decided he had had enough of freighting, and sold out to the strangers.

This was not the end of the story; for California Joe's kindness in sparing Anderson almost cost him his own life. As soon as the latter recovered he promptly disappeared. Vic had not been seen since the day of the trouble; and Joe forgot both. After disposing of his freighting business the scout spent his time in hunting, an occupation he always enjoyed. One September morning while Joe was riding through a canyon several miles from Laramie, the crack of a rifle broke the silence, and a bullet missed him by only a hair's breadth. He was taken completely by surprise, but quickly threw himself from his horse and ran out of range. Believing that his assailant was a renegade Indian, he decided to investigate.

Keeping under cover he climbed up the side of the canyon from which the shot had been fired, and carefully circled back. Using all his skill and cunning he cautiously searched the brush and timber until he finally discovered two men about four hundred yards away. One was tall and the other short, but he could not tell at that distance whether they were whites or half-breeds. Resting his big Sharps rifle across a fallen tree, he took aim and fired. The big man pitched forward on his face, while the other took to his heels and disappeared in the timber, with the scout in pursuit. Failing to find him at the end of an hour, Joe returned to his victim, and received the surprise of his life, for the dead man was none other than his former partner, Charley Anderson. After this affair California Joe returned to Cheyenne, where he spent the winter.

Cheyenne in those days was a roaring frontier town. Joe cared little for the riotous life that went on day and night in one continuous whirl, and he spent most of his time at Fort D. A. Russell, a few miles away. Much of his life had been spent in the army, and the company of soldiers was congenial to him. It was while at Fort D. A. Russell that he had his first and only fight with soldiers; and fortunately the affair ended without a killing. One afternoon four raw recruits returned from Cheyenne, very much under the influence of the fighting brand of frontier whiskey dispensed at that place. Joe was talking to some teamsters at the time, and did not notice them until they began to make sport of his long hair and general appearance. He took it all in good sport until one seized his hair and attempted to pull out a handful. The scout promptly knocked him down; and the other three made a rush at him. Joe, a powerful man and a good fighter in the rough and tumble method of the frontier, knocked his assailants down as fast as they could scramble to their feet. Finally one ran to the barracks for a gun, and was returning when he was stopped by an officer.

"Do you know who that man is?" the officer asked.

"No, I don't," replied the recruit, somewhat taken back.

"Why, you damned fool, that is California Joe, and he will kill you if you show that gun."

Ordering the soldier to put the weapon away, the officer hastily stopped the fight. Joe and the four soldiers afterwards became good friends, and had many a laugh over the incident.

A joke played on two dance hall girls by California Joe that winter in Cheyenne was the cause of a fight between these women before a crowded house. Kate Shay, a snappy little Irish girl, and Nora Woods were bitter enemies. Both were employed in a dance hall near Allen's Gold Rush saloon, one of the most popular in Cheyenne. A ball was scheduled for a certain Saturday night, and Kate purchased one of the most expensive dresses ever seen in old Cheyenne. She had a double motive; to attract the men, and to arouse the jealousy of Nora Woods; and she boasted among her friends that this new dress would make Nora, her arch enemy, turn green with envy.

Joe decided to have some fun at the expense of both girls. The night before the ball he went to Kate Shay's room while she was at the dance hall, secured the coveted dress and presented it to Nora Woods with his compliments. Nora did not suspect that the

beautiful garment belonged to the other girl and she
thanked Joe very graciously, promising to wear it
the next night.

Kate was wild with rage when she missed her
dress, but she could find no trace of it and was compelled to attend the ball in an old one. The first
sight that greeted her eyes when she entered the hall
was Nora Woods strutting through the crowd, proud
as a peacock, attired in the missing dress. With blazing eyes the little Irish girl rushed across the floor,
and demanded to know how Nora came to be in
possession of the gown. Her rage knew no bounds
when the latter curtly told her to mind her own
business.

Seizing her enemy roughly by the shoulders, Kate
ordered her to take the dress off then and there. She
refused to believe Nora when the latter explained
that it was a present from California Joe; and the
Irish girl immediately attempted to recover her
property by force. Instantly Nora flew at her, and
the battle was on. There were no rules of the game.
The crowd howled with delight, and made room for
them to fight it out to a finish. Like two wildcats
they went at each other, scratching, pulling hair,
biting and slapping. Finally, when they had stripped
each other almost naked the crowd stopped the fight
and declared it a draw.

California Joe and several of his friends who knew
the inside facts were interested spectators. When it
was all over, the former told how he had started the

whole affair. The two girls, with scarcely enough rags clinging to their bodies to conceal their nakedness, looked at each other for a moment, and then burst out laughing as they realized that they had both been victims of a joke. At the scout's suggestion they shook hands and became friends.

XV

Ews of the discovery of gold in the Black Hills country reached Cheyenne late that winter, and on March 3, 1875, California Joe in company with John Hickey, Nelse DeLude, and George Barnes started for the new fields. After an uneventful journey they arrived in the Black Hills and established a permanent camp where Crook City, South Dakota, was afterwards built. They were no sooner settled than Joe found signs of Indians, and, well knowing their fate if discovered by the Sioux, he advised that they leave at once. Hickey and Barnes, inexperienced in Indian fighting, were at first opposed to the idea; but Joe's counsel prevailed and they made ready for flight.

Before they had broken camp, however, a war party of fifteen Sioux suddenly swooped down upon them, shooting and yelling as they came. DeLude fell dead at the first fire and two packhorses were wounded. Joe and his two remaining comrades emptied three saddles, but in spite of this deadly fire the Sioux rode right through the camp. The packhorses galloped off in a wild stampede, scattering the contents of their packs over a wide area, while the three white men escaped by running to their saddle horses tied in a nearby clump of aspen trees. Joe killed two more Indians as the Sioux came yelling down upon the prospectors, and his third shot struck a warrior's rifle with such force that he was knocked from his horse only a few feet away. Leaping to his feet, with his tomahawk in his hand, the Sioux struck at Joe's head; but the scout was a fraction of a second quicker, and with one mighty sweep crushed his enemy's skull with his big Sharps rifle. Hickey and Barnes had not been idle, and three more Indians fell before their guns. The remainder of the band, having had enough of such deadly fighting, quickly withdrew out of range.

Taking advantage of this respite the white men stuffed some food and ammunition into their saddle bags; and, without waiting to bury DeLude, started for the nearest fort. They had no time to lose, for they well knew that the defeated Sioux would soon be on their trail with a much larger party. Before they had gone far Joe discovered that they were being pursued, and presently a party of at least twenty-five Indians came in sight. Then began a thrilling race for life. Employing every ruse and all the cunning of his long experience, the scout finally succeeded in eluding the Indians, and after a long, weary flight he and his comrades rode into Fort Laramie.

The Jenny Geological and Topographical Surveying Expedition was then at Fort Laramie, preparing to explore the Black Hills country. Professor Walter P. Jenny, chief geologist, had a corps of eminent scientists under his direction. This included Mr. Newton, assistant geologist; Mr. Tuttle, astronomer; Dr. V. T. McGillicuddy, engineer and topographical officer; and Mr. Patrick, botanist. The civilian members of the Expedition were limited to sixteen, but this permitted several assistants to the experts, as well as laborers.

By direction of President Grant, General George Crook, commanding the Department of the Platte, ordered a military escort under Lieutenant-Colonel Richard J. Dodge to accompany the expedition. This force, which was ample to cope with any body of Indians, consisted of six companies of three hundred and sixty-three men, selected from the Second and Third Cavalries, and parts of two companies of ninety-one men from the Ninth Infantry, with one twelve-pound howitzer. Four ambulances, sixty-one wagons, and three hundred and ninety-seven mules besides the cavalry horses, were required to transport this little army; while a herd of one hundred and thirty-four beef cattle, with one butcher and three herders, was taken along to supply fresh meat.

The expedition left Fort Laramie on May 25, 1875, and returned to that post on October 13. Among the army officers, besides Lieutenant-Colonel Dodge, were First Lieutenant M. C. Foote, adjutant; First Lieutenant I. F. Trout, acting assistant quar-

termaster and acting assistant commissary; Second
Lieutenant I. G. Burke, topographical officer; As-
sistant Surgeons J. P. Jaquette and J. R. Lame;
Captains A. S. Burt, William Hawley, Samuel Mun-
son, and E. J. Spaulding; First Lieutenants Joseph
Lawson, M. C. Foote, C. T. Hall, and A. D. King;
Second Lieutenants Hayden, J. C. Conte, Charles
Morton, F. W. Kingsbury, J. E. H. Foster, and L. A.
Craig. One guide was also allowed, and when Cali-
fornia Joe rode into Fort Laramie at the end of his
flight from the Black Hills he was employed in this
capacity at a salary of one hundred dollars a month.

Two days before the time set for the departure
Joe disappeared, and as another man who knew the
country could not be secured on such short notice
the Expedition left without him. Colonel Dodge
could not account for this mysterious action, and he
was afraid the scout had met with foul play. Travel
over that unknown country without roads or trails
of any kind was slow work; and it was July 20 before
the column reached the middle fork of Rapid Creek,
where a permanent base was to be established, Colonel Dodge had ridden ahead that day to select the
site for the camp; and when he returned he was
astonished to find California Joe talking to the officers. When the commander demanded an explanation of his guide's strange conduct, the latter replied: "Oh, I just wanted to get here first, and see
where all the gold is that there's so much talk about."
But he admitted in answer to Colonel Dodge's inquiry

as to his success, that he had not found a trace of color. Joe then promised to act as guide for the remainder of the explorations; and he served in this capacity until the Expedition was disbanded at Fort Laramie in the fall. Camp Crook was established July 21 and occupied as a base until August 13; but beyond the search for scientific knowledge of the country, nothing worthy of note occurred while the Expedition remained there. On August 14, the column moved to a new location. In his official report, from which we quote the following, Colonel Dodge paid a high tribute to California Joe's wonderful ability as a guide:

"On August 18, at Camp Terry, I ordered California Joe to remain at headquarters for the time being to assist me in 'hunting road,' which I found in the territory entirely too laborious for one man . . . In descending the mountains from Camp Terry to the westward over a rugged country, it was found necessary to construct a road . . . This road is a marvel of skill and road craft, for which California Joe deserves great credit."

This feat is all the more remarkable when it is known that California Joe had never been in this section before; and it is some of the roughest country in all the West. Harry S. Young, one of the teamsters of the Jenny Expedition, was for several years prior to his death a friend of Joe E. Milner, and he contributed much of interest on California Joe's ability as a guide and scout while with that command, always referring to him as "the great mountaineer and guide in the Black Hills." We can do no better than quote the following from Mr. Young's account of the Jenny Expedition in his book *Hard Knocks*, in which he relates his frontier experiences:

"Our guide on this expedition was California Joe, a very noted man in the West. This man was one of the greatest mountaineers the West ever produced, not excepting Fremont. I will also speak more of this great man later on.

"In due time we arrived at the outskirts of the Black Hills, and made our first permanent camp on French Creek. The town of Custer City is now located there, named in honor of General Custer.

"As mentioned previously, I stated that California Joe was our guide. To give the reader some idea of the task this man was attempting in an unknown country, I will explain that there were one hundred and six mule teams and ten companies of soldiers, part of which were cavalry. The mules and cavalry horses had to have grass and water to subsist on. The men also had to have water, and the commissaries that sustained these men had to be transported with them. Bear in mind that there were no roads in this country, and suitable ground had to be selected by the guide in order that the teams and soldiers could get through. Not once on the whole trip did this man make a mistake, and never one dry camp did we have to make.

"After entering the Black Hills, California Joe

traveled entirely on foot, accompanied by a large
black hound. Wearing an old cavalry overcoat, cavalry pants tucked in his boot tops, his gun in hand,
and on his head an old black, broad-brimmed slouch
hat, he would start out about the break of day, and
before the command was ready to move, Joe would
ascend to a hilltop and with his hands shading his
eyes would scan the country in all directions. He
would then return to camp and report to Colonel
Dodge, telling him the direction he wanted the teams
to travel that day and that at times he would inter-
cept us, if he wanted the route changed. This much
accomplished, California Joe would then fill a buckskin sack with food enough to last for twenty-four
hours for both himself and his dog, carrying the sack
himself.

"We usually followed the ridges, sometimes descending to the river bed, and a few times it would
be necessary to rough-lock with chains the wagon
wheels, and with a rope attached to the hind axle,
then taking a turn with the rope around a tree; in
this way securing the wagon, as otherwise it would
have been impossible to have gotten down to the
river bed. We never, at any time, turned back. Joe
would appear on an average of twice a day to see how
we were getting along.

"I remember one afternoon, after having had a
pretty hard time of it all the morning, Colonel Dodge
stopped the command to rest, when Joe happened to
come along. Being driver of the headquarters wa-

gon, I was always close to Colonel Dodge and his officers, and overheard Dodge ask Joe where we were going to camp that night.

"Joe replied: 'Colonel, do you see those two mountains off to the west? There we will find the headwaters of some river.'

" 'How do you know this, Joe? You say you have never been in here before.'

"All the reply Joe would make was: 'I can tell by the lay of the country.'

"Dodge smiled and said: 'Joe, where is due north and south?'

"Immediately Joe broke off a piece of dry grass and holding it between his thumb and finger, said: 'Colonel, take out your store compass and if this piece is not pointing due north, I will eat my old hat.'

"Sure enough it was. The Colonel looked at Joe a moment, and then said: "Joe, I would follow you through the wilds of Africa.'

" 'Well,' said Joe, shrugging his shoulders, 'I could take you and the outfit through there.'

"To which Dodge replied: 'I believe you.' Then turning to the bugler, he ordered him to blow the march. We then moved on and in three hours we found the headwaters of Red River, and a beautiful spot it was. Surrounding it was a small, open valley, with plenty of grass, and to the astonishment of Professor Jenny, he found timothy hay growing there three feet high. How the seed ever got there was always a mystery."

One of the noted frontier characters with the
Jenny Expedition was Calamity Jane. Her presence
was due to her infatuation for Sergeant Frank Siech-
rist, who smuggled her through in men's clothing.
This was the only military expedition she ever remained with from beginning to end. One story is
that Colonel Dodge, advised of her presence, summoned her to his tent. She admitted her identity, but
was allowed to remain. If this was true it is because the column was too far away from the fort
to send her back. However, some of the survivors
claim that she succeeded in concealing her identity
from the commander to the end. This is a more
plausible explanation.

From a letter written to the authors by Dr.
V. T. McGillycuddy we quote the following with
reference to this strange woman:

"Calamity Jane, who was the daughter of a private soldier named Dalton, was born at Fort Laramie
about 1861. When her father was discharged from
the army he located a ranch on the LaBonte about
forty miles northwest of Laramie, and a year afterwards was killed by a war party of Sioux. His wife,
packing her baby on her back, managed to get back
to Fort Laramie, walking at night, and died the next
day of exhaustion. Jane was then adopted by Sergeant Basset, and given the additional name of Calamity. When we started for the Black Hills, Jane
attached herself to our party, and traveled with us
that season, returning to Fort Laramie in the fall;

and for the remainder of her life became a scout, camp follower, and dance hall girl."

Martha Canary, known over the frontier as "Calamity Jane," was one of the strangest female characters ever produced by the Old West. Living with men, often dressed in male attire for its greater freedom of action and as a disguise to conceal her sex when with some military expedition, she saw and lived all phases of western life, from a dance hall girl and gambler to an Indian fighter and soldier. As a man she could out-swear and out-drink the best of them; and as a woman she quickly degenerated into a dance hall girl, then a camp follower, and finally a common prostitute. And yet, under it all she had traits of character that made the name of Calamity Jane dear to the early settlers of the Black Hills country. Generous to a fault, she would give her last dollar to any man who was broke; for she figured that she could always make more and he could not. Her courage was without question, and during a diphtheria epidemic she entered the cabins of the settlers where she had never been welcomed before, and nursed their children. Later, when the smallpox swept the Black Hills she fearlessly nursed victim after victim, until they were either dead or on the road to recovery; and so it is little wonder that she always found a welcome in the homes of the early pioneers.

Many tales have been told of her life, the most of which are pure fiction due to the fact that she her-

self seldom told the truth. The story in Dr. McGillycuddy's letter is an example, and it was generally
believed as correct in the early days; but later investigations have brought out the fact that there is not
a word of truth in it. She never served as a scout for
Crook, Custer, or any other army officers, as is so
often claimed. In fact, she was not permitted in
camp after her sex was discovered; but the troops
did succeed in smuggling her out in men's clothing.
On one occasion while with a party in the Black Hills
country, her sex was discovered by an officer who saw
her in swimming with a crowd of soldiers. It is just
possible that this was the Jenny Expedition.

According to her own story she was born at
Princeton, Missouri, May 1, 1852, a daughter of Robert and Charlotte Canary. Her father was a farm
boy who had married her mother in a bawdy house
in Ohio to reform her, but never succeeded in making a good job of it. The family emigrated to the
Montana gold fields in 1864; and from that time
until her death forty years later her life was one wild
whirl of drunkenness and prostitution.

While on the Jenny Expedition Calamity Jane
tried to steal California Joe's dog. As soon as he
missed the animal Joe started to search and finally
found it tied to the wheel of a wagon under which
Jane had her bed. The scout knew that unless he did
something rather drastic she might succeed in weaning the dog away from him, and he decided to punish
her in such a manner that she would let his pet alone.

Finding her among the teamsters, he seized her, and before she realized what he intended to do, he stood her on her head and then lifted her up by the feet. After repeating this several times to the great delight of the teamsters and soldiers, he released her with the warning to let his dog alone, a warning which she was careful to obey.

California Joe's rescue of Charley Wiles, a teamster, after he had been tied up to an ambulance wheel, was told on the frontier for many a year afterwards. This occurred during the Jenny Expedition. Standing over six feet, Wiles was a powerful man, and noted as one of the best fist fighters in the West. He was not of a quarrelsome disposition, but was always ready to meet any man who disputed his pugilistic ability.

One morning he had a little trouble with the wagon master of the supply train, and refused to follow out the latter's instructions. The master reported to the officer of the day, who immediately ordered Wiles tied up spread-eagle fashion to the rear wheels of an ambulance. An hour later when the officer returned to release the prisoner, Wiles cursed his superior in typical frontier fashion. The officer immediately retaliated by telling him that as further punishment he would have to remain there until six o'clock that evening; and when Wiles continued his abuse the officer removed his hat, at the same time giving orders that the teamster was to remain bareheaded in the boiling sun.

California Joe, who had been hunting that day, returned to camp about four o'clock with a deer over his shoulder. The instant he saw the teamster he strode up and asked: "Wiles, who tied you up like that and how long have you been there?"

"The officer of the day," was the reply, "and I've been here over six hours."

Without another word Joe drew his knife and freed Wiles. Then he advised him to shoot it out with anyone who tried such a thing again. Hastening to Colonel Dodge, the scout related the incident; but when he told of his own actions the Colonel promptly informed him that he had exceeded his authority. However, Dodge sent for the officer of the day and reprimanded him.

After circling entirely around the Black Hills and penetrating them at several points, the Expedition returned to Fort Laramie, where it was disbanded on October 13.

Joe was immediately selected as guide for a cavalry column to be sent from Fort Laramie to the Red Cloud Agency, Nebraska, where five thousand Sioux were gathered ready to go on the warpath against the miners who were invading their sacred Black Hills in violation of their treaty with the government. Shortly after his arrival at the Red Cloud Agency Joe received a letter from his son, George, which he answered immediately. This letter from the scout, which is now in possession of the Milner family, follows:

Nov. 1, 1875
Red Cloud Agency, Neb.

Dear sons i received your kind letter yestiddy and was glad
to hear from you all i returned from the Black Hills 10 days
ago after having a six months travel through the prettyes
country that i have seen for many days it would take me a
month to described it to you so i give you the outlines in short
as for gold there is good wages from 5 to 25 dollars a day by
good work the mining destrict is 40 miles long by 25 wide
plascer diggings there is some quartz but not developed as yet
for a stock country the world can't beat it some of the creeks
is the best for ranches i ever saw timber and water splendid if
you all want to start in a new country this is about your last
chance i wish you was all here anyway in the spring there will
be a grand rush there in the spring the country not treated yet
so the government is trying to keep the miners out but they
keep going in and the soldiers keep bringing them back the
Indians talk fight but it is all talk there is three companies of
soldiers stationed in the Black Hills to keep miners out it is 100
miles from here there 30 soldiers start from here tomorrow and
i am going up with them i want to make some new locations
because i know where the best pay is my opinion is that the
first man gets on the ground in the spring will hold it you say
that you want to come up i would be more than glad to see you
all you Charley and Eugene aught to come for this is a better
country to make money in than Oregon but wait until i rite
again i will rite in time for you to come and tell you how to
come if the indians dont get me on this trip i saw five thousand
indians yestiddy drawing their rations the happyest days i see
is after deer with my pony gun and dog direct Fort Laramie
W. T. to California Joe your affectionate father.

M. E. MILNER.

On November 2, 1875, California Joe left the Red Cloud Agency as scout and guide for a detachment of thirty soldiers sent to aid Major E. W. Wynkoop in keeping the miners out of the Black Hills until a new treaty could be concluded with the Sioux. This was the same Major Wynkoop who, as commandant of Fort Lyon, Colorado, had first hired Joe as scout and interpreter for that post in 1864, prior to the Sand Creek Massacre. He was now in command of what was known as the Black Hills Rangers, a detachment of troops patrolling that county to enforce the terms of the old treaty that set this land aside for the exclusive use of the Sioux.

The trip gave the scout an opportunity to meet General Custer, his old commander, whom he had not seen since they parted at Fort Hays six years before; for shortly after his arrival at the ranger camp in the Black Hills, Major Wynkoop asked him to carry dispatches to Custer, then stationed at Fort Abraham Lincoln, near the present city of Bismarck,

North Dakota. It was from this post that Custer marched a few months later on the campaign which ended in the death of himself and half of his entire command on the Little Big Horn River, Montana.

It was a long, dangerous journey of seven hundred miles through a country infested by Sioux Indians who at that particular time were keen to add to their already large collection of white scalps. Joe declined the escort of ten men offered by the Major, explaining that he could get through better and make faster time alone. In journeys of this kind California Joe probably excelled any other scout in all the West.

He arrived safely at Fort Lincoln; and Custer, delighted to meet his former scout of the Washita campaign, immediately offered him the position of chief of scouts for the Seventh Cavalry during the coming summer. Service under Custer meant plenty of action, and Joe accepted; for it was a foregone conclusion that the roving bands of hostile Sioux under Sitting Bull, Crazy Horse, and Gall would go on the warpath if the Black Hills should be opened to settlement, as was expected. After a week's visit at Fort Lincoln, Joe went back to Major Wynkoop, promising to return in the spring. Before he left Custer presented him with a large black and tan deerhound.

Shortly after the Rapid Creek fight in April, 1876, Joe returned to Fort Lincoln, only to find that Custer was in Washington as a witness in the Belknap scandal trial. In fact, it was because of his

straightforward testimony on that occasion that the
General incurred the displeasure of President Grant,
who not only demoted him, but relieved him tempo-
rarily of his command, because he had dared to tell
the truth; and it was only at the last minute when
Custer appealed to Grant as a soldier that the President restored him in time to lead the Seventh Cavalry
on his last campaign. When Joe learned that Custer's movements were uncertain, with a possibility
that he might not return to the West, the scout went
back to the Black Hills. It was one thing to scout for
Custer and quite another for some officer he did not
know. He was certain of an exciting time with his
old commander, but that was to be denied him.

We will now return to California Joe's arrival at
Major Wynkoop's camp in November, 1875. At
that time Captain John W. Crawford, famous
throughout the West as "Captain Jack, the Poet
Scout of the Black Hills," was chief of scouts for the
rangers; and during the following winter a warm
friendship developed between these noted frontiersmen. Crawford was one of the best known army
scouts produced by the Indian wars of the seventies.
In speaking of him to his two sons a few months
later, Joe declared that of all the plainsmen he had
met during his long experience Jack Crawford was
the most courteous and gentlemanly; and every man
who knew him held the same opinion.

Joe scouted for Major Wynkoop that winter; but
in the spring filed on three hundred and twenty acres

on Rapid Creek. The present town of Rapid City, South Dakota, a place of some four thousand people, owes its origin to California Joe. He fully intended to start a ranch there; but by the time he had completed his cabin the gold rush to the Black Hills was at its height, and he laid out his land in a townsite, which he named Rapid City. It was shortly after Joe's settlement at Rapid Creek that the miners there were attacked by Indians; and as Captain Jack Crawford took part in this fight we quote the following from his story, *A Camp Fire*:

"About the middle of April, 1876, I received a note from California Joe, who had a fine ranch on Rapid Creek, and was trying to induce newcomers to settle there and build a town to be called Rapid City. The note was written in lead pencil and ran thus:

'Rapid City, April 10, 1876.

'My Dear Jack:—If you can be spared for a week from Custer City, come over and bring Jule and Frank Smith with you. The Reds have been raising merry old Hell, and after wounding a herder and miner named Sherwood, got away with eight head of stock, my old Bally with the rest. There are only ten men of us here all told, and I think if you can come with the two boys we can lay for them at the lower falls and gobble them next time. Answer by bearer if you can't come; and send me fifty rounds of cartridges for the Sharps big fifty. Hoping this will find you with your top-knot still waving,

'I remain as ever your pard.

'Joe.'

"I immediately saw Major Wynkoop, commanding the Rangers, got permission and arrived at Rapid
Creek on the following night with four comrades,
besides myself. After two days and nights watching
at the lower falls, Jule Seminole, one of my scouts, a
Cheyenne, came in at dusk, and informed us that
there were between twenty and thirty Indians
camped at the box elder, about twenty miles away,
that they were coming from the direction of the Big
Cheyenne and would probably move to Rapid during
the night. Jule could almost invariably tell what an
Indian was going to do, if he could only get his eyes
on him, and he was correct in this instance.

"About three o'clock the next morning Joe went
up to his cabin and started a big log fire; also two fires
in different cabins. These cabins were over a mile
from where we were in ambush, while our horses
were all picketed a quarter of a mile down the creek,
which was narrow at its point of entrance from the
prairie, but widened into a beautiful river half a mile
farther.

"Just as day was breaking one of the Indians was
discovered by Frank Smith wading up the creek.
Frank reported to Joe and me, and Joe remarked, 'Let
him go; he will soon signal the others to follow.'

"In fifteen minutes more the shrill bark of a coy-
ote proved Joe's judgment to be correct. Twenty-
three well-armed Indians—Sioux—rode up along the
willow bank in Indian file. There were seventeen of
us, Zeb Swaringer and Ned Baker, two old miners,

having joined us the night before. We had six men on one side, near an opening we knew the Indians would break for on receiving our fire from the opposite side, and farther up.

"When the Indians had got parallel with our main body, we took aim as best we could in the gray of the morning and fired nearly together; then before they recovered gave them another volley, and leaving our cover, followed on foot those who did not stay with us. We were disappointed in their taking the opening, but the boys were in fair range and did good work, killing one, wounding two and unhorsing three others who took to the woods. We got fifteen ponies, our fire never touching horsehair, but emptying several saddles. Out of the twenty-three Indians fifteen escaped. Joe killed three himself with his big Sharps rifle, the last one being nearly five hundred yards away when he fired from a rest on Frank Smith's shoulder. Joe had a piece taken out of his left thigh. Franklin was wounded in the left arm, and the writer (Jack Crawford) slightly scratched near the guard of the right arm. Nobody was seriously hurt, and we had eight scalps to crown our victory.

"But I did not intend when I commenced, to write all these particulars; I merely intended to speak of a campfire story as told by Joe at the campfire on the night following the incident related. The following lines as nearly as I can recollect, tell the story of Joe's courtship and marriage. I must add that Joe was killed at Red Cloud in December of the same year, while acting as Black Hills guide. He was a brave, generous man, and his only fault was liquor."

The story referred to was the poem by Crawford entitled *California Joe*, which has already been given. However, Captain Jack used considerable license in enlarging upon this, for the courtship and marriage as related in the poem are not in keeping with the facts. Crawford is also mistaken in saying that Joe was killed at Red Cloud in December, as will be shown in a subsequent chapter.

One of the miners in the fight at Rapid Creek was Franklin W. Hall, now living in Houlton, Maine, who, with his two brothers, joined the gold rush to the Black Hills in 1876. He became well acquainted with California Joe while at Rapid Creek, and has contributed much valuable information to the authors.

Shortly after this fight California Joe returned to Fort Abraham Lincoln to enter Custer's service, as already related in this chapter. While there he met Charley Reynolds, brother of Maggie Reynolds, the little girl whom he rescued from the Indians years before. Reynolds was delighted to see the scout again and tried to persuade him to await Custer's return. Not long after his arrival at Rapid Creek, Joe was joined by his two sons, George and Charley, from Oregon. In the meantime news of rich strikes throughout the Black Hills reached the little settlement. Most of the men there joined the stampede to Deadwood Gulch, and California Joe's dream of founding a city vanished in a night.

With his son, Charley, he started on a prospecting trip. Finding their provisions were running low, they decided to secure a fresh supply, and on June 20, 1876, arrived in Deadwood, then one of the wildest mining camps in the entire West. Soon after their arrival they entered the famous Sixty-Six Saloon, and one of the first men Joe saw in the crowd in front of the bar was his old friend, Wild Bill Hickok.

Before his death some years ago, Harry S. Young, a bartender in the old Sixty-Six, gave Joe E. Milner some interesting information about this saloon, the most famous resort in Deadwood's early history. Various writers have referred to it as the Number Six, the One Hundred One and the I X L, but the correct name was the Sixty-Six. It was destroyed in the first big fire that swept Deadwood, and the I X L saloon was erected on its ashes, thus giving rise to the mistake in the name of the original.

Mr. Young related the story of the manner in which it received this name. Among the first men in Deadwood was a grizzled frontiersman with long hair and full beard, a picturesque figure that attracted attention even in that picturesque throng of gold-seekers, the majority of whom were young men. Who the veteran was or where he came from no one ever knew. Like many another odd character found in the camps of the Old West, he came in on the high tide of the gold rush, and after his short act on the stage of frontier life drifted out into the unknown. He was an interesting old fellow, well liked by all who knew him. Most of his time was spent in this saloon, and as he seemed to have plenty of money he was popular with the proprietors. One day when he was the center of attraction before the bar, someone asked him his age.

"I'm sixty-six years old," was the reply, "but I can out shin-dig anyone in the saloon, ladies included."

A roar of laughter greeted this, and someone else asked, "What's your name, dad?"

"I was born on the plains, and I never had a name as far as I knows of," was the answer.

From that hour he was known among the miners as "Old Sixty-Six"; and in a short time they fell into the habit of calling the saloon where he was generally found the "Sixty-Six." The building was no different from many others in old Deadwood, except that it was a little larger than most, being sixty-five feet long by forty feet wide and built of logs. In one corner was a strong-room for the storage of liquor; and as it was the safest place in town, the proprietors kept gold dust there for the miners until it could be shipped out. Mr. Young told how Wild Bill, after a night spent at poker, would frequently request Mr. Young to lock him in this strong room so that he could sleep without fear of assassination. When he was ready to come out he would knock three times.

IN COMPANY with Charles Utter, known as "Colorado Charley," Wild Bill had joined the stampede to the Black Hills only a short time before this meeting with California Joe. Some years after the noted gun fighter's death, Calamity Jane claimed to have been his sweetheart during the early Deadwood days, and her story was accepted as truth by writers of a generation ago, but this, like many of her other tales, was invented on the spur of the moment for a drink of whiskey and a little publicity. Wild Bill had been married shortly before going to Deadwood; and, although his wife did not accompany him on his last rush, he had nothing to do with Calamity Jane. She was present as Colorado Charley's companion. Several versions of Wild Bill's last days have been written, and Buel's account seems to be fairly correct. However, details of some interesting events that occurred during the weeks prior to his murder by Jack McCall, were given to the authors by Charles Milner, of Portland, Oregon, son of California Joe, who was with his father during those thrilling days in old Deadwood. After the meeting in the Sixty-Six Saloon on June 20, 1876, Wild Bill invited California Joe and his son to make their headquarters at the camp which he occupied in partnership with Colorado Charley, about two hundred yards down the gulch. Thereafter Wild Bill, California Joe, Colorado Charley, young Charley Milner, and Ed Reece, who dealt faro in the Sixty-Six, were constantly in each other's company. The authors, therefore, present the facts from one who speaks from personal association.

For three score years Wild Bill's wonderful marksmanship has furnished material for countless arguments and stories. Noted plainsmen who knew him at his best have agreed that many men could beat him at a target; but when it came to shooting at a man who was trying his best to kill him, Wild Bill had no equal. The secret of his success, according to Charley Milner, was "on the draw." He was through shooting before his adversary got into action, in spite of the fact that he always gave his opponent the advantage of the first move.

In a shooting match at Cheyenne, Wild Bill was defeated by Frank North, Johnny Owens, and a man named Talbot; and while camped together at Deadwood during that summer of 1876, California Joe beat him almost every day at target shooting with a rifle. Charles Milner set up the tin cans for them. Frequently they would shoot for the drinks. Joe used a fifty caliber Sharps rifle, and Wild Bill a "needle gun"; but both used Colt's revolvers of the frontier pattern. After firing several rounds Joe would always say: "Bill, I can beat you with your own gun." Then they would exchange, and the result was always the same. But Wild Bill was more at home with a six-shooter; and he was the only man who ever defeated California Joe with this weapon.

The day Joe met Wild Bill in the Sixty-Six Saloon Calamity Jane was the victim of another rough joke at the scout's hands. She entered while the two men were talking, and after edging her way through the crowd before the bar, said: "Hello, Joe; don't you want me to dance for you again, standing on my head?"

In relating this incident more than half a century later, Charles Milner said with truth: "This was the only time that any man ever put the fear of the Lord in Calamity Jane's heart; and it was also the only time anybody ever made her dance to the tune of a six-shooter."

Looking at the woman rather scornfully for a moment, California Joe suddenly whipped out one of his revolvers with the command: "Now you dance for this crowd until I tell you to quit."

Calamity Jane's only reply was a mocking laugh.

"Start in and dance," thundered the scout, at the same time firing several bullets very close to her feet. This was too much for even the hardened Calamity to withstand, and she immediately began to shuffle her feet over the floor. Whenever she showed signs of stopping Joe would hasten her movements with another bullet, to the delight of the crowd of miners. After several minutes he suddenly lifted her to the bar where he made her continue her nimble steps, firing a warning shot over her head when she showed signs of quitting. In the end he permitted her to stop, but warned her to keep away from him unless she wanted to dance every time they met.

Early in July the news of Custer's massacre with over half of his command reached Deadwood. Joe was dazed by the catastrophe; but said to his son and several others present: "If I had waited at Fort Lincoln for Custer to return, and gone with him as his chief scout, I don't think such a thing would have happened."

It is interesting to speculate on the result of Custer's campaign with California Joe as his chief of scouts. It is possible that the latter's superior knowledge of Indians and their methods of warfare might have saved the day; and again he might have fallen with his beloved commander.

During a hunting trip early in July, California Joe made another of the long-distance shots for which he was famous. Wild Bill, Colorado Charley, California Joe, and his son, Charley Milner, left Deadwood for a few days' sport in the Black Hills. They had stopped for dinner at noon of the third day, and as California Joe was bending over the camp fire he suddenly said to his son, "Hand me my rifle."

Charley Milner handed the weapon over from the opposite side of the fire. His father took it with one hand and at the same time lifted the pot of boiling coffee from the flames with the other. Then he suddenly snapped the gun to his shoulder and fired. As unconcerned as though nothing had occurred, he turned around and placed the rifle on the ground.

"What did you shoot at, Joe?" asked Wild Bill. "I didn't see a thing."

Pointing towards a bluff some five hundred yards away, California Joe coolly replied: "Take a little stroll up to that bluff, an' yo' can have the feathered Indian I just shot."

His comrades all believed that he was joking. But Wild Bill was still curious, and when he mentioned it again after the meal was over, Joe was so sincere that Wild Bill, Colorado Charley, and Charley Milner proceeded to investigate. Just over the edge of the hill their found the body of an Indian warrior wearing a large war-bonnet, which they brought back as a trophy.

"Why did you shoot him, Joe; he wasn't bothering anyone?" asked Wild Bill upon their return.

"I didn't like the pitch of his war-bonnet," was the laconic reply.

When Bill declared that this was the longest shot he had ever seen on the plains, the scout boasted in his droll, matter-of-fact tone: "I could have cut off a feather from his war-bonnet, an' not even disturbed him, if I'd wanted to."

More than half a century has passed since the killing of Wild Bill in Deadwood; but it was not until long afterwards that the real reason for the murder became known. It was believed at the time that Jack McCall committed the deed while drunk, and for the glory of having killed a man of Wild Bill's reputation. But Charles Milner tells a different story, which is confirmed by other old-timers. According to his testimony Will Bill's assassination was the result of a plot. In support of this we again call the reader's attention to the fact that Mr. Milner and his father were camped with Wild Bill and Colorado Charley, and were on the most intimate terms with them. Therefore he was in a position to know the truth.

The day following their return from the hunting trip just described, Wild Bill was informed by friends that the tough element was plotting to kill him because he was being talked of for town marshal. At that time the toughs and outlaws ran things to suit themselves, robbing and killing without restraint; and law and order were unknown in Deadwood. The manner in which Wild Bill had brought peace to both Hays City and Abilene, Kansas, was known throughout the West, and the law-abiding people of the new camp believed that he was the man to clean up Deadwood.

Wild Bill only laughed at the warning. "There's no one here going to shoot me," he said. "I would not take the marshal's job." It must be remembered in support of this that Bill's last victim had been Jim Williams, his own friend, whom he had shot accidentally during the fight in which he had killed Phil Coe in Abilene. But the rumor persisted to such an extent that it finally affected his iron nerve, which probably accounts for his premonition of death the night before the murder. After a discussion of the possibility of an assassination, Wild Bill, Colorado Charley, and California Joe decided to start without delay on a prospecting trip. In the meantime they kept a sharp watch on all suspicious characters. A day or two later Wild Bill, California Joe, and young Charles Milner were sitting on a bench in the Sixty-Six Saloon, when two tough-looking strangers entered. Apparently the best of friends, they started to quarrel after a few drinks, and suddenly drew their revolvers. With guns ready for action, they continued their verbal battle, hurling epithets angrily back and forth, until suddenly California Joe roared out: "Why in hell don't you shoot?"

The effect was startling, for without another word both men put up their guns and left the saloon. After Bill's murder California Joe expressed the opinion that this pair had faked the quarrel to get the drop on Wild Bill, but that crafty gunman had watched them so closely that they did not have the nerve to chance a shot at him.

According to the plans for the prospecting trip referred to, California Joe and his son left Deadwood with the packhorses on the morning of August 2, Wild Bill and Colorado Charley intending to join them later. The Milners ate lunch at Crook City; but as they were saddling up to resume their journey the big hound given to Joe by General Custer snapped at one of the horses, which promptly kicked the scout in the side, knocking him down and injuring him severely. Charley did everything possible under the circumstances to ease his father's suffering, and then started for Deadwood to secure some liniment.

As he galloped into town he heard a shot; but the discharge of firearms was of frequent occurrence in old Deadwood, and he paid no attention until, when he dismounted a few minutes later, he saw men running from all directions towards the Sixty-Six Saloon. He joined the crowd in front of the building, which had quickly grown to at least a thousand men, for the news that Wild Bill Hickok had just been killed traveled like wildfire. Both doors had been locked to keep out the curious; but when Carl Mann, one of the owners, recognized young Milner he admitted him, for he was known as one of Wild Bill's partners.

The greatest excitement prevailed in the saloon. Young Milner saw the body of Wild Bill lying on the floor where he had slumped when the fatal shot was fired, and sitting in a corner under guard of half a dozen armed men was his murderer, Jack McCall, who had been captured in front of the Sixty-Six just after the shooting.

The murder of Wild Bill in the Sixty-Six Saloon at Deadwood, on August 2, 1876, was the most noted killing of that time and section, due to the fact that the victim had a reputation as a killer which has never been surpassed. No man, no matter how quick on the draw or how certain his aim, had ever faced Wild Bill in a gun fight and lived to tell the story. There were a few others as quick and as deadly, among whom were John Wesley Hardin, of Texas, and Billy the Kid, of New Mexico; but Wild Bill and Hardin never met as enemies, and the Kid did not begin his career until after the noted fighter's death.

Among the legends of old Deadwood one runs to the effect that as Wild Bill and Colorado Charley first rode into camp the former remarked, "I have a hunch that I'll never leave this gulch alive."

That men sometimes have a premonition of approaching death is also borne out by the story still told that on the evening before the murder, Tom Dosier found Wild Bill leaning against the doorway of the Sixty-Six Saloon with a despondent look upon his handsome face, and when asked what was wrong he replied: "I have a presentiment that my time is up and that I'm going to be killed."

Whether all this actually occurred or not cannot be definitely established after the passing of more than half a century; but there is ample evidence in the letter Wild Bill wrote to his wife on the night before his murder, that he was in a melancholy mood. The general tone of this letter indicates that he felt that they might never meet again.

The authors are indebted to the late Harry S. Young, bartender in the old Sixty-Six Saloon when Wild Bill was killed, for details of the murder. For several years prior to Mr. Young's death at Portland, Oregon, on November 12, 1926, Joe E. Milner was personally acquainted with him, and heard his story many times.

Wild Bill's acquaintance with Jack McCall probably began on the night of August 1, when they engaged in a poker game. When Young went on duty the next morning he found them still playing. McCall's sack of dust (gold dust was legal tender in the early mining camps of the West) was behind the bar, and shortly after Young started to work Wild Bill asked him how much was left.

The bartender reported that it contained one hundred and seven dollars' worth, and Bill said to McCall: "You've overplayed yourself by ten dollars."

"All right, I'll make it good next Saturday night," was the reply.

Then as the two men arose from the table McCall said, "I haven't enough money to buy my breakfast."

Bill handed him seventy-five cents and told him that if he was hungry later in the day he would help him out. After a parting drink at the bar McCall left.

About half past one in the afternoon of the same day, Charles Rich, Carl Mann, one of the proprietors of the Sixty-Six Saloon, and Captain Massy, a former riverman, started a three-handed poker game; and when Wild Bill and Colorado Charley came in a little later, Mann invited Bill to make it four-handed. Bill accepted the invitation, but requested Rich, who was sitting with his back to the wall, to give him his seat. As a precaution Wild Bill always sat with his back to a wall so that an enemy could not approach him from the rear; and knowing this habit, Rich arose to give him his seat. But Bill had won from Massy the previous night, and the latter now protested, saying that he wanted Bill opposite him, and that no one was going to shoot him in the back.

"All right, you old grouch, I'll sit here," replied the latter, pulling the stool from under the table; and for the first time in his life Wild Bill Hickok, the master killer, sat down with his back to a door. He was facing the front entrance, but the rear door was behind him.

Some twenty minutes later Massy had his revenge for the game of the night before by beating Bill's king full with four sevens, and winning his stack of chips. Bill then requested Young, who was still on duty, to bring him fifty dollars' worth of checks, and Colorado Charley, who had been sitting a little back from the table watching the game, remarked: "Bill, I'll go and get something to eat."

As Young placed the chips on the table, Bill remarked: "The old duffer (meaning Massy) broke me on the hand." Those were the last words he ever spoke.

The saloon was almost deserted, and the four men were laughing and joking with no thought of death hovering so near. A few minutes before, McCall had entered and walked up to the bar in a careless manner that betrayed no hint of the murder in his heart. He watched the game in progress for a time and then walked across the room. No one paid any attention to his movements, for few knew him or cared about him. When a few feet behind Wild Bill where the latter could not see his movements, McCall suddenly whipped out a Colt's forty-five and fired, at the same time shouting, "Take that." Without waiting to see the effect of his shot he turned and fled, snapping his gun at Young as he dashed out of the door. But his second shot missed fire, and the barkeeper lived to tell the story.

Wild Bill never knew who killed him. As the bullet crashed through his brain at a downward angle he crumpled in his seat and fell lifeless to the floor. The slug passed entirely through his head and wounded Captain Massy in the left wrist. It was all so sudden that the latter did not know who fired; for he leaped to his feet and ran into the street shouting that Wild Bill had shot him. The murdered man never moved after he toppled from his stool. His cards slipped from his fingers, showing a pair of jacks and a pair of eights; and from that day to this jacks and eights have been known in western parlance as "the dead man's hand."

As young Charles Milner entered the Sixty-Six Saloon a few minutes after the murder, Colorado Charley rushed up to him and asked: "Where is Joe? Did he come in with you?"

When the young man explained that his father had been kicked by a horse a few hours before and badly hurt, Utter told the boy to get him into Deadwood as soon as possible. As soon as young Milner secured the liniment he hastened back to his father, and when he related the details of the murder California Joe was wild with rage. Declaring that he would return to Deadwood and avenge his dead comrade he tried desperately to mount his horse, but it was useless. His injury would not permit him to ride, and he was unable to make the journey until the fifth of August.

After Wild Bill's murder his remains were taken to Colorado Charley's campfire where funeral services were held the next afternoon at three o'clock. The first interment was in the old Ingleside burial ground on the mountainside nearby, where the body remained until August 3, 1879, when the growing city of Deadwood made it necessary to remove this frontier graveyard. On that date the coffin was exhumed and buried in Mount Moriah Cemetery, where a large marble monument in the form of a life-sized figure of the murdered man, erected by Colorado Charley and Lewis Shoenfield, is pointed out to this day among the relics of old Deadwood. The first headstone over the grave was carried away piece by piece by relic hunters, and in order to protect the new monument from vandalism it was necessary in 1892 to completely enclose it in a heavy wire cage. Thus passed

Wild Bill Hickok, the most noted gun fighter of the
Old West.

Immediately after the murder, Jack McCall was
captured in the street near the Sixty-Six Saloon, and
placed on trial before a miner's court. His only defense was that Wild Bill had killed his brother, Jack
Strawnhan, a notorious desperado, in Drum's saloon,
at Hays City, Kansas, on October 19, 1869. There
was not a word of truth in this, for McCall had no
brother; and he afterwards admitted that he had
known of Strawnhan because he was in Hays City at
the time the latter was killed by Wild Bill; but he
was acquitted by a miners' jury, and left Deadwood
immediately. It later developed that he had been
hired by the tough element of the camp to commit the
deed for two hundred dollars; and it was broadly
hinted that the jury was bribed. According to one
story it was Timothy Brady and John Varnes who
paid McCall for the killing. The outlaw element was
afraid that the noted gunman would be appointed
marshal of Deadwood.

When California Joe reached Deadwood on August 5, he was met by Colorado Charley, who told him
the particulars of the killing and the farce of a trial
that had freed McCall. As they were standing in
the street talking a young man carrying a Winchester
rifle walked past. Six-shooters were considered perfectly legitimate in old Deadwood and as necessary
as a man's clothing, sometimes more so; but a rifle
was a different matter. Those were exciting times

and feeling had reached a very high pitch during the days following Wild Bill's death. Believing that this young man was one of the gang that had plotted his friend's murder, Joe demanded his reason for carrying such a weapon on the street.

Hot words passed between them, and when the youth told Joe to mind his own business the scout took the rifle from him and threatened to shoot him if he saw him in town again with a gun. Charles Milner, who was with his father at the time, heard this conversation. This young man was Thomas Newcomb, who three months later murdered California Joe at Fort Robinson. Newcomb was from Gervais and Silverton, Oregon; and in 1875 had joined in the rush to Deadwood.

After Wild Bill's murder Colorado Charley took possession of his dead comrade's personal effects; but the slain gun fighter had possessed little of this world's goods. All that he left behind were two forty-five caliber Colt's six-shooters, a needle gun, and the derringer with which he had killed Dave Tutts in the duel at Springfield, Missouri, in 1865. The needle gun and not the Sharps rifle, as has been stated by writers, was buried in the casket with him, and the derringer is now one of the prized possessions of the Business Men's Club of Deadwood. Wild Bill had been presented with many guns by different arms companies for advertising purposes; but he had given these to friends.

When California Joe announced his determination

to follow McCall, Colorado Charley handed him one of Wild Bill's six-shooters, with the remark: "If you can kill him, do it with one of Bill's own guns." The scout accepted the weapon at the same time handing Utter one of his own in exchange.

Joe was still feeling the effects of his injury of a few days before; but in spite of this he left Deadwood on August 6, to find McCall. The trail led direct to Laramie, Wyoming, where he learned that his man had been arrested; but when Joe informed the jailer that he would save the expense of a trial if he could just see the prisoner for half a minue, he was not allowed in the jail, for the authorities well knew his quick temper. Under the belief that his acquittal at Deadwood made him immune from a second arrest, McCall boasted of his deed as soon as he reached Laramie, admitting that Wild Bill had never killed his brother. But the miners' court at Deadwood was not a duly constituted tribunal under the law of the land, and Jaçk McCall was promptly arrested for his crime. As he had no money, General W. H. H. Beadle and Oliver Shannon were appointed to defend him. His trial was started at Yankton on November 27, 1876. Although his attorneys made a hard fight, on the grounds that a man could not be placed in jeopardy of his life twice for the same offense, the court refused to recognize the jurisdiction of the miners' tribunal, and he was found guilty of murder in the first degree. An appeal was taken to the territorial supreme court, but the verdict was affirmed; and on March 1, 1877, McCall was hanged.

XVIII

WHEN California Joe found that the law had claimed Jack McCall for the murder of Wild Bill he went to Cheyenne to secure medical attention for his injury, which was still troubling him; but as soon as he was able to ride he started north in search of General Crook's expedition against the hostiles in the Big Horn Mountain country of Wyoming. The government records show that Moses E. Milner joined Crook's command as scout and interpreter on October 3, 1876, and was discharged at Fort Robinson, Nebraska, October 25, 1876. A story of the manner in which California Joe met Crook's column was told by Buffalo Bill in his later autobiographies, and it has been generally accepted as fact for many years; but like many of Cody's stories it was not correct in any particular. Cody places the date as 1874, two years earlier than the year Crook actually led the Big Hole expedition.

According to Buffalo Bill's account he was guide for Colonel Anson Mills, with a detachment of the Fifth Cavalry, in the Big Horn country, in 1874. His story of this alleged meeting follows:

"One day when we were on the great divide of the Big Horn Mountain, the command had stopped to let the pack train close up. While we were resting there quite a number of officers and myself were talking to Colonel Mills, when we noticed coming from the direction in which we were going a solitary horseman about three miles distant. The colonel asked me if I had any scouts in that direction, and I told him I had not. We naturally supposed it was an Indian. He kept drawing nearer and nearer until we made out it was a white man, and as he came on I recognized him to be California Joe. If California Joe had any other name but few knew it; he was a grizzled trapper and scout of the old regime. He was the best all-around shot on the plains. He was the first man to ride with General Custer into the village of Black Kettle of the Cheyennes, when that chief's band was annihilated in the battle of the Washita in November, 1868, by the United States Cavalry and the Nineteenth Kansas. Joe was murdered in the Black Hills several years ago.

"When he got within hailing distance I sang out, 'Hello, Joe,' and he answered, 'Hello, Bill.'

"I said, 'Where in the world are you going to, out in this country?' (We were then about five hundred miles from civilization.) He said he was just out for a morning's ride. I introduced him to the colonel and the officers, who had heard and read of him; he had been made famous in Custer's *Life on the Plains*. He was a tall man, about six feet and three inches, very thin, nothing but bone and sinew and muscle. He was riding an old cayuse pony, with an old saddle, and a very old bridle, and a pair of elkskin hobbles attached to his saddle, to which hung also a piece of elk meat. He carried an old Hawkins rifle. He had an old shabby army hat on, and a ragged blue army overcoat, a buckskin shirt, and a pair of dilapidated greasy buckskin pants that reached only a little below his knees, having shrunk in the wet; he also wore a pair of old army government boots, with the soles worn off. That was his makeup. I remember the colonel asking him if he had been very successful in life. He pointed to the old cayuse pony, his gun and clothes, and replied, 'This is seventy years' gatherings.' He was of great assistance to me, as he knew the country thoroughly. He was a fine mountain guide, but I could seldom find him when I most needed him, as he was generally back with the column, telling frontier stories and yarns to the soldiers for a chew of tobacco."

California Joe at that time (1876) was forty-seven years of age, and could hardly pass for a man of seventy; and he had not carried a Hawkins rifle, which was of the old muzzleloading type, for many years. His favorite at that time was the Sharps fifty caliber.

Cody relates further that one day they found a grave which Joe said was that of Amos Billings, whom he had helped to bury with a lot of gold many years before. That night the teamsters and soldiers opened the grave in search of the gold, but their only reward was a few bones; and the next day Joe had a good laugh over the incident.

This story of the meeting between Buffalo Bill and California Joe sounds very much like the Cody pressagent production of later years. Buffalo Bill's early autobiography contains no mention of such an incident, and it was only in later years when the press agents of the Wild West show wrote Cody's life and adventures over his name, that this mention of California Joe was made.

In later years Joe E. Milner was personally acquainted with Buffalo Bill, and when he inquired as to the truth of this story and other statements Cody was alleged to have made about California Joe's life, the scout replied that it had been so long ago that he could not remember. It is now a matter of doubt as to whether Buffalo Bill ever took part in many of the thrilling incidents of border life attributed to him by his biographers; and only recently Richard J. Walsh in *The Making of Buffalo Bill* has proven that many of the great showman's adventures on the old frontier actually fell to others.

The manner in which California Joe joined the Crook command in 1876, was related to Joe E. Milner by both Holdout Johnson, who has already been mentioned in connection with the Washita campaign in

1868, and Robert Heckle, famous over the frontier as "Texas Bob,"* who was General Crook's scout and dispatch bearer. Ever since the days of the Washita eight years before, Johnson had followed the frontier, frequently serving as a teamster with some military expedition. We give his version told many years ago to Mr. Milner, and we have every reason to believe that it is correct:

"I had not seen Joe for eight years. Then one morning just as we teamsters and soldiers were getting ready for breakfast, Texas Bob Heckle, a scout and dispatch bearer, came riding into camp, and I was greatly surprised to see my old friend California Joe with him. He appeared to have been injured, and as I greeted him for a few minutes he told me that he had been shot in the left shoulder in a brush with some Indians the day before. He then went with Texas Bob to report to Colonel Mills, who at once ordered him to the care of a surgeon. The wound proved to be only in the flesh and was not dangerous. In two or three days he was ready for scout and guide duty, serving in this capacity with an excellent record until the expedition ended. I saw a great deal of him until we disbanded at Fort Robinson late in October, for he spent most of his time with the teamsters and soldiers when he was not on duty. He was never with-

---

* Texas Bob Heckle died in 1931 at Mesa, Arizona, at the age of eighty-five. The last years of his life were spent as a cattle-raiser, first near Oracle and later at Mesa.

out his big Sharps fifty caliber; it was a part of him even in camp."

With reference to the manner in which Buffalo Bill claims to have met California Joe riding alone through the mountains, Johnson said:

"Buffalo Bill Cody was out with several scouts, and did not know that California Joe was with the command until along about noon of the day Joe came in with Texas Bob. Buffalo Bill first saw Joe down in the teamster's camp, and I happened to be there at the time. It was getting pretty cold at that time of the year (this was October in Wyoming) and Joe, who had been in Cheyenne under a doctor's care, had bought a good supply of winter clothing before he left. I well remember that he wore a very fine, heavy buffalo-hide overcoat; and he was well mounted on a black mare he had purchased in Cheyenne."

California Joe's story of Amos Billings' grave as told by Johnson, differs from Cody's version:

"Joe was popular with everybody in the command; and he was always playing jokes on the teamsters and soldiers. The grave of a prospector or trapper was found one afternoon when we camped; and that night when some of the soldiers and scouts were gathered around the mule-skinners' campfire, Joe winked at one of the teamsters, and then told about the grave, for the benefit of the soldiers.

"He declared that a few years before he and several other men had been on a successful prospecting trip in that country. Each one had secured ten thousand dollars in gold dust, and as they were coming out one of the party died. They had buried him in the grave we had found that evening; but as none of the others would have the dead man's gold they buried it with him.

"Nothing more was said, but after everybody had gone to bed, Joe and two other teamsters and myself crawled out and watched the grave. Presently five soldiers crept out with picks and shovels, and for hours they dug in that grave, but all they ever found were some bones. Joe afterwards told the joke to the officers. Cody knew nothing of the grave or what had occurred that night until he heard Joe tell the story."

Johnson declared that while Buffalo Bill was with the Crook command he was always bragging about his own exploits. California Joe would quietly listen with a smile, but one day he remarked to Johnson: "I wonder if Cody ever killed an Indian in all his life. I don't think he ever did. He talks too much."

Both of the authors were personally acquainted with Texas Bob Heckle. He was one of the first Texas cowboys to go north with a trail herd, after which he rode the cattle ranges from Montana to Mexico, and in 1875, '76 and '77 served as a scout and dispatch bearer with the regular army operating against the hostile Indians in the Northwest. After spending over seventy years in the saddle, drifting here and there with the vanishing frontier, always searching for some spot just beyond civilization's last outpost, he settled in the Salt River Valley, in Arizona. His story of the manner in which California Joe joined Crook's expedition follows:

"One morning just at sun-up, as I was nearing the command, which was between the Powder River and Fort Reno, I heard several shots in the direction in which I was going. I was carrying dispatches from Fort Reno at the time. There were many roving Indians in that vicinity, and I at once prepared for trouble. Keeping a sharp lookout I soon saw a lone horseman about three-quarters of a mile away. He seemed to be in trouble of some kind, for he was trying to tie a buffalo overcoat behind his saddle. As soon as I was within hailing distance I called to him to wait until I came up and I would help him.

"When I rode up and asked him his name and inquired about the firing I had heard, he told me that he was known as California Joe, but that his real name was Mose Milner. He informed me that he had killed an Indian a short time before but that four others had escaped. He had been shot in the left shoulder in the scrimmage, but did not believe the wound was serious. I tied his coat on his saddle, and he accompanied me to the command, which we reached about two hours later.

"As soon as Colonel Mills learned that my companion was the noted California Joe, he hired him as a scout and interpreter. His wound was dressed by the surgeon, and in a short time he was ready for duty. During the days that followed I was in California Joe's company most of the time when I was not carrying dispatches. He was a good story teller and good company, and we all liked him. Later, while we were on the way to Fort Fetterman during the month of October, California Joe and myself with a few other men were ordered to flank the train of some two hundred wagons.

"That was the last time I ever rode with California Joe, as I was ordered to accompany a detachment of soldiers sent to Medicine Bow to look for deserters. After I left Joe at Fort Fetterman he was assigned to the command of Colonel Ranald S. Mackenzie, of the Fourth Cavalry. On the night of October 22, Mackenzie surrounded Red Cloud's and Red Leaf's bands. The Indians, numbering about four hundred warriors, were taken completely by surprise, and the next morning surrendered without firing a shot. They were disarmed and with their families and all camp equipment were taken to the agency.

"After holding a council with Spotted Tail, General Crook was satisfied that this chief intended to remain loyal to the government, and he placed him in charge of all the Indians at both the Red Cloud and Spotted Tail Agencies, thus deposing Red Cloud whose followers had shown anything but peaceable intentions. These Indians were the same who had killed a large part of the garrison of Fort Phil Kearny

in 1866, and who had in 1874 threatened to massacre
the people of the Red Cloud Agency because they had
attempted to hoist the United States flag."

During the brief period California Joe served
with Crook's command he became intimately acquainted with Baptiste Garnier and Frank Gruard,
two noted scouts of the Indian wars in the Northwest. Garnier was known in the army as "Little
Bat" to distinguish him from Baptiste Pourier, another scout, who was called "Big Bat." After the
close of hostilities he was granted a pension of one
hundred dollars a month, upon recommendation of
General Crook. This man, who gave the best years
of his life in the service of advancing civilization, was
murdered in the later nineties in a saloon at Crawford, Nebraska, by James Haguewood, the bartender,
and was buried in the post cemetery at Fort Robinson,
where he still sleeps a few feet from the grave of
California Joe. Little Bat's services for the white man
during the Indian wars was entirely forgotten, and
his murderer was acquitted, despite the fact that he
was guilty of a cold-blooded killing. Garnier, the
son of a French trapper and a Sioux squaw, was
looked upon as only an Indian, while his murderer
was a white man. The color of the skin was a decid-
ing influence whenever the question of right and
wrong was left to a white jury.

Frank Gruard was one of the most noted scouts
in the United States Army during the Indian wars in

the Northwest. Captain John G. Bourke in his book, *On the Border With Crook,* thus describes him:

"Frank Gruard, a native of the Sandwich Islands, was for some years a mail rider in northern Montana and was there captured by the forces of Crazy Horse; his dark skin and general appearance gave his captors the impression that he was a native Indian, whom they had recaptured from the whites; consequently they did not kill him, but kept him a prisoner until he could recover what they believed to be his native tongue, the Sioux. Frank remained for several years in the household of the great chief, Crazy Horse, whom he knew very well, as well as his medicine man, the since renowned Sitting Bull. Gruard was one of the most remarkable woodsmen I have ever met; no Indian could surpass him in his intimate acquaintance with all that pertained to the topography, animal life, and other particulars of the great region between the head of the Piney, the first affluent of the Powder on the west, up to and beyond the Yellowstone on the north; no question could be asked him that he could not answer at once. His bravery and fidelity were never questioned; he never flinched under fire and never growled at privation."

In recognition of his services to the army General Crook recommended at the close of the Indian wars that Gruard be given a pension of one hundred and fifty dollars a month for life.

With the close of the
Big Horn Expedition California Joe's days on earth
were few indeed. It was certainly a strange trick of
fate that this man, who had braved the dangers and
hardships of the wild western wilderness from the
time of the old fur traders and trappers down through
the years of Indian warfare and gold rushes, should at
last fall before the bullet of an assassin. No man in
all the West ever faced death oftener or knew the
mountains and plains better than he. His fame as an
army scout was not surpassed by any other man of
his time; and today his name is a legend throughout
the Western land.

After the close of the Big Horn Expedition, Colonel Ranald S. Mackenzie was ordered to prepare for
a winter campaign against the Cheyennes under Chief
Dull Knife; and California Joe was engaged as scout
and guide. This is known in history as the Powder
River Expedition. On October 25 Joe was paid off
at Fort Robinson, Nebraska, for his services with
General Crook, and ordered to join Colonel Macken-

zie's column which was to leave Fort Fetterman, Wyoming, on November 15. Following the custom of frontiersmen of that time, who always enjoyed a few days of recreation at the nearest saloon after a hard campaign, Joe and several other men went to Red Cloud Agency, a few miles from Fort Robinson, on October 26. After a few drinks with some friends they entered the commissary building, where a number of Indians (some say about a dozen) were sitting on a bench against the wall. The weather was very cold, and the warriors were enjoying the warmth from the large stove in the center of the room.

The whisky had had its effect on Joe, and the instant he saw the Indians, who had been disarmed a few days before, he shouted, "I'll show you how you killed Custer."

Seizing a pine limb from the wood box, he struck one after another, knocking them to the floor before they could recover from the surprise of the sudden attack. As they scrambled to their feet and made a dash for the door with Joe at their heels, swinging the heavy club, he knocked the stove pipe down.

When the Indians finally escaped, their assailant turned back to find two young bucks lying unconscious on the floor. Without a word he picked them up and threw them bodily into the snow. Then with the help of the other men he replaced the stove pipe.

California Joe never would have been guilty of such a rash act had he not been under the influence of liquor; and only the prompt action and coolness of the officers in command at the Agency prevented an outbreak, for the Indians immediately prepared to avenge this unwarranted assault. Although the warriors had been disarmed, serious trouble might have resulted, for they had concealed a number of rifles and side arms; but when the Sioux saw the troops assembled, ready for action before they could make any plans, the counsel of cooler heads prevailed and they dispersed without trouble.

Fort Robinson, the scene of the last act in California Joe's adventurous life, was one of the most historic army posts in the old Northwest. Established in 1874 on the White River, in what is now Dawes County, Nebraska, it was named in honor of Lieutenant Levi H. Robinson, of the Fourteenth Infantry, who, with Corporal Coleman, was killed by Indians on February 9, 1874, while in charge of the lumber train returning from the government sawmill near Laramie Peak, Wyoming. This was the beginning of a series of depredations by Indians from the Red Cloud and Spotted Tail Agencies, located one hundred and twenty and one hundred and fifty miles respectively northeast of Fort Laramie; and on account of their distance from an army post it was considered advisable to build a fort near at hand.

No army post in all the Northwest played a more important part in the conquest of the once powerful Sioux and their allies, the Northern Cheyennes. From the day it was first established under the guns of Red Cloud's and Crazy Horse's warriors, down through the Indian wars of the seventies and eighties to the outbreak of 1890, which forever broke the power of the Sioux, Fort Robinson was the center of exciting events. Close at hand General Crook surrounded Red Cloud's and Spotted Tail's warriors and compelled them to return to the reservation after they had been disarmed without the loss of a man on either side. And it was from Fort Robinson that Colonel Ranald S. Mackenzie departed one chill October day in 1876 on the winter campaign which resulted in the destruction of Dull Knife's village on the Crazy Woman Fork of the Powder River. As the troops marched away from the post that day they paid a last tribute to the memory of California Joe, who was to have accompanied them as chief of scouts.

It was at old Fort Robinson that Crazy Horse, the young war chief of the Ogallala Sioux, was killed by soldiers September 7, 1877, while resisting an attempt to place him in the guardhouse after he had been arrested. Crazy Horse was the most warlike and skillful general the Sioux nation ever had, and with his death armed opposition to the white race collapsed. His body was carried away by his warriors and buried in secret; and to this day the location of his grave remains unknown.

Again in 1879, Fort Robinson was the scene of the massacre of Dull Knife's Northern Cheyennes, when they made a desperate effort to escape after learning that they were to be returned as prisoners to a strange land where many had already left their bones. After their defeat by Colonel Mackenzie on November 25, 1876, and their subsequent surrender, the Northern Cheyennes were removed to Oklahoma, where they were held as prisoners under military guard; but many of them died in this strange climate, and the survivors longed to return to their old home. Finally, on the night of September 9, 1878, a band led by Dull Knife, Wild Hog, and Little Wolf broke away from Fort Reno and started on the long flight back to their native hills in South Dakota.

There followed one of the most remarkable pursuits in the history of Indian warfare. Only the retreat of Chief Joseph with his Nez Perces the year before surpassed this feat of the Northern Cheyennes. With hundreds of troops, cowboys, and settlers closing in on them, this little band of homesick Indians fled across Kansas and Nebraska, eluding every attempt at capture, and slipping through every trap set for them, until they were finally surrounded in the sandhills of northwestern Nebraska on October 23, by Captain J. B. Johnson, with Troops B and D, Third Cavalry. One hundred and forty-nine, including Dull Knife, Old Crow, and Wild Hog, surrendered, but the remainder escaped under Little Wolf's leadership.

The prisoners were conducted to Fort Robinson, and driven to desperation when they learned they were to be taken back to Oklahoma, refused absolutely to move. Their fuel and food were cut off in an effort to bring them to terms; and on the night of

January 9, 1879, they attempted to escape. Twenty-
eight were shot down as they broke from their prison;
and the next day the remnants of the band were surrounded in Hat Creek Basin, where most of them
were slaughtered by troops. Thus another Indian
problem was settled by the white man in his own way.

Its past glories departed, Fort Robinson's useful-
ness as a military post ceased with the end of the Indian wars and the passing of the frontier in the early
nineties. It is now used as a remounting station for
cavalrymen.

Several versions of California Joe's tragic death
have been published during the past half-century,
none of which are correct; and for the first time we
give the true account. Buffalo Bill and even Captain
Jack Crawford placed it at the Red Cloud Agency,
while Buel declared he was shot from ambush by an
unknown assassin sitting in front of his cabin at
Red Cloud. His two sons, Charles and George Milner, who were in the Black Hills at the time, did
not hear of their father's murder until three weeks
later, and it was many years before they learned the
truth. Indeed, not until Joe E. Milner first met
Holdout Johnson at Sheridan, Wyoming, in 1902,
and heard the story from him, did the family know
the facts. Johnson was at Fort Robinson at the time,
and witnessed the shooting. In corroboration of his
testimony we present a letter written by Dr. V. T.
McGillycuddy to Joe E. Milner under date of April
8, 1927. Dr. McGillycuddy, who is still living at

Berkeley, California, was also at Fort Robinson at that time, and from his account, which coincides with Johnson's, the authors are able to give for the first time the true story of California Joe's murder.

After the affair with the Indians in the commissary at Red Cloud Agency, Joe returned to Fort Robinson on the evening of October 28, and spent the night with Holdout Johnson. It will be remembered that they had been friends since the Washita campaign in 1868, in which Johnson served as a teamster, and they were together the greater part of the next day, talking over their experiences with Custer. Neither had been drinking, as the seriousness of Joe's conduct while under the influence of liquor at Red Cloud three days before was still fresh in his mind. Consequently he was on his good behavior; for he was not yet certain just how the military authorities would regard his attempt to avenge Custer, and he wished to accompany Mackenzie as a scout. About two o'clock in the afternoon Joe decided that one drink would not hurt him. He and Johnson went to the sutler's store, and while they were standing at the bar with a number of other men, Tom Newcomb entered. The instant he saw the scout he drew his six-shooter, for the memory of their last meeting in Deadwood three months before was still fresh. It will be remembered that at that time Joe had disarmed Newcomb and threatened to shoot him the next time he saw him carrying a rifle on the street.

Dr. McGillycuddy throws light on the mystery

by giving what is probably the real reason for the bad feeling between California Joe and Newcomb. It seems that Joe had accused the latter of circulating a story that he, Joe, had killed John Richard, a squaw man, the previous winter, and naturally Newcomb was afraid of the scout. This was no doubt the real cause for Joe's action when he met the former on the street in Deadwood the previous August. Dr. McGillycuddy's letter to Mr. Milner, which gives the details of the meeting in the sutler's store, the subsequent murder, and the reason for the enmity between the two men, follows:

Hotel Claremont,
Berkeley, California,
April 8, 1927.

Mr. Joe E. Milner,
Portland, Oregon.

My dear Mr. Milner:—

Gen. Geo. Crook's command, to which I was attached as surgeon of the Second and Third U. S. Cavalry, and California Joe as scout, arrived at Ft. Robinson, Nebraska, late in October, 1876, for the purpose of disbanding and going into winter quarters after the long and arduous summer expedition, or campaign against the hostile Sioux, which practically ended in the Custer Massacre, and the retreat of the hostiles into British America.

In the later afternoon of October the 29th, on entering the Post Trader's, I observed California Joe lined up at the bar with a number of men drinking, and while they were doing so, an employe of the post butcher shop, Tom Newcomb by name, entered. There had been bad feeling between himself and Joe for some time, and on observing Joe he drew his gun. California Joe turning around and observing him, did likewise, which naturally resulted in the crowd scattering; but Joe finally called out, "Put up your dam' gun, Tom, and come up and have a drink," which Newcomb did, and shook hands with Joe. A short time afterwards I left the trader's accompanied by Joe, who was on his way to the Quartermaster's corral. Enroute I stopped off at the hospital, Joe remarking on the good times ahead of him, as was to leave the next morning as scout with the Fourth Cavalry under command of General Ranald Mackenzie for the winter expedition to round up the scattered bands of marauding Sioux and Cheyennes who were raiding in the Big Horn country.

Half an hour later while sitting on the porch of the hospital I heard a shot in the vicinity of the Quartermaster's corral, and shortly afterwards a private rushed up with the information that Joe was shot; and proceeding to the corral I found Joe dead, lying on his back on the ground on a lower bench below the corral, a ball having passed through his chest from the rear. I ordered the remains taken to the hospital for a post-mortem examination.

It appears that Joe was talking to three or four men with his back to the corral, when Newcomb suddenly came around the corner from a point about a hundred feet away, with a Winchester rifle, and called, "Look out, boys." They scattered, but before Joe could turn, Newcomb fired. Joe threw up his hands saying, "What is it?" whirled around and dropped to the ground.

Newcomb was arrested and put in the guardhouse, and the nearest civil authorities four hundred miles away were notified to come and get the prisoner; but they not appearing at the end of four days, we had to under the law, turn him loose; and there being no frontier town near by there was no one to lynch him. So he went free; and I heard of him about twelve years ago at Gardner, Montana, where he was acting as a guide for eastern hunting parties.

At the post-mortem that night I found letters in his clothes showing that his true name was Joseph or Moses Milner, of Kentucky; and under that name I buried him the next day on the banks of the White River.

The bad feeling between Joe and Newcomb had its origin as follows: The previous winter Joe had come down to the Red Cloud Agency from the Black Hills, and he and John Richard, a French squaw man, had gone into camp on the Niobrara River, south of the Agency, in Nebraska. They had considerable liquor, and the camp was visited a good deal by Indians and half-breeds. After a time Joe returned to the Black Hills. Some time after, Richard was murdered and his body found in the camp, moccasin tracks in the fresh snow indicating that he was killed by Indians; but a report was circulated, for which Joe held Newcomb responsible, that he, Joe, was responsible for the murder; hence the bad feeling.

When the Fourth Cavalry under Mackenzie marched past the hospital next morning on the winter expedition Joe was laid out in his coffin on the porch with the flag draped over him.

I saw much of Joe as a scout on the previous expedition (the Jenny Expedition), and I question if he had his equal as a scout in natural ability, reliability, and wide experience over the frontier.

V. T. McGillycuddy.

Holdout Johnson's story corroborates Dr. McGillycuddy. We give it in detail as related to Mr. Milner:

"We had both been drinking together (in the sutler's), and as we were talking in walked Tom Newcomb. Just as he saw California Joe he pulled his forty-four Colt's revolver out of his holster. Joe, seeing this, made a fast draw and covered Newcomb. Why California Joe did not fire and kill Newcomb has always remained a mystery in my mind, as he had him covered. About an hour later that error cost him his life. When this gunplay took place the large crowd naturally got out of the way, and I done the same.

"When California Joe had Newsomb covered he said: 'Tom, put up that damned gun and come and have a drink.'

"When Newcomb came up they both shook hands and had several drinks together, and talked about half an hour. The conversation was mostly about the murder of John Richard, the squaw man, and it seems their bad feeling towards one another was all settled in a peaceful way, for just as Newcomb was about to leave he shook hands again with Joe, and said, 'Now, Joe, everything is all right.'

"I noticed particularly Newcomb's actions, and I will say he was partly under the influence of liquor at the time. A few minutes after Newcomb left, Joe went out in company with Dr. McGillycuddy. That was the last time I saw him alive; for in about half an hour he was shot in the back and instantly killed by Newcomb, who had watched to get the drop on him.

"Newcomb sneaked up to the quartermaster's corral with a Winchester, and, taking a rest on a wagon wheel, shot a man who, a short time before, had spared his life and shook hands with him. There were several attempts to lynch Newcomb; but the cool-headed officers of the post told the crowd the law would have to take its course.

"At the time of his murder, California Joe was not attached to any command. This made him a civilian, and his murderer must be tried by the state courts. The next day Joe would have been attached to Mackenzie's command as a scout, and if the murder had been committed then, the military authorities could have tried Newcomb.

"Holt County, a couple of hundred miles east of the fort, was the nearest point of state law, and the sheriff there was properly notified by Major Jordan, of the Ninth Infantry, the post commander; but the officers were delayed by a terrific blizzard, and did not reach the fort in time to secure the prisoner. You see, according to the law at that time, the military authorities were compelled to release Newcomb after holding him several days, four I think, if the sheriff did not come for him. Well knowing the feeling against the prisoner, the officers released Newcomb secretly, for they did not wish to run the risk of receiving a reprimand from the War Department which was certain to follow a lynching."

Thus ends Holdout Johnson's story. After his release Newcomb went to Deadwood; but when he openly boasted of his crime he was imprisoned in the log jail and held fourteen days, while an effort was made to locate Charles and George Milner so that they could secure the warrant from Holt County and have him taken there for trial. The brothers could not be found for more than three weeks; but as soon as they heard of their father's murder they hastened to Deadwood. In the meantime the excitement had died down, and Newcomb had again been released; but this time he had disappeared completely. Winter was at hand, and as travel was difficult at that season, the brothers remained in the Black Hills until the trails were open in the spring when they set out in search of their father's murderer, but no trace of him was ever found.

California Joe's long association with the army entitled him to a military funeral; and he was buried with all honors at the post cemetery at Fort Robinson. In that long-neglected graveyard he has slept peacefully for more than half a century. In that barren spot on the lonely prairies of western Nebraska are many graves of soldiers and civilians who gave their lives in the Indian wars, forgotten by the country they served so well.

Concealed amid the tangle of briers and weeds is the grave of California Joe, marked by one of the granite headstones furnished by the United States Government for its soldiers, and upon it is this simple inscription:

MOSES MILNER
SCOUT

That is all; nothing to tell the stranger that one of the men who gave the best years of his life and the best that was in him in the fight to make the West safe for civilization today peacefully sleeps the years away in this forgotten corner, awaiting the end of time. Perhaps he would have it so; perhaps it is best thus; but surely the West owes him a more pretentious monument and a more fitting resting place.

CUSTER'S LAST FIGHT

COLONEL WM. H. C. BOWEN

Colonel Bowen was stationed at Fort Buford when Sitting Bull and the remnants of his band (one hundred and eighty-seven in number) returned from Canada and surrendered at that post. In describing Sitting Bull's appearance at that time, Colonel Bowen said: "He did not appear to be a well man, showing in his face and figure the ravages of the worry and hunger he had gone through. He was getting old. Since the sixties he had been the hero of his race. Giving in to the hated whites and the final surrender of his cherished independence was a hard blow to his pride, and he took it hard. He was much broken."

CUSTER'S LAST FIGHT

By Colonel Wm. H. C. Bowen, United States
Army, Retired

J UNE 25, 1926, marked
the fiftieth anniversary of a most sanguinary Indian
battle, the so-called Custer Massacre. In this fight
some twenty officers and two hundred and forty-five
enlisted men and scouts of the United States Army
were killed. Moreover the commanding officer with
all of the men under his personal command went
down to death, not one man escaping to give the details of the fight.

George A. Custer had graduated from West Point
in 1861, shortly after the outbreak of the Civil War,
and rapidly rose in rank during the following four
years until in 1865 at the end of the war he had
reached the rank of Major General of Volunteers. At
the reorganization of the regular army in 1871 he
was made a Lieutenant Colonel and assigned to duty
with the Seventh Cavalry, organizing the regiment
and commanding it. He saw much duty in Kansas
and Indian Territory, against hostile Indians, and in
Kentucky and Louisiana during reconstruction times,
and in 1873 was transferred with his regiment for

duty at posts on the Missouri River at and below Bismarck, Dakota Territory.

For a decade there had been ever-increasing trouble between the Indians of the plains and the settlers. Treaty after treaty was made by representatives of the government and alleged legal representatives of the Indians, but many of the tribes claimed that their chiefs or head-men had no authority to sign away their rights, in other words their lands; that these lands belonged to the tribes; and that if they were to be sold or given away, each and every male member of the tribe of warrior-age must be present and transfer his individual right to his "undivided" portion of the terrain. These Indians claimed that each tribe was pure democracy, not a republic, and that their chiefs were elected or appointed for other purposes than to make "treaties" of any kind or nature with tribes or nations. And, again, the experiences of the Indians had proved to them that, no matter what the white man promised, as soon as he desired any portion of the land of the red men, that portion was taken, as witness two notable occasions: The one in Georgia during the "reign" of Andrew Jackson, and the second the taking of the lands of the Nez Perces in Idaho in 1877, against the desires of the tribe. Both cases led to Indian wars.

In 1866 Forts Phil Kearny and C. F. Smith were established in Wyoming and Montana to guard the roads leading to the mining regions of Western Montana. In 1866 occurred the massacre at the former station, known in history as the Fetterman Massacre, where the commanding officer of the troops, Captain Fetterman, Eighteenth Infantry, and some eighty officers and enlisted men were killed. This affair led to the abandonment of the two forts. Another "treaty" was made, in which it was promised that the lands in controversy were to be "forever" Indian lands.

One of the regions covered by this "treaty" was the section known as the Black Hills in Dakota. In 1874, gold was discovered in this section by Custer and his command, who had been sent there on an exploring expedition. After his official report, which was soon made public, hundreds of white adventurers and prospectors flocked into these hills, for what will keep a white man from *gold*? Of course the answer is obvious.

The best-known leader of the hostile bands of Indians in Dakota and Montana was Sitting Bull, or Ta-tan-Ka-I-yo-tanka, in the Sioux language. Sitting Bull had always been a "hostile." He never visited an agency and never received supplies directly from the Indian Bureau. His personal following was some sixty lodges, possibly numbering a total of three hundred persons, warriors, squaws, and children. But he had a reputation as a great medicine man, and the discontented from all the region about visited his camp, bringing presents and asking advice. Now a medicine man not only ministers to the sick and ailing in body, but he also ministers to the soul. Thus as

the years passed Sitting Bull's fame grew, and he drew
to himself the discontented of all the Sioux tribes, as
well as those from the Northern Cheyennes, and other
tribes, with leaders of fame such as Rain-in-the-Face
(Ita-yo-mo-go-zua), and White Bull (Ho-too-ah-
wo-kum).

The discontented element among the tribes became more and more daring, and in their visits to the
agencies they were arrogant and fomenters of dissen-
sion and strife until finally depredations were made
upon the commerce to the Black Hills and a number
of lives were lost, the blame of which fell upon the
hostiles under Sitting Bull.

Among these discontented and arrogant young
warriors Rain-in-the-Face especially fell under suspicion. He visited at one of the army stations on
a day when Captain Tom Custer was officer of the
day. He was so violent when arrested that the order
was given to put him in chains, and when the leg-
irons were placed upon him he threatened Captain
Custer that if he ever caught him out in the open he
would cut his heart out and eat it. After several
days of confinement he managed to free himself from
the irons and escaped. Custer never saw him again
until the day of the fight.

It is true that the government did its best to clear
the land of the invading hordes, but without success.
Then came more killings of white men by the Indians.
These killings called for reprisals, and soon the government found a first class Indian war upon its hands.

In March, 1876, forces of troops from the Department of the Platte, with headquarters at Omaha, Nebraska, under the command of the veteran Indian fighter, General George Crook, met a decided repulse. Orders were then issued for a regularly organized expedition from the south under Crook, and from the north under Terry, to take the field. Between them it was expected to make a final "clean-up." On June 17, 1876, the forces under Crook were again badly handled by the Indians, on Goose Creek, Wyoming, perhaps fifty miles south of the place in Montana where on the twenty-fifth occurred the fight which annihilated Custer.

Custer with his regiment, the Seventh Cavalry, left Fort Lincoln, Dakota, opposite Bismarck, May 17, to join Terry with the balance of his command on the Yellowstone River. This junction took place early in June, as contemplated, at a supply camp located near the mouth of a stream called Powder River, emptying into the Yellowstone. From this camp scouting parties were sent out to try and locate Indian villages, or to find fresh trails. It must not be forgotten that this whole region was unmapped. There were no roads and no telegraph lines. Up and down the Yellowstone the shallow river-boats made the matter of supply and communication comparatively easy, but as soon as one left the river, men and animals depended on wagons or pack-animals for supplies of all kinds.

The command of General Terry consisted of the

entire Seventh Cavalry, twelve troops, averaging fifty
men to a troop, six hundred men in all; four troops
Second Cavalry (a squadron) under command of
Major Baker; several companies of the Seventh Infantry, under Colonel John Gibbon, late Major-Gen-
eral of Volunteers and commander of the celebrated
Iron Brigade during the Civil War; and some detached
companies of infantry, besides a hundred or so Indian
scouts, and a few white scouts. Most of this infantry
besides the Second Cavalry squadron had marched
from Western Montana. With the infantry were
two Gatling guns, the machine-guns of that day.

On June 10 Major Reno with six troops of the
Seventh Cavalry was sent from the supply camp at
the mouth of the Powder river to scout up that stream
to its junction with the Little Powder, thence across
to Tongue River, then down that river to the Yellowstone where a new camp was to be formed. Reno
found a large trail about three weeks old leading south
and east towards the Big Horn Mountains, and as no
other trails were found by other troops sent out in
other directions, it was believed that the whole collection of disaffected Indians were in one or more camps
located on a branch of the Big Horn River called by
them the Greasy Grass; Little Big Horn by the white
scouts.

On or about June 20 this report was brought to
General Terry at the supply camp locating a comparatively fresh trail of the enemy. He now formulated
a plan to defeat them. This plan contemplated sur-

rounding the Indians wherever they might be found, and either forcing them back to their reservations or into the hands of Crook, somewhere to the south. From reports of Indian scouts, the hostile Indian camp was supposed to be located on the banks of the Little Big Horn River. This stream was a branch of the Big Horn River, one of the tributaries of the Yellowstone, heading in the Big Horn Mountains, which could be seen dimly in the distance to the south. Custer and his regiment were ordered to march across country and be in the valley of the Little Big Horn on the twenty-seventh instant. Terry, with a steamboat carrying the supplies, supported by the troops which marched along the shore, was to go up the Yellowstone to the mouth of the Big Horn, then up that river to the mouth of the Little Big Horn, to reach "the valley of the Little Big Horn not later than the twenty-seventh."

Please remember that there were no maps and no reliable data as to distances. Much depended upon guess-work, good luck, and good judgment. Of course much also depended upon secrecy of movement. Therefore Custer must move forward with caution and not allow the fact of his presence in the country to be discovered too early, otherwise the enemy might flee between the two commands and the work have to be done over again. No one gave a thought of defeat; only the possible escape of the troublesome Indians. Nothing, of course, was known of Crook or his fight which had taken place on June 17, less than a week before this movement of the forces under Terry. The command, as a whole, kept together as far as the mouth of the Rose Bud. There it separated, Custer branching off to his left-front to march across country, starting at noon of the twenty-second of June.

Between the Rose Bud and the Big Horn Rivers comes in another branch of the Yellowstone called Tullock's Fork. White scouts accompanied Custer in order that one or more of them could proceed down Tullock's Fork and communicate with Terry. The distances were not great for seasoned troops and trained horses, but many of the enlisted men were raw recruits, and many of the horses were new and untrained to the appearance and odor of Indians, to the sounds of shooting and to the smell of gunpowder. On the twenty-second Custer's command marched only ten miles; on the twenty-third he left camp at five A. M. and marched until five P. M., covering about thirty miles, not an excessive march by any means. On the twenty-fourth he again marched all day, covering about thirty miles, bivouacked until ten P. M., and then marched off and on all night.

This night marching, especially in a new and unknown country, is trying and fatiguing to seasoned troops and horses. How much worse then for raw men and animals, for it is a matter of rest, not distance, which affects the vitality. Remember, too, there were no roads.

About daylight on the twenty-fifth a halt was

made to await reports from the scouts who had been sent forward to find out what was ahead. The troops availed themselves of this opportunity to unsaddle and rest the horses, and to make coffee for themselves, but the water was so full of alkali that it was undrinkable, even the horses refusing it. At eight o'clock the march was continued, and about noon the trees along the Little Big Horn were seen from the high ground. Not only was the command more than a day ahead of time, but its presence in the country had been discovered, for during the previous night's march a pack on one of the mules had become loose and a box of hard-bread had fallen off, and when some of the men went back on the trail to recover it, two Indians were seen trying to break it open. They escaped and naturally returned to their camp to report the presence of the troops.

At the point where the Little Big Horn was first seen the Indian camp was discerned. Here Custer divided his command into four parts. Reno, the major and second in command, was given Troops A, G, and M. His orders were to march straight forward, down a small water-course easily seen and which led into the Little Big Horn River. He was to cross the river and attack at once. Benteen, the senior captain, was given Troops D, H, and K. He was to keep to the left of Reno, cross the river wherever he might reach it, and come up on Reno's left, attacking whatever he found in his front. Custer himself took Troops C, E, F, I, and L. He was to

follow Reno and "support him." The twelfth
troop, B, under its captain, McDougal, was to escort
the pack-train, commonly called the packs. With
the packs, in addition to Troop B, was the Old Guard,
consisting of five men from each troop, and also one
or two cooks from each troop, the non-commissioned
officers in charge of the mess, and the sick. It will
thus be seen that there were not more than forty men
ready for active service with each troop.

Reno was, naturally, the first to reach and cross
the river. He formed a skirmish line as soon as he
had crossed, extending the line to his left, having the
trees which grew thickly along the banks of the
stream, to his right. He entered into action almost at
once. The firing had hardly commenced when, from
a high hill on the river bank, Custer was seen waving
his hat and seeming to cheer the men on. He then
disappeared from view behind a high range of hills
which ran parallel to the river. This was the last
ever seen of him or his command, alive, with the exception of the one man who was sent back to Benteen
with a message. This man did not return to Custer,
but remained with Benteen after he had delivered his
message. He therefore knew nothing of Custer's contact with the Indians.

It was about noon when the command was divided, and as the distance to be covered to the river
was about twelve miles, first contact with the enemy
could not have been before three P. M. The Little
Big Horn River is a rapid mountain stream from

twenty to forty yards wide and with a firm pebble
bottom, but with abrupt soft banks where the mountain torrent cuts it way through the soft alluvial soil.
The water was from two to five feet deep at the
ordinary stage, but at this time of year, June, the
melting snows from the mountains, so near at hand,
rendered it much deeper. The general direction of its
course lay northeasterly down to the battle-field,
whence it turns suddenly northwesterly to its confluence with the Big Horn. Between the two rivers is
an undulating plateau or high prairie, while between
the Little Big Horn and the Rose Bud is a broken
country of considerable elevation called the Little
Chetish or Wolf Mountains. The command had followed a trail up these mountains to within about a
mile of the summit. It was from these highlands that
the trees along the river had first been seen, and scouts
had discovered the smoke from the early morning
fires in the Indian villages. From the great number
of these "smokes" they had estimated the numbers of
the enemy at from two thousand to nine thousand
warriors.

It was well known to the Indians that troops were
in the field against them, but the proximity of those
to the north, Terry's command, was not known by
them until the return of those who had found the
boxes of hard-bread on the early morning of the
twenty-fifth. Reno pushed forward as rapidly as
possible until he reached the river. There a halt of
some fifteen minutes was made to water the horses

and fill canteens. He then moved forward perhaps half a mile in column of fours, and formed a skirmish line to the left, still mounted, with the Indian scouts on his left. These scouts, Rees, numbered about one hundred. After drawing about a mile further he came into contact with the enemy. The horses of two of his men became unmanageable and ran away, carrying them into the Indian camp; the details of their death are not known. Their bodies were never recovered.

The enemy, which now developed great force, opened a brisk fire, and a large number, mounted, made a dash against Reno's Indian scouts, who hastily broke and turned tail, not to be seen again until days afterward, at the supply camp. Reno was quickly forced backwards. His left being "in the air," caused his line to become an irregular one, all being with their backs to the trees. Then the order was given to dismount to fight on foot, the led horses being taken by the horse-holders deep among the trees with the "line" in the outer edge. Shortly afterwards the troopers were ordered to mount and retreat to the bluffs across the river.

The hostile strength had so pushed Reno's line that he could not recross the river at the point where he had entered it. A mile further down stream, however, he found a fordable place. It was while recrossing the river that Lieutenant McIntosh was killed. Dr. DeWolf was killed while climbing the bluff after the crossing had been made. Lieutenant Hodgson was wounded in the leg and his horse was killed. He took hold of a comrade's stirrup and managed to get across the river, but there another bullet caught and killed him. During the retreat Bob Davern, Troop F, had a hand-to-hand conflict with an Indian; he killed his man, caught his pony (his own horse having been killed), and escaped.

Reno's command finally recrossed the river, climbed the hills, and eventually reached the top after heavy losses. There he was soon joined by Benteen and his command who, because of rough ground, had been unable to reach the river. Soon thereafter the packs and escort arrived, making a fairly homogeneous command and one strong enough to entrench and hold back any number of attacking foes. This was successfully done, but not without loss, for during the remainder of daylight the fighting was continuous, also during all day of the twenty-sixth and until the arrival of Terry about noon of the twenty-seventh.

Now as to Custer. From what was told by the messenger before referred to, that officer kept to the right of the range of hills which for four miles bordered the river before finding a valley or opening leading to it. Before reaching the river he was attacked in force. He had no time even to form a regular line, for each unit seemed to have a separate battle of its own on its hands. From Indian accounts, and it is only from Indians that we have any data, the fight was not over until every white man was dead. One person who was with the command did

escape, a Crow Indian scout named Curley, but no
one ever believed he was in the fight at all. Every
officer and civilian knowing anything of Indian life
believes that he "hid out" until dark, when he made
his way down the river, finally reaching Terry's command in the early morning of the twenty-seventh.

Terry and the troops with him after forced
marching reached the valley of the Little Big Horn
on the twenty-sixth late in the night. It later came
out that the point reached was fully ten miles from
the scene of the Custer fight and fourteen miles
from Reno Hill, but still in the valley of the Little
Big Horn. Terry could hardly believe that Custer
and his command had been killed as reported by Curley, but took up the march soon after daylight the
next morning to find out just what had happened.

Within four hours he found the site of the Indian
village, and about noon came within sight of Reno
Hill and the scene of the early part of the Reno fight.
Custer Hill was found by the scouts. The rest of the
day was given up to the burial of the dead and the
care of the wounded. The Indians had "silently
folded their tents, like the Arabs, and as silently had
stolen away."

Of the dead, besides Custer himself, there were
Captain Tom Custer and Boston Custer, brothers;
Archie Reed, a nephew; Lieutenant Cook, the adju-
tant; Dr. Lord, the surgeon; Kellogg, a newspaper
man; Captains Smith, Keogh, and Yates; Lieutenants
Harrington, Sturges, Porter, Riley, and Crittenden.

The total killed with Custer and Reno was two hundred and sixty-five; wounded (all with Reno, of course) fifty-two. Of the killed there were two hundred and twelve buried; fifty-three were missing. Among the missing were Dr. Lord and Lieutenants Harrington, Porter, and Sturges, the last named a son of the colonel of the regiment, who at the time of the campaign was absent on detached service, leaving the command to Custer, its lieutenant-colonel.

"Why did Custer divide his command into four parts, with each part so widely separated?" is a question frequently asked. Custer thoroughly believed that his regiment could whip any number of Indians brought against him. He had had some experience with the southern Indians in that part of the country then known as Indian Territory, now the State of Oklahoma. In those encounters the Indians were armed only with bows and arrows, inferior muskets and rifles of the muzzle-loading type, and with spears and knives. During the years following the Fetterman Massacre at Fort Phil Kearny in 1868 the Indians of the northern tribes had become armed with the Henry sixteen-shot rifle, now called the Winchester. With these arms they were superior to the army, who were armed with the Springfield .45, single-shot. The Indians were also fine marksmen at short range, for their living depended on their hunting qualifications, and almost all of their hunting was at ranges less than two hundred yards, whereas target practice for the army did not begin until the eighties, when Indian warfare had come to an end.

But of this superiority in arms and ability to use them, no account seems to have been taken by the authorities. Believing that he could, without doubt, whip the Indians, Custer wanted to prevent their escape. He therefore decided to attack them on three sides, the only open side being towards the mountains with the Big Horn River between, for if they fled in front of Reno before he, Custer, cut them off, he hoped to drive them direct into Terry's command.

Again, the country was broken and unknown. Reno's advance was to a terrain easily seen from the point where the division had been made, but the country to the left was hidden. Benteen was sent that way to spy out the land and to prevent a surprise by an enemy possibly camped in that direction. When he reached the river and crossed it he was to come upon Reno's left flank.

As it turned out the country was too broken for cavalry horses to get through and Benteen was pushed further and further to his right until he struck Reno's trail just before the latter had crossed the river. Before Benteen reached the river, however, he met part of Reno's command on his own side of the river and joined it, just in time to prevent its complete defeat. Thereafter until Terry came up on the twenty-seventh the two commands acted as one.

This plan of Custer's was a good one for a large

command, but under the circumstances was bad judgment. A blunder is worse than a crime.

Now a word about the message sent back by Custer to Benteen. It must not be forgotten that Custer was in an unmapped and unknown country. Shortly after he waved his hat to Reno and seemed so jubilant he must have reached another point which overlooked the whole Indian encampment. He now saw that he had been in error in sending Benteen so far away, but he still thought Reno could, at least, hold his own. He therefore turned to his orderly who, for the day, was Trumpeter John Martin, and gave this order: (I quote Martin's own words) "Orderly, I want you to take a message to Captain Benteen. Ride as fast as you can and tell him to hurry. Tell him it's a big village, and I want him to be quick and bring the ammunition packs." The adjutant, Cook, who was riding with Custer, then broke in: "Wait, orderly, I'll write the message for you." The adjutant stopped his horse, took a small book from his pocket and wrote in a hurry. He then tore out the leaf and handed it to Martin, saying: "Now, orderly, ride as fast as you can to Colonel Benteen. Take the trail we came along on. If you have time and there is no danger, come back, otherwise stay with your company." This was the famous message which was worded as follows:

"Benteen, come on, big village, be quick, bring packs.
    P. S. Bring packs."

Martin, on his ride to Benteen, saw Reno and his men fighting in the bottom across the river, but his duty was to find Benteen. This he did a little later, joined him and remained with him until the coming of Terry.

"But," you ask, "why didn't Benteen obey his order and 'come quick'?" As a matter of fact, Benteen was barely able to join Reno as the latter reached the hills after having been driven by the Indians from the bottom where he had been defeated. This united band was soon surrounded by thousands of exultant, blood-thirsty and victorious Sioux. Go to Custer? They might as well have tried to reach the North Pole. From their stand on Reno Hill, as was afterwards proved by measurements, they were more than four miles from the hill where Custer and his heroes had fallen, for in the meantime Custer and his immediate command had been annihilated, their part in the fight having lasted less than an hour.

The number of Indian warriors in this fight has never been accurately ascertained. No estimate places their numbers at less than two thousand. Some authorities have estimated them as high as nine thousand. This was the estimate of Frank Gruard, chief of scouts for Crook's command, himself a half-breed Indian, who made the official statement: "the biggest Indian village ever known on the American continent."

"Did any human being escape of those who accompanied the personal command of Custer?" is a question that has been asked me many times during the past fifty years. In the list of casualties as given earlier in this account attention is invited to the "missing." What became of them?

One Indian tale recites that eleven escaped from the immediate scene of slaughter and were followed for nearly fifty miles before they were overtaken and killed in a part of the mountains called by the Indians Wolf Mountains. No remains of these men have ever been found. Another tale tells of the escape of one horseman down the river. After he had been followed several miles the chase was abandoned. Just at this moment he turned in his saddle, saw the Indians, evidently became panic-stricken, placed the muzzle of his revolver to his head, and blew his brains out. He was stripped, his horse and arms taken, and his body left where it fell. Such is the tale.

Another story is as follows: The command, on reaching the Yellowstone on its return march, found in a small grove the body of a horse, recently killed and fully equipped. No dead trooper or scout was found. The horse had been shot through the head. He could not have wandered so far, some forty miles, more or less. Search was made for the rider, but without success. What became of him? No satisfactory answer has ever been given regarding this silent evidence of a terrible tragedy.

"The mutilation of the bodies of the dead in the Custer fight does not seem to have been universal." Such is the testimony of Lieutenant James H. Bradley, Seventh Infantry, Gibbon's chief of scouts, and the first white man to see the dead on the Custer field after the fight. "Custer's body was wholly un-mutilated," is his statement. He also states: "Several bodies were entirely clothed. Half a dozen at least. The real mutilation occurred in the case of Reno's men killed near the village, where the squaws and boys had a chance at them. Fortunately not many were exposed to such a fate."

One body was sadly mutilated, that of Tom Custer. Early in this account I have told of Captain Custer and Rain-in-the-Face. Tom Custer's heart had been cut out and was not found. Rain-in-the-Face stated afterwards that he had cut it out and had eaten a part of it.

According to Indian accounts their whole loss in dead was less than one hundred, with a few very slightly wounded. During all the years that followed they never varied from this statement.

Ten years after the Custer fight there was a re-union of some of the survivors of the Reno command on the battlefield. Among those present were Colonel Benteen, Captain Godfrey, Captain McDougal, and a few others, including Chief Gall, who had led the combined fighting forces of the Indians. The writer was present as lieutenant of Company K, Fifth Infantry, the host of the day. He heard Gall give his account of the fight and of the losses. He heard the interpreter explain as Gall gave his testimony. One statement impressed itself especially on the writer's mind and that was this. Gall was questioned as to the number of fighting men with him.

He stood up to his six feet of splendid manhood, and with his back to the monument, hands extended forward, slowly raised his arms towards the heavens, at the same time glancing upwards, and uttered these words, slowly and impressively:

"My young men were like the grass that comes up in the spring." As these words were spoken his arms were slowly raised with fingers fully extended. When his arms were at an angle of about sixty degrees, head thrown back and eyes still glancing upward, he stood rigid for fully a minute. Then he slowly lowered his arms to his sides, and sat down, his back still to the monument. At this time he stated that the Indian losses in dead were less than one hundred, slowly opening and closing both hands ten times to indicate the number.

The following detailed account of what happened to Custer and his command was given me by Colonel Benteen in 1894, at his home in Atlanta, Georgia, where he lived after his retirement from active service. It reflects the judgment of expert soldiers after having seen the dead on the field, and after they had interviewed hundreds of Indians who had been in the fight.

"The Indians state that Custer's column was never nearer the river or village than his final position on the ridge. On the battlefield in 1886 Chief Gall indi-

cated Custer's route to me, and it was on the high
ridge east or back of the field.

"The ford theory arose from the fact that there
were found there numerous tracks of shod horses, but
they evidently had been made after the Indians had
possessed themselves of the cavalry horses, for they
rode them after capturing them. No bodies of men
or horses were found anywhere near the ford, and
these facts are conclusive to my mind that Custer did
not go to the ford with any body of men.

"As soon as Gall had personally confirmed the report brought him that a body of cavalry was coming
from another direction than that of Reno's approach,
he sent word to his warriors battling against Reno,
and to the people in the village. The greatest con-
sternation prevailed among the families and orders
were given for them to leave at once. Before they
could do so, the great body of warriors had left Reno
and hastened to attack Custer. This explains why
Reno was not pushed when so much confusion at the
river crossing gave the Indians every opportunity of
annihilating his command.

"Not long after, the Indians began to show a
strong force in Custer's front. Custer turned his
column to the left and advanced in the direction of
the village to near a place now marked as a spring,
halted at the junction of the ravines just below it, and
dismounted two troops, Keogh's and Calhoun's, to
fight on foot. These two troops advanced at double

time to a knoll, now marked by Crittenden's monument.

"The other three troops, mounted, followed them a short distance to their rear. The led horses remained where the troops dismounted. When Geogh and Calhoun got to the knoll the other troops marched rapidly to the right; Smith's troops deployed as skirmishers, mounted, and took position on a ridge which, to Smith's left, ended in Keogh's position. Smith's right ended on a hill on which Custer took position with Yates and Tom Custer's troops, now known as Custer's Hill, and marked by the monument erected by the government to the command. Smith's skirmishers, holding their grey horses, remained in groups of fours.

"The line occupied by Custer's battalion was on the first considerable ridge back from the river, the nearest point being about a mile from it. His front was extended about three-quarters of a mile. The whole village was in full view. A hundred yards from his line was another but lower ridge, the further slope of which was not commanded by the line. It was here that the Indians under Crazy Horse, from the lower part of the village, among whom were the Cheyennes, formed for the charge on Custer's hill. All bodies of Indians had now left Reno. Gall collected his warriors and moved up a ravine south of Keogh and Calhoun. As they were turning their left flank they discovered the led horses without any guard other than the horse holders. They opened fire upon these horse holders, using the usual devices for stampeding the horses, such as yelling, waving blankets, etc. In this way they succeeded in turning the horses loose, and the squaws and boys following the warriors caught up the frightened animals. In this disaster Keogh and Calhoun probably lost all their reserve ammunition, which was usually carried in the saddle-bags.

"Gall's warriors now moved on foot to the knoll held by Calhoun. A large force had dismounted and advanced up the slope far enough to be able to see the soldiers when standing, but were protected when squatting and lying down. By jumping up, firing quickly, then dropping from sight again, they exposed themselves only for an instant, but this drew the soldiers' fire, causing a waste of ammunition. In the meantime Gall was massing his mounted warriors under the protection of the slope. When everything was in readiness, at a signal from Gall, the dismounted warriors rose, and fired, and the mounted warriors gave voice to the war whoop, put whip to their ponies, and the whole mass rushed upon and crushed Calhoun. By their own momentum the Indians were carried forward over Calhoun and Crittenden, down into the depressions where Keogh was with only about thirty men; and all was over on that part of the field.

"In the meantime, the same tactics were pursued and executed on Custer Hill where the warriors under Crow-King, Crazy Horse, White Bull, Hump and others, moved up the ravine west of the hill. The bloody work was soon finished and the accomplishment of the massacre completed. This part of the fight lasted only thirty or thirty-five minutes."

This short article on the Custer fight should end with a remark of Sitting Bull while in Canada, where he went during the winter of 1876 or spring of 1877:

"They tell me I murdered Custer. It is a lie. I am not a war-chief. I was not in the battle that day. His eyes were blinded that he could not see. He was a fool and rode to his death. He made the fight, not I."

BIBLIOGRAPHY

Buel, James William, *Heroes of the Plains*, Philadelphia, 1883.

Cody, William F., and Colonel Henry Inman, *The Great Salt Lake Trail*, Topeka, Kansas, 1898.

Connelly, William E., *Doniphan's Expedition and the Conquest of New Mexico and California*, Kansas City, 1907.

Crawford, *Captain Jack, The Poet Scout*, San Francisco, 1879.

Custer, Elizabeth B., *Following the Guidon*, New York, 1901.

Custer, General George A., *My Life on the Plains*, New York, 1874.

Inman, Colonel Henry, *The Old Santa Fe Trail*, Topeka, Kansas, 1899.

Jackson, Helen Hunt, *A Century of Dishonor*, New York, 1885.

Sabin, Edwin L., *Kit Carson Days*, Chicago, 1914.

Visscher, William Lightfoot, *Buffalo Bill's Own Story of His Life and Deeds*, Chicago, 1917.

Wilstach, Frank J., *Wild Bill Hickok*, New York, 1926.

Young, Harry (Sam), *Hard Knocks; A Life Story of the Vanishing West*, Chicago, 1915.

APPENDIX

THE CUSTER BATTLEFIELD
NATIONAL CEMETERY

Compiled by Earle R. Forrest

T HE FOLLOWING LIST of the men killed and wounded with General George A. Custer and the killed and wounded with Major Marcus A. Reno was compiled from many sources, and for this reason some duplications will be found, due to a difference in spelling in various lists or errors in the troop to which certain men belonged. In order that this record may be complete I have included all.

The first published casualty list appeared in the extra issue of the Bismarck, North Dakota, *Tribune*, of July 6, 1876, and this in the main is correct. From this and from the official reports of the battle furnished the War Department the following list was compiled. The notes following various names of killed and wounded were compiled from the many stories of survivors found in the source material at the end. I believe that this is the first time such information has been given in this form.

The records of the service and brevets awarded the various officers are from official records.

The authors wish to make special acknowledgment of their indebtedness to Mr. Rudolph W. Fickler, of Chicago, Illinois, for casualty lists and other valuable information; to Dr. Thomas B. Marquis, of Hardin, Montana, for personal information on the Custer Battlefield; to W. H. Banfill, newspaper reporter, of Billings, Montana, for interviews and personal information on the Custer Battlefield National Cemetery; Victor A. Bolsius, of Crow Agency, Montana, Superintendent of the Custer Battlefield National Cemetery, for personal information furnished.

Mr. Fickler, who has been a collector of Custer records and

literature for the past thirty-five years, kindly placed his extensive collection at my disposal.

On June 25, 1877, exactly one year after the battle, a squad from Fort Keogh, Montana, under command of Captain H. I. Nowlan and accompanied by Colonel Michael Sheridan, visited the battlefield for the purpose of securing the remains of seven of the officers whose graves had been marked the year before. In this party were Captain Hugh L. Scott, later Major General. Sheridan and Nowlan located the officers' graves by means of a chart that the latter had prepared while quartermaster for General Terry in 1876, when the bodies were originally buried four days after the battle. This party in 1877 exhumed the remains of all except Lieutenant Crittenden, and they were reburied in other sections, as noted in this list.

The condition of the Custer battlefield at that time is well described by Thomas H. Leforge.[1] During the year following the battle he frequently visited the field and "found many a grinning skull, ribbed trunk or detached limb bone on top of the ground and but partly covered up."

The original graves of the officers were only a few inches deep, and the bodies of the enlisted men had been left to rot in the rain and snow and wind; their bones had been bleached by a summer's sun, and in many cases wolves and coyotes had aided the elements in the gruesome work of destruction. This neglect after the battle was unavoidable, for neither Terry's nor Gibbon's men were equipped with proper digging implements; but a burial expedition could have been sent to the field after the wounded were taken to Fort Abraham Lincoln. It is unfortunate that nothing of this kind was ever done. The men were dead and could be of no further use to the army, so why bother with a lot of bones A year passed before the field was visited by a burial squad of any kind; and this small expedition of June 25, 1877, which Leforge accompanied, had so little time at its disposal that it could only bother with the officers' graves.

General Scott thus describes his work with this squad:[2] "There was no time to dig deep graves, and I was told to cover the bones made into little piles where they were lying. This I did, but the soil was like sugar, and I have no doubt that the first rain liquefied it and exposed the bones later. We had neither the force nor the time to rebury the whole command in deep graves, as we were obliged to join the main command."

As a matter of fact, only the officers of Custer's battalion were ever buried. Neither Reno's men nor the relief column had the tools for such work, and it was necessary to get the wounded to a hospital as quickly as possible. Four days after the battle the bodies of the officers were buried, but the men were left scattered over those bleak hills in that lonely land by the Little Big Horn, to rot under the blazing sun.

The squad of 1877 was sent for the sole purpose of securing the remains of the officers. General Custer was removed to West Point; Captain Myles Keogh to Albany, New York; and Captains Tom Custer and George W. Yates, with Lieutenants Algernon E. Smith, Donald McIntosh, and James Calhoun were reinterred at Fort Leavenworth, Kansas, where tablets to their memory were placed by the Seventh Cavalry in the post chapel.

Dr. Thomas B. Marquis says[3] that human bones were seen by all visitors to the battlefield in the early days. This condition existed until 1885, when there was a general cleanup, and all bones that could be found on the surface were gathered and buried in a square pit at the base of the monument on Custer Hill. Other remains have been found from time to time since then. In 1932 workmen unearthed some bones in the vicinity of the slabs near the monument; and Dr. Marquis relates an interesting incident that occurred a short time prior to this. While repairing one of these slabs, human bones were found just under the top soil. The interesting feature of this discovery is that the bones of an officer were supposed to have been removed from this spot by the squad of 1877. There was certainly a mistake somewhere.

The white slabs seen on the battlefield were not placed at the graves of soldiers. They mark the spots where Custer's men are believed to have died; but in many cases even this is in doubt. General E. S. Godfrey states that when the bones were gathered up the locations were marked by stakes. Years later when the marble slabs were erected, it was found that the stakes had rotted away; and wild animals had undoubtedly dragged the remains of some of the men from their original locations. In some cases the death ground of soldiers was identified by the fact that at that particular spot the vegetation had grown heavier, indicating that animal matter had decayed there; and from the extent of ground covered by the ranker vegetation and the indications of the soil it was determined whether it had been a man or a horse.

None of those white slabs contain the names of the men who died there, with the exception of the officers, who were identified after the battle, and three civilians: Mark Kellogg, correspondent of the Bismarck Tribune, Boston Custer, and Arthur Reed. The officers supposed to have been identified were General Custer, Captain Tom Custer, Captain George W. Yates, Captain Myles Keogh, and Lieutenants A. E. Smith, Donald McIntosh, James Calhoun, John J. Crittenden, W. W. Cooke, William W. V. Riley, and Benjamin H. Hodgson.

McIntosh was removed with others in 1877 to Fort Leavenworth, Kansas, and it is doubtful if the marker at Hodgson's supposed grave is correct. Dr. J. M. DeWolf's grave is not known, although a marker is at its supposed location.

Of the twenty-nine men killed during Reno's retreat from the river bottom, the grave of only one is known. This was a skeleton found in the spring of 1926 on the site of Reno's first fight; and during the fiftieth anniversary celebration of the Custer battle these bones were buried with ceremony as the "unknown soldier" of the Battle of the Little Big Horn. A heavy flat stone covers the grave at the side of the road, a mile from the spot where it was discovered; and so twenty-eight other soldiers are known to be buried somewhere in that river bottom.[3]

The eighteeen men killed in the subsequent fighting on Reno Hill were buried secretly on the night of June 26, 1876, in one common grave; but its location is unknown. A wooden cross was placed at the spot where Scout Charley Reynolds was killed in the river bottom.

Another skeleton with buttons,[3] fragments of cloth and the remnant of a gun scabbard were discovered in a gully a quarter of a mile southeast of the battlefield in 1928 by a Crow Indian. Nineteen empty shells and one loaded cartridge were picked up within a few feet of the bones; and an iron arrow point in the vertebrae of the neck showed the manner of death. This may have been Sergeant James Butler, of Troop L. The skeleton was buried in the national cemetery.

An interesting story which is told of Gustave Dorn, blacksmith in Captain Keogh's troop, has an element of truth. When Custer's command was near the scene of the battle this trooper stopped to tighten his saddle girth. When he overtook his command the fighting had started; his horse became frightened at the sound of firing and bolted, and after a wild ride in which the animal was wounded five times, Dorn succeeded in reaching Reno after that officer had taken his position on the bluff. Gustave Dorn was one of the first men killed at the Battle of Wounded Knee fifteen years later.[4]

The Custer battlefield was reserved as a national cemetery by an executive order issued December 7, 1886. The cemetery contains seven and one-half acres and the reservation is one mile square; while the Reno reservation contains 160 acres. Since the national cemetery was created, the bones of 1,421 soldiers and civilians have been reburied at this shrine of the old frontier. From graveyards at long abandoned forts and battlefields all over the Northwest, the remains of men killed in battle or who died of wounds and disease during the Indian wars in the days when the Old West was young, were removed to that bleak land where Custer and his men fought and died long ago.

The records of the War Department show that up to March 31, 1931, a total of 1,668 interments had been made in the Custer Battlefield National Cemetery, including 247 of Custer's men. Of this total number there are 1,392 known and 276 unknown. The following list of army posts of the old Northwest, with the number of bodies removed from each, is from the official records of the War Department:

```
Fort Phil Kearny, Wyoming_____111
Fort C. F. Smith, Montana_____ 17
Fort Sisseton, Dakota _____ 40
Fort Totten, North Dakota_____ 27
Camp Poplar River, Montana_____ 13
```

Fort Pembina, North Dakota	25
Fort Maginnis, Montana	22
Fort Rice, South Dakota	146
Fort Abraham Lincoln, North Dakota	160
Fort Bennett, South Dakota	25
Fort Shaw, Montana	77
Fort McKinney, Wyoming	61
Fort Custer, Montana	70
Fort Buford, North Dakota	151
Fort Keogh, Montana	173
Fort Logan, Colorado	7

The last removals were seven bodies from Fort Logan, Colorado, on November 25, 1931.

The Custer Battlefield monument on Custer Hill contains the names of 265 killed; but there are only 209 marble slabs on the field. The various points at which the others died are not known.

Much interesting history of the days of Indian warfare in the old Northwest could be written around the bones of those 1,421 soldiers and civilians gathered from army posts scattered over a far-flung frontier, most of them long abandoned and neglected; but I will confine myself to some of the most important.

One of the bodies removed from Fort Shaw was that of Captain William Logan, who was killed by a squaw on August 9, 1877, at the Battle of the Big Hole, Montana, when General Gibbon was defeated by the Nez Perces under Chief Joseph, during their historic flight to join Sitting Bull in Canada.

In October, 1892, the bones of seventeen soldiers and civilians who died at old Fort C. F. Smith, Montana, during the two thrilling years of its existence, were exhumed and taken to the Custer Battlefield National Cemetery. Henry C. Klenck, now in the soldiers' home at Columbia Falls, Montana, but at that time in the quartermaster department at Fort Custer, had the contract for the removal; but for some reason this work was actually done by a detail of ten Negro soldiers from the Tenth Cavalry, then stationed at that post. These men were in command of Second Lieutenant C. T. Johnson, with Captain Horace A. Bivens,[5] a Negro veteran of the regular army, now living at Billings, Montana, as sergeant in command of this squad. In describing the work for the author, Captain Bivens stated that the graveyard was located about half-way between the ruins of the old fort and the Big Horn River, a distance of about 200 yards. Some of the bones were only about a foot and a half below the surface, and in the course of time would have been washed out; but they were probably buried much deeper than that in the beginning.

Standing in the center of this ancient burial ground was a large stone shaft, twelve feet high, built in three sections, the base being twenty inches square. It was erected in memory of their comrades by five companies of the Twenty-seventh Infantry that were stationed at Fort C. F. Smith during two years of bitter warfare with Red Cloud's Sioux. Sixteen names appear on the shaft, eight killed by Indians, three drowned, one died of wounds, one died of disease, one died of injuries, one died in the hospital (cause not stated), and one was killed by accident. The seventeenth body was that of Mrs. Julia Roach, who was drowned in the Big Horn River. Her name does not appear on the monument.

These seventeen bodies were buried in a row with Lieutenant Sigismund Sternberg at one end and Mrs. Roach at the other, and the monument erected in the center. Each grave is marked with a white marble slab, placed by the government, with the name and rank of each person thereon.

The inscription on the west side follows; but parts of it have been obliterated by the elements:[6]

In memory of
Second Lieut.
Sigismund Sternberg,
killed while . . . . . de-
fending the . . . . . .
part of 27 . . . . soldiers and citizens as

> . . . . . forces of 600
> Sioux Indians at the
> hayfield . . . . . . from
> July 1st to
>   Aug. 1, 1867.
>   Erected by
> Cos. D, E, C, H and I,
>   27th U. S. Inf.

On the north side:

>   Sacred to the
>   memory of
>   Alvah H. Staples
> Corp. Co. D, 27th Inf.
>   killed by Indians
>   Sep. 20th, 1866.

>   Charles Hackett,
>   pvt. Co. D, 27th inf.
>   killed by Indians
>   Sep. 21st, 1866.

>   John Murphy
> Sergt. Co. C, 27th inf.
>   drowned in river
>   Aug. 24th, 1867.

>   Thomas Navin
>   pvt. Co. H, 27th inf.
>   killed by Indians
>   Aug. 1st, 1867.

>   Jeremiah Osier
>   pvt. Co. D, 27th inf.
>   died of disease
>   May 15th, 1868.

On the south side:

Sacred to the
memory of
James Strong
teamster
died of injuries
Dec. 8th, 1867.

J. C. Hollister
citizen
killed in action
Aug. 1st, 1867.

Charles Riley
pvt. Co. D, 27th inf.
died in hospital
Apr. 27th, 1868.

Robt. Clair
pvt. Co. D, 27th inf.
killed by accident
June 27th, 1867.
Thomas Fitzpatrick
pvt. Co. D, 27th inf.
killed by Indians
Sep. 20th, 1866.

On the east side:

Sacred to the
memory of
James Brennon
guide,
killed in action,
Oct. 19th, 1866.

Wm. Bruce Smith
citizen
died of wounds
Oct. 12th, 1866.

Geo. W. McGee
wagonmaster
drowned in river
Aug. 11th, 1866.

Charles Bowman
citizen
killed by Indians
Sep. 14, 1866.

Daniel Grouse
citizen
drowned in river
Sep. 9th, 1866.

I am informed that Mrs. Roach is one of two women buried in the Custer Battlefield National Cemetery.

The date of the erection (June, 1868) was just a few weeks before Fort C. F. Smith was abandoned, following the treaty with Red Cloud. What a job it must have been in those remote days to have had that monument carved and hauled over the long miles from the nearest white settlement. Those five companies of the Twenty-seventh Infantry certainly did their best to see that the comrades they had left behind in that dreary land did not sleep in forgotten graves; and through that monument their memory has been perpetuated all these years.

One of the most desperate and heroic battles between red men and white on the old frontier is perpetuated on this monument in the death of Lieutenant Sigismund Sternberg, Private Thomas Navin, and J. G. Hollister, a citizen. This was the famous Hayfield fight, near Fort C. F. Smith, on August 1, 1867.

Fort C. F. Smith was one of the two army posts established on the Bozeman trail, the other being Fort Phil Kearny, ninety miles to the south, in Wyoming, that resulted in two long years of Indian warfare. Continuously from the beginning until they were finally abandoned, both forts were under seige by Red Cloud and his warriors; and no man was safe beyond the stockade. Fort C. F. Smith was established August 12, 1866, on the Big

Horn River, Montana Territory, not many miles from the spot where Custer and his men were to die in the greatest of all Indian battles ten years later. It was abandonded July 29, 1868, under the terms of the treaty of peace with Red Cloud.

On August 1, 1867, nineteen men at work cutting hay on Warrior Creek, two and one-half miles from the fort, were suddenly attacked by an overwhelming force of Sioux. A survivor of the battle[7] declared in later years that they were outnumbered a hundred to one; but while this was exaggerated, the whites were greatly outnumbered. The inscription on the monument gives the number of attacking force at 600, which is probably correct. This means that the whites were outnumbered more than thirty to one. There were eleven soldiers under Lieutenant Sternberg, and eight civilian employes from the fort.

That heroic little band of nineteen retreated to a corral at the first sign of an attack, and held off the savage horde launched against them by Red Cloud in as desperate a battle as was ever fought between Indians and whites. The loss was three killed and four wounded, three of the latter being soldiers; but there may have been four deaths, for a survivor[7] speaks of a sergeant who died. However, this man cannot be accounted for on the list of names on the monument.

The known killed as shown by the monument were Lieutenant Sternberg, Private Thomas Navin, and J. G. Hollister, a citizen. The loss of the Sioux was never known; but it must have been heavy to have forced them to retire from the field, for the commander of the fort refused to send relief to the beleagured force; and the next day a squad from the post counted the bodies of fifty dead Indians.

On June 24, 1896, the bones of eighty-two victims of the Fetterman disaster, with three of the Wagon-Box fight and twenty-six others, were removed from the old military graveyard at Fort Phil Kearny, Wyoming, to rest with Custer's men on the hills of the Little Big Horn. For thirty years they had slept in unmarked graves, and when the skeletons were exhumed ninety-eight were reburied in the Custer Battlefield National Cemetery as unknowns. This number included eighty-two killed with Fetterman, who had been interred in one common grave.

Five of the others removed were civilians. This record shows that only seven of the soldiers were identified; and today all their graves may be seen in two rows in the Custer Battlefield Cemetery, each marked with a white headstone.

The establishment of Fort Phil Kearny on July 15, 1866, aroused Red Cloud's fighting spirit as nothing else could, for this was an invasion of the Sioux hunting grounds set aside to them by treaty; and he hurled his legions of fighting warriors against the whites so successfully that the fort was abandoned in August, 1868.

It was on December 21, 1866, that a detachment of seventy-six enlisted men under command of Captain William J. Fetterman, with two other officers and four civilians, were wiped out by Red Cloud's warriors in one of the most sanguinary battles in the history of Indan warfare. The Fetterman disaster was very similar to the Battle of the Little Big Horn ten years later; like the men who rode with Custer that day, not one of Fetterman's command lived to tell the terrible story.

The killed included three commissioned officers, Captain William J. Fetterman, Captain Frederick H. Brown, and Lieutenant George W. Grummond, all of the Eighteenth Infantry; forty-nine enlisted men from the same command; twenty-one from Company A, nine from Company C, six from Company E, and thirteen from Company H; with twenty-seven from Troop C, Second Cavalry, and four civilians.

This makes a total of eighty-three, all of whom were buried in the little graveyard adjoining Fort Phil Kearny; but in January, 1867, the body of Lieutenant Grummond was exhumed and taken east. This left eighty-two, sleeping there together until thirty years later, when their bones were removed to the Little Big Horn.

Another heroic battle of the old frontier, one that even surpasses the famous Hayfield fight or the defense of Adobe Walls in the Texas Panhandle, was fought near Fort Phil Kearny, August 2, 1867. This is known as the Wagon-Box fight, for the reason that the troops engaged took shelter in a corral constructed from the beds of fourteen wagons. Some authorities claim that these wagon-boxes had been lined with heavy sheet iron; but this is denied by survivors.[7]

Actually outnumbered 300 to one, no defense in all history was ever more desperate, and the loss inflicted upon the Indians was a staggering blow to Red Cloud's fighting legions. Thirty-two men, including the soldiers and civilians, actually fought against 3,000 Sioux warriors, the best fighters on the plains.

This battle took place at a wood-chopping camp about six miles from Fort Phil Kearny. Company C, Twenty-seventh Infantry, commanded by Captain James W. Powell, had been detailed only the day before to take its turn at guarding the woodchoppers to and from the fort. The Indian loss was so staggering that Red Cloud would never talk of the battle afterwards; and it was estimated that his killed and wounded amounted to about half the number of warriors engaged.

The whites lost three killed: Lieutenant John C. Jenness, and Privates Henry Haggerty and Tommy Doyle. Their bodies were buried in the post graveyard at Fort Phil Kearny, but were removed to the Custer Battlefield National Cemetery with Fetterman and his men.

CASUALTY LIST OF THE BATTLE OF THE LITTLE BIG HORN

In going over the following casualty list it is well to remember that when General Custer divided his regiment he took Troops C, E, F, I, and L; Troops A, G, and M and Arikara scouts were assigned to Major Reno; while Captain Benteen had Troops D, H, and K and Captain McDougal commanded Troop B, guarding the pack train.

KILLED WITH CUSTER

Field Staff

Lieutenant-Colonel George Armstrong Custer, commanding the Seventh Cavalry; body found near the north extremity of what is now known as Custer Hill, where the monument now stands. He was stripped, but had not been scalped or mutilated. Two bullet wounds, one in the temple and one in the left breast, were hardly noticeable. Lieutenant James H. Bradley,[8] of Gibbon's scouts, described the general's expression as peaceful like one who had fallen asleep.

Only a few feet away were the bodies of Captain Tom Custer, his brother; Captain George W. Yates, and Lieutenant Algernon E. Smith; and close by were Lieutenants Cooke and Reily, Boston Custer, another brother; and Arthur Reed, a nephew. Grouped around these officers were the bodies of some two score soldiers who had rallied to the support of "Custer's last stand." (See Troop E in this list.)

It has long been claimed by some authorities that Custer shot himself when he saw that all hope was gone; but this has never been proven, and it is not now believed. He was found in the midst of a heap of dead soldiers, his legs across the body of one, his head resting on another. Rain-in-the-Face afterward declared that Appearing Elk had some of Custer's weapons, and he was pointed out by the Sioux as the man who killed the general. Appearing Elk never admitted this.[9] As a matter of fact the Indians never knew who killed Custer. In the excitement and confusion of the battle it would simply be impossible to know; and not until long afterwards did the Indians know who was in command of the soldiers at the Battle of the Little Big Horn.

On June 25, 1877, the first anniversary of the battle, a squad in charge of Captain Nowlan and accompanied by Colonel Michael Sheridan, visited the battlefield to secure the remains of Custer and other officers. Custer's were taken to Fort Abraham Lincoln, where Colonel Joseph Tilford, of the Seventh Cavalry, locked himself in a room, and cut a lock of hair from the head in order that Mrs. Custer might have some certain proof of identification.

Thomas H. Leforge[1] says that he was present when Custer's grave was opened, and that only one thigh bone and the skull attached to some part of the skeleton trunk, were found.

Custer's remains were taken from Fort Abraham Lincoln to New York City, and then to a receiving vault at Poughkeepsie. On October 10, 1867, all that was left of the immortal Custer was buried in the cemetery at West Point, in compliance with a request once made to his wife. The funeral was attended by high army officers and thousands of people.

On August 30, 1879, the Custer monument, in the form of a statuesque portrait of Custer in his last battle, designed by Wilson McDonald, was unveiled at the Military Academy grounds at West Point. It is eight feet high and stands on a granite pedestal six feet high.

The last chapter of the Custer tragedy was not written until nearly fifty-seven years after the battle, when the widow of the "Boy General of the Civil War," faithful to his memory all those years,[10] followed him to the grave and was buried at his side. She died in New York City, April 4, 1933, in her ninety-second year, the last of those soldiers' wives of the old frontier who were made widows by the Sioux and Cheyenne on that hill by the Little Big Horn.

CUSTER'S CIVIL WAR RECORD

Born at New Runley, Ohio, December 5, 1839; appointed from Ohio to West Point, July 1, 1857; graduated in 1861, thirty-fourth in his class; commissioned second lieutenant, June 24 and assigned to Company G, Second United States Cavalry; left West Point, July 18, and three days later was in the first Battle of Bull Run, July 21, on the staff of General Phil Kearny; assigned to the Fifth Cavalry, August 3, 1861.

In February, 1862, he was assigned to the staff of General W. F. Smith, in charge of balloon reconnaissance with the Army of the Potomac, and during the campaign on the peninsula between the York and James Rivers he made balloon observations. At the Battle of Williamsburg, Virginia, May 5, 1862, General Hancock made special mention of Custer for leading the way for the Union forces.

On May 22, 1862, he waded the Chickahominy River, showing its depth, and devised a plan of attack on the Confederate picket-post. At his own request Custer was given command of three companies with which he attacked the pickets, according to his plan, and captured the first battle flag for the Army of the Potomac. As a reward for this exploit General McClellan placed him on his staff as additional aide-de-camp with the rank of captain, dating from June 5.

During the Peninsula campaign that followed he served on McClellan's staff, participating in the Battle of Fair Oaks, May 31 to June 1, and the various engagements of the Seven Days' battle, beginning June 25 and ending with bloody Malvern Hill, July 1. At Gaine's Mills, June 27, he marked out the positions for the Union forces.

When McClellan was removed as commander of the Army of the Potomac after the close of the disastrous Peninsula campaign, July 8, 1862, Custer lost his rank as captain; but on July 17 he was promoted to first lieutenant of Company M, Fifth Cavalry. With this command he fought at South Mountain, Maryland, September 14, and at Antietam, the bloodiest battle of the war, September 16 and 17.

He took part in the battle of Chancellorsville, Virginia,

from May 1 to 5, 1863, after which General Hooker sent him on a special mission into enemy territory with seventy-five picked men, during which he captured a number of prisoners and a Confederate officer, all of whom were taken to Washington, and Custer was thanked by Hooker. He was then placed on the staff of General Pleasanton.

At Aldie, Virginia, June 17, Custer saved the day for the Union cavalry by turning what looked like defeat into victory. On June 29, 1863, upon recommendation of General Pleasanton, he was commissioned brigadier general of volunteers and placed in command of a Michigan cavalry brigade. Thus he became the "Boy General" of the Union Army at the age of twenty-three.[11]

At Gettysburg, July 1, he was opposed to Wade Hampton's brigade; and during the three days of fighting he prevented the Confederates from turning the Union flank. While leading a charge his horse was shot and his life was saved by a boy in his command who killed a Confederate about to shoot him; and Custer rode to safety behind this same lad. At Two Taverns, July 3, the "Boy General" again distinguished himself, in what has gone down in history as one of the most brilliant cavalry charges of the war, by leading one Michigan regiment to victory against four of the enemy; and thereby foiling General J. E. B. Stuart. For gallant and meritorious service on this occasion he received the brevet of major in the regular army. During the three days at Gettysburg his command lost 542 killed, wounded and missing, and he had two horses shot under him.

On July 5, during Lee's retreat, Custer with only four companies captured an entire Confederate brigade; and between Gettysburg and the Potomac he destroyed an enemy train of 400 wagons, capturing 1,800 prisoners.

In charge of the left end of the line of advance on Culpepper Court House, Virginia, September 13, 1863, Custer with only a few men galloped into the town ahead of the main column and captured two guns.

At Brandy Station, Virginia, October 11, Custer and his brigade were outnumbered and surrounded; but with two regiments he cut his way through. Turning on the Confederates in a series of raids and skirmishes he once forced his old enemy, General Stuart, to flee.

While on a furlough home he married Miss Elizabeth Bacon, of Monroe, Michigan, February 9, 1864. Accompanied by his bride to the front, their honeymoon was spent on the battle line; and nineteen days after the wedding he led the famous Custer Raid through Albemarle County, Virginia. With 1,500 men he destroyed one railroad bridge and three flour mills filled with grain, and captured 500 horses and six caissons loaded with ammunition. Cut off by Stuart on the return he charged with such fury that he cut his way through the Confederate line and captured fifty prisoners, reaching the Union lines March 18, after covering 100 miles in a day and a half.

With Sheridan's corps, Custer's brigade fought at the Battle of the Wilderness, May 5-7, 1864. On May 8, when Sheridan started towards Richmond, Custer was placed in advance to ride around the enemy, and on May 9, at Beaver Dam Station he captured three trains and two engines, and released 400 Federal prisoners. In the Battle of Yellow Tavern, seven miles north of Richmond, May 11, in which the famous Confederate cavalry leader, J. E. B. Stuart, was killed, he captured a battery, and was breveted lieutenant colonel for gallant and meritorious service. In this raid Sheridan almost reached the gates of the Confederate capitol.

Sheridan started on his last raid around Lee's left at Cold Harbor, Virginia, June 7, 1864, and four days later at Trevillion Station, Custer captured many wagons, ambulances and caissons, 800 men and 1,500 horses, in addition to burning the station and tearing up the tracks. Another brigade that was to support him could not keep up the terrific pace, and Custer was nearly surrounded. The train, moved by a frightened quartermaster without orders. was captured by the Confederates with much of Custer's property; and when his color bearer was killed Custer tore the flag from the staff held in the death grip of the bearer, and saved it by wrapping it around his body. A horse was killed under him. Finally, when out of ammunition and food, he ended his raid and rejoined Sheridan on June 25.

When Sheridan was sent to the Shenandoah Valley of Virginia, Custer and his brigade went along. At Winchester, September 19, 1864, Custer won the battle for the Union forces by breaking the Confederate main line of defense in a charge with 500 men in which he captured two guns, 700 prisoners, including fifty-three officers, seven battle flags, two caissons, and many small arms. For this he received the brevet of colonel.

After a desperate fight at Woodstock, October 9, Custer in command of the Third Division, routed the Confederate cavalry under General Rosser, his old classmate at West Point. Custer's pursuit of the enemy for twenty-six miles gave this battle the name of the "Woodstock Races"; and all artillery except one piece was captured with 300 prisoners.

The Union victory at Cedar Creek, October 19, famous in history for "Sheridan's Ride," was largely due to Custer's brilliant defense. With General Merritt he was transferred from the right of the Union army to the left where the fighting was heaviest; and with between 6,000 and 7,000 cavalry, part of an infantry division and a few batteries, they stopped the advance of 20,000 Confederate infantry flushed with victory. This was the first time during the war that such a defense had occurred. With the enemy held back by Custer and Merritt, General Wright reorganized his forces, and about 2 p. m. Sheridan dashed in from his famous ride from Winchester.

Placing his cavalry on the flanks, Sheridan shouted: "Go in, Custer." With his entire division Custer led one of the most brilliant charges of the war, and the entire Union army followed to victory. Custer's men captured twenty-five of the forty-nine guns taken and several hundred prisoners. He was given the honor of carrying the report of the battle to Washington with the captured battle flags. For his brilliant work and also for his gallantry at Winchester, September 19, and at Fisher's Hill, September 22, Custer was rewarded with the brevet of major general of volunteers, dating from October 19.

In spite of danger, Mrs. Custer accompanied her husband to the battle front whenever possible; and when he returned from Washington to the Shenandoah, his wife went along, spending the cold winter of 1864 and 1865 with him at headquarters in Winchester.

With 9,489 troops, General Sheridan started on his last great cavalry raid on February 27, 1865. The goal was Lynchburg, but if possible he intended to join forces with Sherman in North Carolina. Custer, in command of 4,600 men, pushed through a driving rain, and on March 2 attacked General Early, who, with two brigades of infantry and Rosser's cavalry, was fortified in a strong position at Waynesboro. Planning his attack before the enemy had time to think, Custer charged right over the Confederate works, and through the streets of Waynesboro to Early's rear. The latter only escaped by leaping upon a locomotive; and Rosser and three other general officers narrowly escaped being captured; but eleven guns, 200 wagons, 1,600 prisoners, and seventeen battle flags fell into Custer's hands.

While Sheridan rested at Charlottesville, Custer and Merritt raided the countryside, destroying railroads and public property, until Sheridan gave up his plan of reaching Sherman, and decided to join Grant who was hammering at Petersburg. At a telegraph office Custer picked up a message from Early, stating that he intended to attack early the next morning, and with the advantage of this knowledge Custer attacked first, routing the Confederates and almost capturing Early. His next exploit was to burn a railroad bridge within eleven miles of Richmond; and on March 26 Sheridan joined Grant in front of Petersburg, thus ending the last great cavalry raid of the war.

Then began the series of battles that ended the Rebellion. At Dinwiddie Court House, on March 31, Custer reached the field as the Union forces were gradually giving way, and threw his entire division against the enemy with such fury that the Confederate advance was not only checked but the lost ground was regained.

The next day, April 1, Custer and Diven led the attack at Five Forks. The fighting was severe, and the cavalry was dismounted, but they drove the enemy from two lines of defense to the last stand. Then, with Sheridan leading and Custer driving straight for the Confederate line, General Pickett surrendered. Starting in pursuit of General Lee's retreating army on April 2, Sheridan entered Richmond on the 3rd. When Merritt and Crook failed to break the enemy's line at Sailor Creek, April 6, Sheridan ordered Custer in, and his troopers leaped their horses over the enemy breastworks. Sixteen pieces of artillery, thirty-one battle flags, and 7,000 prisoners were the results of that day's work. The captured Confederates included seven general officers, among whom was Custis Lee, son of General Robert E. Lee; and General Ewell.

When General Kershaw surrendered he asked the privilege of delivering his sword to General Custer personally, for this Confederate considered him one of the best cavalry leaders this or any other country ever produced.

Custer was nearest to the enemy on April 9, and it was he who received Lee's flag of truce, which was presented to him by General Sheridan after the surrender, with this letter: "I know of no one whose efforts have contributed more to this happy result than those of Custer." Mrs. Custer preserved this flag until her death. Sheridan also presented to Mrs. Custer the table upon which Grant and Lee signed the articles of capitulation of the Army of Northern Virginia.[12]

After Appomattox, Custer was promoted on April 15 to the full rank of major general of volunteers. Only twenty-six years old, he was the first man of his age to be so honored since Lafayette; and next to Grant, Sherman, Thomas and Sheridan he was the outstanding general of the war, and one of the most popular heroes of the American people. In addition to this honor he was awarded the brevet of brigadier for gallant and meritorious service at Five Forks, April 1, 1865, dating from March 13, 1865, and major general for gallant and meritorious service in the campaign ending in the surrender of the Army of Northern Virginia, April 9, 1865, dating from March 13.

With the exception of one, he participated in every battle of the Army of the Potomac. Eleven horses were shot under him; bullets passed through his hat and once he lost a lock of hair, but he went through the entire war with only one wound— in the thigh from a spent ball.

His division never lost a gun, never lost a color, and was never defeated, and captured every piece of artillery opened upon it. During the last six months of the war his division captured 111 pieces of field artillery, sixty-five battle flags, and 10,000 prisoners, including seven general officers. During the last ten days and included in the above, were forty-six guns and thirty-seven battle flags. And yet this was the man in whom Major Reno, at his own court of inquiry in 1879, expressed an entire lack of confidence. This was the man Benteen hated with a bitterness that lasted to the grave—a bitterness born of jealousy because Custer was placed in rank ahead of Benteen in the Seventh Cavalry after the war.

Custer's success and rapid advancement from second lieutenant to brigadier general and then major general bred jealousy among other officers of lesser fame whom he passed. "Custer luck," they called this success, and they steadfastly refused to give him credit for military ability. This animosity followed him all through his subsequent career, and was one of the contributing factors that caused his defeat on the banks of the Little Big Horn. This jealousy, which was reflected in Major Reno's testimony at his court of inquiry, and in Captain Benteen's hatred of his commander, was the cause of a controversy over Custer's defeat that has raged for more than half a century.

But Custer had his friends in the army as well as his enemies, and they have gallantly rallied to his defense. They admit that Custer promised to support Reno in the attack on the village; but military experts point out that the general had several miles farther to go before striking the encampment, and that Reno failed to give him time to cover this distance. Custer's friends claim that Reno attacked at once with the idea of riding through the village and gaining a decided victory before his commander could arrive.

Reno was not an experienced Indian fighter, and while his bravery could not be questioned during the Civil War he never displayed any marked military ability. And Benteen refused to obey Custer's last order delivered to him by Trumpeter Martin. It is doubtful if he could have turned the tide of battle; but he did not know that at the time, and the fact remains that he absolutely disregarded his superior's last order. Had Custer lived Benteen's action would undoubtedly have resulted in a court martial or a court of inquiry.

Mrs. Custer was one of the two officers' wives who rode at

the head of the victorious Union troops from Richmond to
Washington; and Custer's Third Cavalry Division was given the
post of honor at the head of the Grand Review by leading the
parade.

On February 1, 1866, General Custer was mustered out of
the volunteer service, and on July 28, 1866 he was appointed
lieutenant colonel of the reorganized Seventh Cavalry.

First Lieutenant William Winer Cooke, adjutant of the regiment; body found with General Custer and the little group of
officers on Custer Hill. His long sideburns of which he was very
proud, had been scalped. Over half a century later Wooden
Leg, a Northern Cheyenne, told Dr. Thomas B. Marquis that it
was he who took Lieutenant Cooke's whiskers.[13]

Army Record: Lieutenant Cooke was not a graduate of
West Point, but a native of Canada and a soldier of fortune.
On January 26, 1864, he was appointed from New York as second lieutenant of the Twenty-fourth New York Cavalry, and
on December 14, 1864, he was commissioned first lieutenant in
the same regiment. Honorably mustered out June 25, 1865,
and commissioned second lieutenant, Seventh Cavalry, July 28,
1866; commissioned first lieutenant, July 31, 1867; served as
regimental adjutant from December 8, 1866, to February 21,
1867, and from January 1, 1871, to June 25, 1876.

Civil War Record: The following brevets were awarded to
him on March 2, 1867, for service on the battlefield: Captain,
for gallant and meritorious service at Petersburg, Virginia, June
17, 1864; major, for gallant and meritorious service at Dinwiddie
Court House, Virginia, March 29, 1865; lieutenant colonel, for
gallant and meritorious service at Sailor Creek, Virginia, April
6, 1865.

First Lieutenant George Edwin Lord, assistant surgeon; his
body was not found by Terry's burial squad after the battle; but
a skeleton discovered some years later, not far from the battlefield, is said to have been identified as that of Dr. Lord.

Army Record: He was a native of Massachusetts, and not a
graduate of West Point; appointed June 26, 1875, from Massa-

chusetts to the Seventh Cavalry, as assistant surgeon with the rank of first lieutenant.

Non-Commissioned Staff

Sergeant Major William H. Sharrow; Chief Trumpeter Henry Voss; Trumpeter William Kramer.

Troop C

The greater number of men of Troop C, with many of those of Troops E and F, were found along the main ridge of Custer Hill, on both sides, but most of them were on the western slope. It was in this locality that Captain Tom Custer, Captain Yates, and Lieutenant Smith were found with General Custer where the "last stand" was made.

Captain Thomas Ward Custer, in command; brother of General Custer; body found in the group on Custer Hill, with that of General Custer, Captain Yates, Lieutenants Smith, Reily and Cooke, and Boston Custer, another brother, and young Arthur Reed, a nephew of the general. On June 25, 1877, the remains were exhumed with those of General Custer, Captains Yates and Keogh, and Lieutenants Smith, McIntosh and Calhoun, and on August 3, 1877, reinterred at Fort Leavenworth, Kansas.

The story that Rain-in-the-Face cut out Tom Custer's heart and ate it was accepted by many writers for years; but it was not true. Captain Custer had arrested Rain-in-the-Face at Standing Rock Agency in January, 1875, for the murder of Dr. Houzinger and a Mr. Baliran during the Yellowstone expedition in the summer of 1873, and the Sioux chief had been imprisoned.[14] The story was given color years later by two reporters who interviewed Rain-in-the-Face at Coney Island. Captain Benteen, one of the men who identified the remains of Tom Custer, denied this story, but stated that the body had been somewhat mutilated. In an interview with Dr. Charles A. Eastman, the Sioux, Rain-in-the-Face, denied cutting out Captain Custer's heart. Some claim that Rain-in-the-Face killed Captain Tom Custer, but this is doubtful. Indian survivors today say that his head was cut off.[18]

Army Record: Captain Custer was not a graduate of West Point, but a product of the Civil War. Entering the service as a private in Company H, Twenty-first Ohio Infantry, September 2, 1861, he served until October 10, 1864, and on November 8, 1864, he was transferred to the Sixth Michigan Cavalry as second lieutenant; honorably mustered out November 24, 1865; commissioned second lieutenant in the First United States Infantry, February 23, 1866; commissioned first lieutenant, Seventh Cavalry, July 28, 1866; regimental quartermaster from December 3, 1866, to March 10, 1867; commissioned captain, Seventh Cavalry, December 2, 1875.

Civil War Record: The following brevets were awarded him for gallant service in action: First lieutenant, captain, and major of volunteers, March 13, 1865, for distinguished and gallant conduct; captain, March 2, 1867, for gallant and distinguished conduct at Waynesboro, Virginia, on March 2, 1865; major, March 2, 1867, for distinguished conduct at Namozine Church, Virginia, April 3, 1865; lieutenant colonel, March 2, 1867, for distinguished courage at Sailor Creek, Virginia, April 6, 1865. Awarded the Congressional Medal of Honor, April 24, 1865, for capture of a Confederate flag at Namozine Church, April 3, 1865; and another Medal of Honor, May 22, 1865, for capture of a Confederate flag at Sailor Creek, April 6, 1865.

Second Lieutenant Henry Moore Harrington: Body never identified; believed to have been shot in the attempt to cross the Little Big Horn when Custer charged down the hill towards the village.[15] The Indians afterwards reported that several soldiers fell into the river when the charge was repulsed.[16] Nothing definite has ever been learned of the fate of Lieutenant Harrington. He was either killed in the river or his body was so disfigured by mutilation that identification was impossible.

Army Record: Lieutenant Harrington was a native of New York. Appointed to West Point from Michigan, July 1, 1868, he graduated four years later, and was commissioned second lieutenant in the Seventh Cavalry, June 14, 1872.

First Sergeant Edwin Bobo (spelled Baba in *Tribune* list);[17] Sergeant Jeremiah Finley; Sergeant August Finckle (spelled Finkle in *Tribune* list); Corporal Henry E. French; Corporal Daniel Ryan; Corporal John Foley; Trumpeter Thomas J. Bucknell; Saddler George Howell; Blacksmith John King.

Privates

Fred E. Allen; John Brightfield; Christopher Criddle; ———— Darris (this is probably a duplication of John Darris, killed with Troop E); ———— Davis (this is probably a duplication of William Davis, killed with Troop E); George Eiseman; Gustave Engle; James Farrand (given on *Tribune* list as Fanand); Patrick Griffin; ———— Hamel (appeared on *Tribune* list, and given on official report of the battle furnished the War Department); James Hathersall (given as Hattisoll in *Tribune* list); ———— Kingsoutz; appeared on *Tribune* list and given on official report of the battle furnished the War Department; John Lewis; Frederick Meier (given as Mayer on *Tribune* list and on official report of the battle furnished the War Department); August Meyer (given as Mayer on *Tribune* list and on official report of the battle furnished the War Department); Edgar Phillips; James H. Russell; Edward Rix; John Ranter; Nathan Short; Jeremiah Shea; Ignatz Stungewitz (not given on *Tribune* list or on official report of battle furnished the War Department; appears on later lists); Samuel S. Shade; Alpheus Stuart; Ludwick St. John; John Thadus (given Thadius on *Tribune* list and on official report of the battle furnished the War Department); Garrett Van Allen; Oscar T. Warren (given on a later list as Warmer); Henry Wyndham (given as Windham in *Tribune* list, and as Wyman in a later list); Willis B. Wright.

Troop E
The Gray Horse Troop

Many of the men of this troop were found with the group of officers on Custer Hill, where some two score soldiers evidently rallied to the support of their commander in the famous "last stand." All we know of what occurred came from the Indian side, and they declared that the Gray Horse Troop stopped Two Moons, and held firm until Crazy Horse led the Sioux in that last charge that swept over the little band.[18] It is claimed by some authorities that Lieutenant Smith and the remnants of his troop tried to cut their way out;[19] but the lieutenant's body was found on Custer Hill. A number of the men of Troop E were found in a group of twenty-eight in a gully leading from the monument to the river. In 1898 Chief Two Moons told Hamlin Garland that these men left the hill after Custer had fallen, and tried to cut their way out. This was near the end of the battle.

First Lieutenant Algernon E. Smith, in command; body found near General Custer in the group on Custer Hill, with Captains Tom Custer and Yates, and Lieutenants Cooke and Reily, Boston Custer and Arthur Reed, with a number of troopers. On June 25, 1877, Lieutenant Smith's remains were exhumed with those of other officers already mentioned, and on August 3, 1877, reinterred at Fort Leavenworth.

Army Record: Lieutenant Smith was a native of New York, and not a graduate of West Point; commissioned second lieutenant in the 117th New York Infantry, August 20, 1862; first lieutenant, April 25, 1864; captain, October 12, 1864; honorably mustered out, May 15, 1865; commissioned second lieutenant in the Seventh Cavalry, August 9, 1867, and first lieutenant December 5, 1868; served as a regimental quartermaster from March 31 to July 7, 1869.

Civil War Record: The following brevets were awarded him for gallant service in action: First lieutenant, August 9, 1867, for gallant and meritorious service at Drury's Farm, Virginia; captain, August 9, 1867, for gallant and meritorious service at Fort Fisher, North Carolina, January 13-15, 1865, and major of volunteers, March 13, 1865, for gallant and meritorious service at Fort Fisher.

Second Lieutenant James Garland Sturgis; his body was never found, and nothing was ever heard in regard to his fate. Terry's burial squad did identify a body as his, and a wooden marker with his name upon it was later placed at the grave; but it was discovered that this identification was a mistake, and it is now generally accepted that his body was never found.

Army Record: He was a native of New Mexico, and was appointed from that territory to West Point, July 1, 1871; graduted in 1875, and commissioned second lieutenant in the Seventh Cavalry, June 16, 1875.

First Sergeant Frederick Hohmeyer; Sergeant John S. Ogden (this is probably the same man whose name appeared on official report of the battle furnished the War Department[20] as Egden and on the *Tribune* list as Egnen); Sergeant William B. James; Corporal George C. Brown; Corporal Blorm (this name appeared on the official report of the battle furnished the War Department); Corporal Thomas Hogan (given as Hagan on the *Tribune* list); Corporal Henry S. Mason; Corporal ———— Meyer (this name appeared on the official report of the battle furnished the War Department, but it is not found on any subsequent list. On later lists the name of Corporal Albert H. Meyer appears with Troop L; no doubt the same man); Trumpeter Thomas McElroy; Trumpeter George A. Moonie or Mooney, as it sometimes appears.

Privates

Robert Barth; James Brogan (spelled Bragew on *Tribune* list, and Brogen on official report of battle furnished the War Department); William H. Baker; Owen Boyle; Edward Connor; John Darris; William Davis; Richard Farrell; Francis T. Hughes (this name did not appear on official report of battle furnished the War Department or on the *Tribune* list; but it was given on a later list); John G. Hiley; William Huber; John Heim (spelled Hime on official report of the battle furnished the War Department); John Henderson; Sykes Henderson; Andy Knecht; Herod F. Liddiard (given as Leddison on official report of the battle furnished the War Department); Patrick O'Connor; Edward Rood; William H. Rees (given as Ruse in official report of the battle furnished the War Department); Albert A. Smith; James Smith, 1st; James Smith, 2nd; Alexander Stella; Benjamin F. Stafford; Charles Schele (given as Schoole on official report of the battle furnished the War Department); William Smallwood; William A. Torey (this is probably the same as ――― Tarr on the official list furnished the War Department); Cornelius Vansant (given as Vanjant on official list furnished the War Department; probably the same as Vaugant, of Troop I, on the *Tribune* list) George Walker.

Troop F

Many of the men of this troop died along the main ridge of Custer Hill, on both sides.

Captain George W. Yates, in command; body found on Custer Hill in the group of officers near General Custer. The remains were exhumed June 25, 1877, and on August 3, 1877, reinterred with four other officers at Fort Leavenworth, Kansas.

Army Record: He was a native of New York, and not a graduate of West Point. At the outbreak of the Civil War he entered the army from New York, and on June 20, 1861, he was commissioned quartermaster sergeant of the Fourth Michigan Infantry, and first lieutenant, September 26, 1862; honorably mustered out, June 28, 1864; re-enlisted and transferred August 24, 1864, to the Forty-fifth Missouri Infantry with the rank of first lieutenant; transferred September 22, 1864, to the Thirteenth Missouri Cavalry with the rank of captain; honorably mustered out January 11, 1866; commissioned second lieutenant in the Second United States Cavalry, March 26, 1866; served as regimental quartermaster from May 12 to October 28, 1867; commissioned captain in the Seventh Cavalry, June 12, 1867.

Civil War Record: The following brevets were awarded him for gallant service in action: Major of volunteers, dating from March 13, 1865, for gallant and meritorious service during the war; lieutenant colonel of volunteers, dating from March 13, 1865, for conspicuous gallantry at Fredericksburg, Virginia, December 11-15, 1862, at Beverly Ford, Virginia, August 23, 1862, and at Gettysburg, July 1-3, 1863.

Second Lieutenant William Van W. Reily; body found on Custer Hill in the group of officers near General Custer, where the "last stand" was made.

Army Record: Lieutenant Reily was a native of the District of Columbia, and not a graduate of West Point; appointed to the regular army from District of Columbia with the commission of second lieutenant in the Tenth Cavalry, October 15, 1875; transferred to the Seventh Cavalry, January 26, 1876.

First Sergeant Michael Keeney; Sergeant Frederick Nursey.

Sergeant John Vickory, color bearer; said to have been the handsomest mounted man in the entire regiment. After the battle he was found with his right arm cut off at the shoulder. The colors had disappeared, and it is believed that the Indians, finding it impossible to wrench the staff from his death grip, amputated his arm to secure the flag.[21]

Sergeant John K. Wilkinson; Corporal Charles Coleman.

Corporal William Teeman; given as Freeman on the *Tribune* list; said to have been a close friend of Rain-in-the-Face. The story is told that one day while on guard at the prison at Fort Abraham Lincoln when that chief was held there, he unlocked the ball and chain from Rain-in-the-Face's leg and said: "Go, friend; take the chain and ball with you. I shall shoot, but the voice of my gun shall lie."[22]

Corporal John Briody; Farrier Benjamin Brandon; Blacksmith James R. Manning.

Privates

Thomas Atchison; Benjamin F. Brown; William Brown; Patrick Bruce; William Brady; Lucien Burham (given as Burnham in *Tribune* list); Armantheus D. Cather; James Carney; Anton Dohman; Timothy Donnelley; Walliam Gardiner; George W. Hammon (given as Harrimon on the official report of the battle furnished the War Department); Gustave Klein (given as Kline on official report of the battle furnished the War Department and on *Tribune* list); Herman Knauth (given as Krianth on *Tribune* list); John Kelly; William H. Lerock; Werner L. Liemann (given as Luman on official report of the battle furnished the War Department and on *Tribune* list); William A. Lossee; Christian Madson; Francis E. Milton; Joseph Monroe; Sebastian Omeling; Patrick Rudden (given as Ruddew on *Tribune* list); Richard Saunders (sometimes spelled Sanders); Francis W. Sicfous; George Warren (given as Wanew on *Tribune* list); Thomas N. Way.

Troop I

Troop I was the second to be struck by the Indians in the general attack (see Troop L).[23] The officers and men were found in platoon formation. It is a rather curious fact that no semblance of battle lines were found on the field except among the men of Troops I and L.

Captain Myles W. Keogh, the fighting Irishman, in command; body found with over thirty of his men in one group. The remains were exhumed June 25, 1877, and reinterred at Auburn, New York.

Army Record: A native of Ireland and a typical soldier of fortune, Captain Keogh is recorded by men who fought with him as the very soul of valor, a noble-hearted gentleman, and the beau ideal of a cavalry commander. He fought in Italy under Lamoriciere for the Pope. Attracted to the United States by the Civil War, he was commissioned from the District of Columbia, April 9, 1862, as aide-de-camp with the rank of captain; commissioned additional aide-de-camp with the rank of major of volunteers, April 7, 1864; honorably mustered out on September 1, 1866; commissioned second lieutenant in the Fourth United States Cavalry, May 4, 1866; transferred to the Seventh Cavalry with the rank of captain, July 28, 1866.

Civil War Record: The following brevets were awarded him for gallant service in action: Lieutenant colonel of volunteers, dating from March 13, 1865, for uniform gallantry and good conduct during the war; major, March 2, 1867, for gallant and meritorious service at Gettysburg, July 1-3, 1863; lieutenant colonel, March 2, 1867, for gallant and meritorious service at Dallas, Georgia, May 21 to June 1, 1864, while with Sherman on his march through Georgia to the sea.

First Lieutenant James Ezekiel Porter; body never found; either so badly mutilated that identification was impossible, or may have been killed in the river.

Army Record: A native of Maine, he was appointed from that state to West Point, September 1, 1864; commissioned

second lieutenant in the Seventh Cavalry, June 15, 1869; first
lieutenant, March 1, 1872.

First Sergeant Frank E. Varden; Sergeant James Bustard;
Corporal George C. Morris; Corporal Samuel F. Staples; Cor-
poral John Wild; Trumpeter John McGucker; Trumpeter John
W. Patton; Blacksmith Henry A. Baily (listed with Troop I in
Tribune and in official report of the battle furnished the War
department; but in a later list his name appears in the roll of
Troop L).

Privates

John Barry, Joseph E. Broadhurst; Thomas Connors; J. Co-
mas (name appears on official report of the battle furnished the
War Department; do not find it on subsequent list); Thomas P.
Downing; Edward C. Driscoll; David C. Gillett; George H.
Gross; Edward P. Halcomb; Marion E. Horn; Adam Hetesimer
(given as Hitismer on *Tribune* list); Patrick Kelly; Edward W.
Lloyd; Frederick Lehman; Henry Lehman; Archiband McIlhar-
gey; John Mitchell; Jacob Noshaug; John O'Bryan; John Par-
ker; Felix J. Pitter; George Post; James Quinn; William Reed;
John W. Rossbury; Darwin L. Symms; James E. Troy (given as
Tray on official report of the battle furnished the War Depart-
ment); Charles Van Bramar; William B. Whaley.

Troop L

This was the first troop struck by the Indians in the general
attack.[24] The officers and men died in their places, in platoon
formation, the same as Troop I.

First Lieutenant James Calhoun, in command; General Custer's brother-in-law; body found with his men near Lieutenant
John J. Crittenden, at a cross-ridge facing nearly east and the
Custer Ford Coulee; his was the first troop to be wiped out by the
Indians.   The remains were exhumed June 25, 1877, and on August 3, 1877, reinterred with four other officers at Fort Leavenworth, Kansas.

Army Record: Lieutenant Calhoun was a native of Ohio,
and not a graduate of West Point; served as a private and sergeant
of Company D, Twenty-third United States Infantry, from Feb-

ruary 22, 1865, to October 24, 1867; commissioned second lieutenant in the Thirty-second Infantry, July 31, 1867; transferred to the Twenty-first Infantry, April 19, 1869; unassigned October 29; 1870; assigned to the Seventh Cavalry, January 1, 1871; commissioned first lieutenant, January 9, 1871.

Second Lieutenant John Jordan Crittenden, of the Twentieth Infantry; body found with the men of Troop L. His father wished him buried where he had fallen, and in respect to this request the squad that visited the field on June 25, 1877, buried his remains in a deep grave. Dr. Thomas B. Marquis says: "That was the only underground individual grave ever dug on the Custer battlefield."[25] This grave was at the end of the ridge where he died until the spring of 1932, when the bones were unearthed by order of the War Department and transferred to the national cemetery adjoining the battlefield. Dr. Marquis says that the bones were found about three feet beneath the surface without evidence of any container.[25] The original grave was marked for many years by a plain white marble slab with this simple inscription: "John J. Crittenden. Born June 7, 1851. Killed June 25, 1876."

Army Record: A native of Kentucky, and not a graduate of West Point. Lieutenant Crittenden was commissioned second lieutenant in the Twentieth Infantry, October 15, 1875; and at the time of the Battle of the Little Big Horn he was on detached duty with the Seventh Cavalry, serving in Troop L.

First Sergeant James Butler; body found on a little roundtop about a mile and a half from the spot where Custer made the "last stand," and towards the river.[26] A soldier of long experience and courage tried on many fields, he was one of the outstanding heroes of the Battle of the Little Big Horn. Many empty cartrides scattered about his body indicated that he had put up a desperate fight; and the Indians afterwards stated that he held them back for some time, killing more warriors than any other white man in the battle, before they finally wiped him out. The theory has been advanced that he was trying to get through with a message for Reno when he was surrounded on this knoll.[27] Others express the opinion that he took this position at the beginning of the fight, and held the Indians back.

This opinion is borne out by the statements of the Indians themselves.

Sergeant Amos B. Warren; Sergeant William Cashan; Corporal William H. Harrison; Corporal James J. Galvan; Corporal William H. Gilbert (this name appeared in a later list as corporal in Troop F); Corporal John Seiler; Corporal Albert H. Meyer; Trumpeter Frederick Walsh; Farrier William Heath; Blacksmith Charles Simon.

Privates

George E. Adams; Anthony Assadely; William Andrews; John Burke; Elmer Babcock; Ami Cheever; John Duggan; William Dye; William B. Crisfield; Charles Graham; Henry Hamilton; —— Hughes; Weston Harrington; Louis Hauggi; —— Keef (probably the Kiefer on the *Tribune* list); Thomas G. Kavanagh (given as Kavaugh on *Tribune* list); Louis Lobering; Peter McGue; Charles McCarthy; Bartholomew Mahoney; Thomas E. Maxwell; John Miller; David J. O'Connell; Charles Perkins, saddler; Henry Roberts; Walter B. Rogers; Christian Reinbold; Henry Schmidt; Charles Scott; Andrew Snow (this name appears with Troop E on a later list in the War Department); Bent Seimonson (given as Semonson on *Tribune* list); Byron Tarbox; Edmond D. Tessier (given as Tessler on *Tribune* list); Thomas S. Tweed; Michael Vetter (given as Veller on *Tribune* list).

Scouts

Mitch Bouyer; half-breed Crow Indian; Custer's chief of Indian scouts and interpreter. Several years afterwards a Sioux warrior told Thomas H. Leforge[1] that after Custer's men had been killed he found Bouyer near the river, still living, his back broken by a bullet. The scout told the Sioux that, although they had killed these few soldiers many thousands more would come and conquer them all. Bouyer then asked the Indian to kill him and end his suffering. The warrior granted this request, after which he removed the scout's vest and threw the body into the river. Bouyer's vest, made of spotted calf skin, was found near the Little Big Horn after the battle.[28] This story is corroborated by Crow Indians. They say that an Arapahoe with the Sioux told that Bouyer and a bugler escaped from Custer Hill, crossed the river to the west side and hid in the brush. They were discovered and Bouyer, desperately wounded, begged to be killed. Both were slain and the bodies thrown into the river. Bouyer was identified by the calfskin vest.[3]

Stabbed, a Crow Indian.[29]

Civilians

Mark Kellogg; correspondent of the Bismarck, North Dakota, *Tribune;* body found some distance from the battlefield, not stripped or mutilated. John J. Finnerty,[30] correspondent of the Chicago *Times,* with General Crook at this same period, says that Kellogg nearly succeeded in making his escape, but the mule he rode was too slow and he was finally overtaken and shot.

Boston Custer; a brother of General Custer, and his guest on the expedition; body found with the group on Custer Hill where the "last stand" was made. After Custer divided his force, Boston Custer returned to the pack train on an errand, and then rode furiously back. Trumpeter Martin,[31] carrying Custer's last message to Benteen, passed Boston Custer as he was hastening back to join the general "to be in at the death of the Sioux."

Arthur (Autie) Reed; nephew of General Custer and just a boy; accompanied the expedition as a herder;[32] body found with the group on Custer Hill.

KILLED WITH RENO

Major Reno was given Troops A, G, and M; Captain Benteen had Troops D, H, and K, leaving Troop B under McDougal to guard the packtrain. Both Benteen and McDougal did not encounter any Indians and joined Reno after the latter had retreated from the river bottom and taken a position on what is now known as Reno Hill.

In the first charge led by Reno in the river bottom only one man had been wounded when he ordered his men to dismount and take position in the trees by the river bank. When Bloody Knife was killed at Reno's side the major ordered a retreat. It was during this retreat across the river bottom that most of the twenty-nine men were killed.

In the following list those not designated otherwise were killed with Reno's battalion in the river bottom and in the subsequent fighting on the hill. Those killed in Benteen's battalion and McDougal's troop are so designated. They were killed after joining Reno on the hill.

Field Staff

Dr. J. M. DeWolf, acting assistant surgeon. In the retreat from the river bottom Dr. DeWolf and Private Elihue M. T. Clair, of Troop K, crossed the river safely, and had started to climb the bluff when both were shot down and scalped in plain view of the fleeing troops. A marble slab on a narrow ridge sloping from the river bottom to Reno Hill marks the supposed location of Dr. DeWolf's grave; but from present indications it seems impracticable to have buried the remains there.[3] He was probably buried on the hill above with other killed or in an unknown grave nearby.

Non-Commissioned Staff

Corporal James Dalious, of Troop A; this name appeared on the first report of the battle furnished the War Department as Henry Dalious, and on the *Tribune* list as Henry Dallans.
Corporal George K. King, of Troop A.

Troop A

Captain Myles Moylan in command.[33]
Privates
James Drinan (given as Drinaw in *Tribune* list); John E. Armstrong; James McDonald; William Moodie (spelled Moody in *Tribune* list); Richard Rollins (spelled Rowlins in *Tribune* list); John Sullivan; Thomas P. Sweetser (spelled Switzer in *Tribune* list).

Troop B

Captain Thomas M. McDougal in command.[34]
Second Lieutenant Benjamin Hubert Hodgson; wounded in crossing the Little Big Horn during the retreat from the river

bottom, but was carried across by hanging onto the stirrup of a trooper. Just as they reached the opposite bank Hodgson was killed by another bullet. The body did not fall into the hands of the Indians, but was recovered and buried. Four men claimed that Hodgson seized their stirrup. One account states that it was Trumpeter Henry Fisher, while Cyrus Townsend Brady[35] gives the credit to Sergeant Criswell (probably Sergeant Benjamin C. Criswell, of Troop B). Years later Private William E. Morris[36] claimed that it was his stirrup; and James Wilbur says[37] that it was Bugler Myers.

A short distance north of the entrenchments on Reno Hill is a marble slab to Lieutenant Hodgson, with the record that he "fell here." But this is a quarter of a mile from the spot where survivors say he died. Major Reno and other officers record that they went down the hill, and buried him beside the river soon after his death.[3] This was when the Indians withdrew from Reno's front to attack Custer. No marker of any kind was placed at the spot, and it is not known today.

Army Record: A native of Pennsylvania, Lieutenant Hodgson was appointed to West Point from the Keystone State, July 1, 1865; commissioned second lieutenant in the Seventh Cavalry, June 15, 1870.

Privates

Richard Doran, killed with McDougal; George B. Mask, killed with McDougal.

Troop D

Thomas B. Weir in command.[88]
Farrier Charles Vincent; with Benteen.[89]

Privates

Patrick Golden, with Benteen; Edward Hansen, with Benteen.

Troop G

Lieutenant Donald McIntosh in command.
First Lieutenant Donald McIntosh. In trying to rally his men in the woods in the river bottom his horse was shot, and he

darted back into the timber for shelter. A trooper then gave him his horse. McIntosh left the woods far behind the main body of retreating troops, and was cut off by the Sioux, pulled from his horse, and killed. The body was found later badly mutilated. On June 25, 1877, the remains were exhumed, and reinterred at Fort Leavenworth, Kansas, August 3, 1877, with four other officers. He left a family at Fort Abraham Lincoln.

Army Record: He was a native of Canada, said to have been an educated half-breed and held in high esteem; not a graduate of West Point, but entered the army from Oregon, and was commissioned second lieutenant in the Seventh Cavalry, August 17, 1867; commissioned first lieutenant, March 22, 1870.

Sergeant Edward Botzer; Sergeant Martin Considine; Corporal Otto Hagemann; Corporal James Martin; Trumpeter Henry Dose; Farrier Benjamin Wells; Saddler Crawford Selby.

Privates

John J. McGinniss; Andrew J. Moore; Benjamin F.. Rogers; John Rapp (given as John Papp on *Tribune* list); Henry Seafferman; Edward Stanley.

Troop H

Captain Frederick W. Benteen in command.[40]

Corporal Julian D. Jones; with Benteen; this name also appears on a later list as a private in Troop G; given as a private in Troop E in *Tribune* list; Corporal George Lell, with Benteen, given as George Lee on *Tribune* list; Private Thomas E. Meador, with Benteen.

Troop K

Lieutenant Edward S. Godfrey in command.[41]

First Sergeant DeWitt Winney, with Benteen, given as Whitney on *Tribune* list; Sergeant Robert H. Hughes, with Benteen; Corporal John J. Callahan, with Benteen; Trumpeter Julius Helmer, with Benteen; Private Elihue M. T. Clair; this name also appears as Clear in some lists. With Dr. DeWolf he crossed the Little Big Horn safely during the retreat from the river bottom, but while climbing this bluff they were shot and scalped in plain view of the fleeing troops.[42]

Troop M

Captain Thomas M. French in command.[43]

Sergeant Myles O'Hara; the first man killed with Reno. He was shot through the breast when the skirmish line changed its front during the first attack on Reno in the river bottom. One account gives the name of the first man killed as Sergeant Hynes, of Troop A; but this is a mistake. Sergeant Hynes was shot in the left knee and not in the breast. His name appears in the list of wounded.

Corporal Henry M. Scollin; killed with Private David Sommers, also of Troop M. during the retreat across the river bottom.

Corporal Frederick Streing; this name is given as Stringer in the *Tribune* list.

Privates

Henry Gordon, killed while climbing to the top of the cut just after crossing the Little Big Horn in the retreat from the river bottom; Henry Koltzbucher, striker for Captain French, shot through the stomach in the first attack in the river bottom; left concealed in the underbrush by his comrades; body found after the battle, and not mutilated, indicating that the Indians did not discover him; George Lorentz; given as G. Lawrence in *Tribune* list; shot in stomach when about to mount his horse at the beginning of the retreat from the river bottom; William D. Meyer; some give this name as Mayer; killed while climbing to the top of the cut just after crossing the Little Big Horn in the retreat from the river bottom. George E. Smith; when Reno made his first attack in the river bottom this man's horse stampeded straight into the Indian lines, and he was never seen again. His body was never identified and his fate is unknown.[44] David Sommers; killed with Corporal Scollin during the retreat across the river bottom. James J. Tanner; killed in an attempt to secure water from the river for the wounded after Reno was besieged on the hill. Wooden Leg, a Cheyenne, afterwards claimed that he shot this man.[18] Henry Turley; killed just as he reached the top of the cut after crossing the Little Big Horn during the retreat from the river bottom to Reno's position on the hill. Henry Voigt.

Civilians

Charles Reynolds, the famous scout, known as "Silent Charley"; killed just after the first attack in the river bottom. He was with Dr. Porter, who was coolly dressing the wound of a soldier with the bullets flying about him. When he paid no attention to his danger, Reynolds sprang to his feet and cried: "Doctor, the Indians are shooting at you." The next instant the scout fell, shot through the heart. A braver man or better scout than "Silent Charley" could not have been found on the frontier.

Isaiah Dorman; Negro; scout and interpreter from Fort Rice; mortally wounded on the skirmish line during the first attack on Reno's men, and left behind when the retreat from the river bottom began. He was known among the Sioux as "Teat," and was personally known by Sitting Bull. He was found by the Indians and was badly wounded. Sitting Bull ordered that his life be spared, and when Dorman asked for water the chief secured some in his own cup made from a buffalo horn.[45] Dorman's body was found after the battle, but whether he died of his wound or was killed by Indians is not known.

Frank C. Mann; killed on the skirmish line during the first attack in the river bottom.

Arikara (Ree) Indian Scouts

Bloody Knife; killed on the skirmish line during the first attack in the river bottom. While at Reno's side he was shot through the head and his brains spattered in the major's face. It was after this incident that Reno ordered the retreat. Bloody Knife was a bitter enemy of Chief Gall, the principal Sioux leader in the battle.

Bobtail Bull; killed on the skirmish line during the first attack in the river bottom.

Little Brave; sometimes called Little Soldier; killed on the skirmish line during the first attack in the river bottom.

WOUNDED

The following list of the wounded with Reno and Benteen was taken from a list made by Major Marcus A. Reno[46] on board the *Far West*, at the mouth of the Little Big Horn River, June 28, 1876, and also from a list that was published in the Bismarck, North Dakota, *Tribune*, extra of May 6, 1876. This list included all of the wounded except fourteen, who had sufficiently recovered to remain with their commands, by the time the boat left for Fort Abraham Lincoln. I have added the names of several of those who returned to their commands.

In his list Major Reno stated that, with the loss of seven first sergeants, it was almost impossible to account for all of the men at that date. The list of wounded that appeared in the *Tribune* was furnished that paper by Dr. Porter, the assistant surgeon with Reno and the physician who went with the wounded on the *Far West* to Fort Abraham Lincoln.

Scouts

Second Lieutenant Charles Albert Varnum; in command of scouts with the Seventh Cavalry; detailed with Reno's battalion; wounded but remained with the command.

Army Record: A native of New York, but appointed to West Point from Florida, September 1, 1868; commissioned second lieutenant in the Seventh Cavalry June 14, 1872; commissioned first lieutenant dating from June 25, 1876; regimental quartermaster from November 14, 1876, to October 31, 1879; captain, July 22, 1890; major, February 2, 1901; retired as colonel and living in San Francisco, California, in 1933, the last of the officers of the Seventh Cavalry who participated in the Battle of the Little Big Horn.

Awarded the Medal of Honor, September 22, 1897, for most distinguished gallantry in action at White Clay Creek, South Dakota, December 30, 1890. This officer was in command of Troop B and part of Troop E, Seventh Cavalry. The regiment was retiring before a superior force of Indians; and while executing an order to withdraw, Captain Varnum saw that a continuance of the movement would result in the exposure of another troop to the danger of being cut off and surrounded. Disregarding orders to retire, he placed himself in front of his men, led a charge upon the advancing Indians, regained a commanding position that had just been vacated, and thus insured the safe withdrawal of both detachments without further loss.

Troop A

First Sergeant William Heyn; in left knee. Some claim that he was shot in the breast when the skirmish line changed its front during the first attack in the river bottom; probably confused with Sergeant O'Hara, of Troop M.

Privates

Jacob Deal; Samuel Foster; in right arm; given as James Foster in *Tribune* list; Frederick Homsted, in left wrist; Francis Reeves, in left side and body; Elijah T. Stroud, in right leg; Charles Wiedman.

Troop B

Corporal William M. Smith, with McDougal; Private James Cunningham, with McDougal.

Troop C

This was Captain Tom Custer's troop. These men were on detached service with Reno.

Privates

Charles Bennett; in the body; died July 5, 1876, of his wound; name given in *Tribune* list as James E. Bennett. John McGuire, in right arm; name appeared on Reno's official list as Maguire. Peter Thompson, in face. Charles Campbell, in right shoulder. Alfred Whitaker, in right elbow.

Troop D

Private Patrick McDonald, sometimes spelled McDonnell; in left leg.

Troop E

This was the Gray Horse Troop, commanded by Lieutenant A. E. Smith; wiped out with Custer. The following were on detached service with Reno: Sergeant James T. Reilly or Riley; in back and left leg.

Troop G

Privates

Charles Camell; appeared on Reno's first list of wounded with Troop G; probably Charles Campbell, of Troop C. James P. Boyle. James McVey, in hips; appeared in *Tribune* list with Troop C; undoubtedly the same man. John Morrison.

Troop H

First Sergeant Joseph McMurray; Sergeant Patrick Connelly; Sergeant Thomas McLaughlin; Sergeant John Paul, in back; Corporal Alexander Bishop, in right arm; Trumpeter William Ramel; Saddler Otto Voit.

Privates

Henry Bishley; Charles H. Bishop, in right arm; John Cooper, in right elbow; Henry Black, in right hand; William Farley; William George, in left side; died July 3, 1876, at 4 a. m., and buried at the mouth of the Powder River; Thomas Hughes; Daniel McWilliams, in right knee; John Muller, in right thigh, received during the fighting after Reno went into position on the bluff; John J. Phillips, in face and both hands; Samuel Severn, in both thighs; William C. Williams; Charles Wendolph.

Troop I

This was Captain Myles W. Keogh's troop; wiped out with Custer. The following were on detached service with Reno: Private David Corey, in right hip; Private Jasper Marshall, in left leg.[49]

Troop K

Privates

Patrick Corcoran, in right shoulder; Michael C. Madden, in right leg; the leg was broken in three places in securing water from the river for the wounded; the leg was amputated immediately; Max Wilke, in left foot.

Troop M

Sergeant Charles White; wounded in right arm and horse killed when retreat from river bottom began; left in the timber and afterwards made his escape; Sergeant Patrick Carey, in right hip; Sergeant Thomas P. Varnerx, in right ear; Blacksmith Daniel Newell; wounded in left thigh during the fight in the river bottom before the retreat began.

Privates

Frank Brunn, in face and left thigh; W. E. Harris, in left breast; John H. Meyer, in back; some accounts state that his horse stampeded and ran into the Indian lines at the first attack, but his name appears among the wounded who returned to Fort Abraham Lincoln.[47] William E. Morris, wounded in left breast while climbing to top of the cut with Turley, Gordon, and William D. Meyer, all three of whom were killed, just after crossing the Little Big Horn in the retreat from the river bottom; Morris recovered. Edward Pigford, wounded through fleshy part of right hip during the retreat from the river bottom; kept on fighting after position was reached on the hill; took part in the advance with Captain Weir's troops towards the sound of the fight between Custer and the Indians;[48] slightly wounded in right forearm by a small caliber bullet on the 26th; did not return to Fort Abraham Lincoln, but remained with his command; died at Lock Three, Pennsylvania, December 6, 1932; buried in the Richland Cemetery at Dravosburg, Pennsylvania; Roman Rutler, wounded in right shoulder on the 26th; James Wilbur, in left leg.

Indian Scouts

White Swan, Crow Indian

Civilian

J. C. Wagoner, packer; wounded in the head while in the corral with horses during the attack on the hill.

Private David Ackinson, of Troop E, was taken on board the *Far West* at the mouth of the Big Horn River, and left at Fort Buford, July 4, 1876; not in the battle, sick.

Sergeant M. Riley of Company I, Twentieth Infantry, was taken on board the *Far West* at the mouth of the Big Horn River, and left at Fort Buford, July 4; not in the battle.

CASUALTIES BY TROOPS

Killed With Custer

Troop

C, Capt. Thomas W. Custer	41
E, Lieut. A. E. Smith	41
F, Capt. George W. Yates	33
I, Capt. Myles W. Keogh	38
L, Lieut. James Calhoun	45
Total	198
Field Staff	3
Non-commissioned Staff	3
Scouts, Crow Indian	1
Interpreter and scout, half-breed Crow	1
Newspaper Correspondent	1
Civilians	2
Total killed	209

Casualties With Reno and Benteen

Troop		Killed	Wounded
A		7	7
B		3	2
C	(detached)	0	5
D		3	1
E	(detached)	0	1
G		14	4
H		3	20
I	(detached)	0	2
K		5	3
M		12	11
Totals		47	56
Field Staff		1	0
Non-commissioned Staff		2	0
Civilian		1	0
Scouts, Arikara		3	0
Scouts, white		1	1
Interpreter, Negro		1	0
Totals		56	57

The reports state that Reno lost twenty-nine men killed in the river bottom and eighteen killed on the hill, giving a total of forty-seven. His wounded are given at fifty-two. The difference in the above is probably accounted for by several men included in this list who did not return to Fort Abraham Lincoln. The total killed in the battle is given at 265, which corresponds with the above figures.

APPENDIX   REFERENCE   NOTES

(NOTE. The numbers here correspond with the numbers found throughout the text of the appendix.)

1 *Memoirs of a White Crow Indian,* by Dr. Thomas B. Marquis.

2 *Some Memories of a Soldier,* By General Hugh L. Scott.

3 *Custer Soldiers Not Buried,* by Dr. Thomas B. Marquis.

4 *The Sioux Wars,* by Charles E. De Land; South Dakota Historical Collections, Volume XIV.

5 Horace A. Bivens served many years in Negro troops in the West. During the Spanish-American War he was with the Tenth Cavalry when it went
to the support of Roosevelt's Rough Riders in the famous charge up San
Juan Hill. Later he served in the Philippines, and during the World War
he received a commission as captain in charge of a Negro labor battalion.

6 The author is indebted for copies of these inscriptions to Dr. Thomas
B. Marquis, of Hardin, Montana, and Mr. Victor A. Bolsius, of Crow Agency,
Montana, Superintendent of the Custer Battlefield National Cemetery.

7 *The Bozeman Trail,* by Grace Raymond Hebard and E. A. Brininstool.

8 Lieutenant James H. Bradley was killed at the Battle of the Big Hole,
Montana, August 9, 1877, between troops under General John Gibbon and the
Nez Perces under Chief Joseph.

9 Raymond Richards in *The Tepee Book.*

10 Twenty-seven women were made widows by the Battle of the Little
Big Horn. Before leaving Fort Abraham Lincoln the last time they all made
a vow among themselves that they would never remarry. In later years
some of them did marry again, one of whom was Mrs. Calhoun, Mrs. Custer's
sister-in-law.

11 This rapid advancement caused much jealousy among older officers
whom he passed and soon outranked. This feeling of enmity followed Custer throughout all his subsequent career, and even to this day is the cause
of the controversy over the Custer defeat.

12 Mrs. Custer deposited Lee's flag of truce and the Appomattox table
in the War Department a number of years ago. In her will, which was pro-
bated in New York City soon after her death on April 4, 1933, she left
these relics to the United States Government.

13 *A Warrior Who Fought Custer,* by Dr. Thomas B. Marquis.

14 See Corporal William Teeman, of Troop F, and Note 22.

15 Military authorities and many writers long accepted the theory that
Custer charged down the hill when he first sighted the village, but was repulsed at the river and never crossed. It is certain that he did not cross,
but the Indians now claim that Custer never charged down the hill; that he
hesitated and stopped on the side of the hill and that the Indians swarmed
across the river and attacked him there. However, this was not the Custer
method of fighting. He always charged as soon as he came within sight of
the enemy, and many military men still hold to this theory. Stanley Vestal
in *Sitting Bull* says that Custer did not charge down the hill as many believe. See Note 23. In this connection, the story has been told recently by
Indian survivors (see *A Warrior Who Fought Custer,* by Dr. Thomas B.
Marquis) that after the battle started many of Custer's men committed

suicide when they saw that the Indians were coming, and some of them shot each other. Stanley Vestal, who interviewed many Sioux survivors, says that they informed him that the soldiers fought hard and were brave to the last.

16 If the theory that Custer did charge is correct, then this is the first Custer charge ever stopped by an enemy.

17 All references to the *Tribune* list are to the first casualty list ever published, which appeared in the extra issue of *The Bismarck Tribune,* of Bismarck, North Dakota, of July 6, 1876.

18 *Fifty Years After the Little Big Horn,* by Colonel Charles Francis Bates. Some authorities now claim that the Indians did not make a last charge, but shot the last men from a distance. This theory is based upon recent statements of Indian survivors.

19 This is also based upon recent statements of Indian survivors.

20 All references to the official report of the battle furnished the War Department are to the first report sent in. A subsquent report was sent which was much more authentic.

21 Raymond Richards in *The Tepee Book.*

22 Rain-in-the-Face escaped from the guardhouse while imprisoned at Fort Abraham Lincoln; but this story of the manner of that escape is not vouched for as authentic.

23 This is based on the theory that Custer charged down the hill to the river before he was stopped. Still. in the event that he did not charge, this could have been the second troop struck in the general attack. (See Note 15.)

24 In the event Custer did not charge down the hill this could still have been the first troop struck and wiped out in the general attack. (See Notes 15 and 23.)

25 *Custer Soldiers Not Buried,* by Dr. Thomas B. Marquis.

26 It is possible that the skeleton found by a Crow Indian in 1928 in a gully a quarter of a mile southeast of the battlefield may have been Sergeant Butler. from the fact that nineteen empty shells were picked up with the bones. If not his remains then this was an unknown hero of the Battle of the Little Big Horn.

27 Sioux survivors say that Sergeant Butler ran out to one side and stood the Indians off single-handed for a long time before they finally killed him. They say that he was the bravest of all the whites. (See *Sitting Bull,* by Stanley Vestal.)

28 *The Teepee Book.*

29 Some accounts give White Swan and Half Yellow Face. Crow scouts. as killed with Custer. When Custer divided the regiment he took Hairy Moccasin, White-Man-Runs-Him, Goes Ahead, Curley, and Stabbed, all Crows. in charge of Mitch Bouyer. As soon as the Sioux attacked, the first three fled; but they always claimed that Custer ordered them or told them to report to Reno. Curley said in later years that he remained until just before all the soldiers were killed when Custer told him to go. and he made his escape on a swift horse. Another story he told was that he escaped by donning a Sioux war bonnet when he saw that the command was doomed. The Sioux always declared that he took no part in the battle. Some authorities say that he concealed himself in a ravine. while others claim that he watched the battle from a distance. Curley died at Crow Agency. Montana. May 22. 1923. of a fever, and was buried with military honors in the Custer Battlefield National Cemetery, members of the American Legion acting as pallbearers.

30 *War-Path and Bivouac,* by John J. Finerty.

31 Trumpeter John Martin was the last man who saw Custer alive. and lived to tell the story. Just after the village was sighted, Custer sent Martin back to Benteen with the famous last order, which that officer received and then proceeded to disregard. Martin died December 24, 1922, aged sixty-nine years, in a Brooklyn, New York, hospital.

32 Richard A. Roberts, still living in 1933 at Charleroi, Pennsylvania, also accompanied the Custer expedition as a herder in company with Arthur Reed. His horse was taken sick, and he remained at the base camp; otherwise he would probably have been with Reed in the battle. Roberts' sister was the wife of Captain Yates.

33 On November 27, 1894, Captain Moylan was awarded the Medal of Honor for most distinguished gallantry in action against the Nez Perces at the Battle of Bear Paw Mountain, Montana, September 30, 1877, in leading his command until he was severely wounded; retired April 15, 1893, as major of the Tenth Cavalry.

34 Captain Thomas Mower McDougall was a native of Wisconsin, but was commissioned from Kansas as second lieutenant of the Forty-eighth United States Infantry, February 18, 1864; honorably mustered out June 1, 1865; commissioned captain in the Fifth United States Volunteer Infantry, June 2, 1865; honorably mustered out August 10, 1866; commissioned second lieutenant of the Fourteenth Infantry May 10, 1866; transferred to the Second Infantry September 21, 1866; first lieutenant, November 5, 1866; transferred to the Twenty-first Infantry April 19, 1869; unassigned October 21, 1869; assigned to the Sevent Cavalry December 31, 1870; received the brevet of captain March 2, 1867, for faithful and meritorious service.

35 *Northwestern Fights and Fighters,* by Cyrus Townsend Brady.

36 *A Trooper With Custer,* by E. A. Brininstool.

37 *The Teepee Book.*

38 Thomas Benton Weir was a native of Ohio. He enlisted from Michigan in the Union Army and on October 13, 1861, he was commissioned second lieutenant in the Third Michigan Cavalry; first lieutenant, June 19, 1862; captain, November 1, 1862; major, January 18, 1865; lieutenant colonel, November 6, 1865; honorably mustered out on February 12, 1866. He was commissioned first lieutenant in the Seventh Cavalry July 28, 1866; regimental commissary of subsistence from February 24 to July 31, 1867; commissioned captain July 31, 1867; died December 9, 1876. Received the following brevets during the Civil War: Major, July 31, 1867, for gallant and meritorious service at the Battle of Farmington, Tennessee, and lieutenant colonel, July 31, 1867, for gallant and meritorious service in the engagement with General Forrest near Ripley, Mississippi, December 1, 1863.

39 When Captain Weir with Troop D left Reno's position and advanced towards Custer late in the afternoon of June 25 in answer to the volley firing heard from the direction of the battlefield, he continued until forced back by the Indians. He lost one soldier killed, about a mile north of Reno's position. This man's body was never found; but he must have been one of these three men: Vincent, Golden, or Hansen.

40 Captain Benteen was a native of Virginia. At the outbreak of the Civil War he entered the Union army as first lieutenant of the Tenth Missouri Cavalry, September 1, 1861, as he was living in Missouri at that time. He was commissioned captain October 1, 1861; major, December 19, 1862; lieutenant colonel, February 27, 1864; and was honorably mustered out June 30, 1865; commissioned colonel of the 138th United States Colored Infantry July 15, 1865; honorably mustered out January 6, 1866; commissioned captain in the Seventh Cavalry July 28, 1866. Failing of promotion in the Seventh Cavalry, he blamed Custer; but he was not advanced to major until December 17, 1882, when he was transferred to the Ninth Cavalry with that rank. Retired as major July 7, 1888. Record of brevets: March 2, 1867, for gallant and meritorious service in the Battle of Osage; lieutenant colonel for leading a charge at Columbus, Georgia; colonel on August 13, 1868, for gallant and meritorious service in action against hostile Indians at Saline River, Kansas, August 13, 1868; brigadier general, February 27, 1890, for gallant and meritorious service in action against hostile Indians at the Battle of the Little Big Horn, June 25 and 26, 1876, and in action against hostile Indians at Canyon Creek, Montana, September 13, 1877; died June 22, 1898.

41 First Lieutenant Edwin S. Godfrey was commissioned captain Decem-

ber 9, 1876, and retired as a brigadier general. Awarded the Medal of Honor for distinguished and gallant service in action against hostile Nez Perces at Bear Paw Mountain, Montana, September 30, 1877, in leading his command into action where he was severely wounded; died April 2, 1932, aged eighty-eight years.

42 It has never been explained how he and several others listed with Benteen's battalion came to be with Reno at this time, when Benteen was miles away. They were probably on detached service.

43 Captain French was retired on February 5, 1880, and died March 27, 1882.

44 Some accounts of survivors state that the horses of two and some say three men of Troop M stampeded into the Indian lines. In some accounts the name of John H. Meyer is given as one whose horse ran into the enemy lines when Reno made his first attack in the river bottom. However, this name does not appear among the killed, but J. H. Meyer, of Troop M, was among the list of wounded.

45 *Sitting Bull* by Stanley Vestal. It is generally conceded that Sitting Bull did not know for some time after the battle who led Custer's battalion. In fact, he believed he was fighting against Crook. Mr. Vestal says that Bad Juice, a Sioux, recognized Custer's body and pointed him out to other Indians as the leader. In that case Sitting Bull must have heard this within a day or two at least.

46 Major Reno was a native of Illinois, who entered West Point from that state September 1, 1851. He was breveted second lieutenant in the First Dragoons July 1, 1857, and commissioned second lieutenant June 14, 1858; first lieutenant, April 25, 1861; assigned to the First Cavalry August 3, 1861; commissioned captain, November 12, 1861; colonel of the Twelfth Pennsylvania Cavalry from January 1 to July 20, 1865, when he was honorably mustered out; commissioned major in the Seventh Cavalry December 26, 1868; dismissed from the service April 1, 1880; died March 30, 1889. Army Record: The following brevets were awarded him for service during the Civil War: Major, March 17, 1863, for gallant and meritorious service in action at Kelly's Ford, Virginia; lieutenant colonel, October 19, 1864, for gallant and meritorious service at Cedar Creek, Virginia; colonel, March 13, 1865, for gallant and meritorious service during the war, and brigadier general of volunteers, March 13, 1865, for meritorious service during the war.

47 General E. S. Godfrey, first lieutenant in command of Troop K, says that two horses stampeded from Reno's command and ran into the Indian lines at the beginning of the fight in the river bottom (see *The Teepee Book*). One was that of George E. Smith, of Troop M.

48 I was personally acquainted with Edward Pigford for some years before his death, and in an interview secured his account of the battle. He told a most unusual story in which he declared that at Captain French's request he and two others advanced ahead of Weir until they reached a hill from which they could see the Custer battlefield; and he declared that he saw the last of the fight when Custer and the few with him were wiped out. The other two troopers were killed by the Indians, who drove Weir back, but Pigford escaped. All I can say for this story is that it was told convincingly, and that it was possible but not probable. His account of details was such that no one not having been with Reno could dispute him.

49 Reno gave this name as James Marshall, of Troop L. *The Tribune* list gives it as Jasper Marshall, but also of Troop L.

SOURCE MATERIAL FOR APPENDIX

Banfill, W. H., newspaper reporter of Billings, Montana; personal information furnished and old soldiers interviewed for the author.

Bates, Colonel Charles Francis, and Fairfax Downey: *Fifty Years After the Little Big Horn;* pamphlet.

Brady, Cyrus Townsend: *Indian Fights and Fighters; 1866-1876.*

———————— *Northwestern Fights and Fighters.*

Brininstool, E. A.: *A Trooper With Custer.*

———————— *Fighting Red Cloud's Warriors.*

———————— *The Bozeman Trail.*

Bolsius, Victor A., Superintendent of Custer Battlefield National Cemetery, Crow Agency, Montana: Personal information furnished.

Bowen, Colonel William H. C.: *Custer's Last Fight,* a chapter from *The Life of California Joe.*

Burdick, Usher: *The Last Battle of the Sioux Nation.*

Burt, Mary E., editor, and Elizabeth Bacon Custer; *The Boy General.*

Byrne, P. A.: *Soldiers of the Plains.*

DeLand, Charles E.: *History of the Sioux War;* Volume 15, South Dakota Historical Collections.

Fickler, Rudolph W., Chicago, Illinois: Personal work and information furnished from records in his collection.

Finerty, John F.: *War-Path and Bivouac.*

Forrest, Earle R.: *Fighting With Custer;* the stories of Edward Pigford, a survivor of Troop M, Seventh Cavalry, with Reno; and Richard A. Roberts, who accompanied the expedition to the base camp: From *The Observer,* Washington, Pennsylvania, October 3-24, 1932, and *Fur-Fish-Game.*

Funeral of General Custer; Harper's Weekly, October 27, 1877.

Graham, Lieutenant Colonel W. A.: *The Story of the Little Big Horn.*

Hebard, Grace Raymond and E. A. Brininstool: *The Bozeman Trail.*

Holloway, W. L.: *Wild Life on the Plains and Horrors of Indian Warfare.*

Marquis, Dr. Thomas B.: *Memoirs of a White Crow Indian.*

———————————— *A Warrior Who Fought Custer.*

———————————— *Sketch Story of the Custer Battle;* pamphlet.

———————————— *She Watched Custer's Last Battle;* pamphlet.

———————————— *Which Indian Killed Custer?* pamphlet.

———————————— *Custer Soldiers Not Buried;* pamphlet.

———————————— Also much personal information furnished on the Custer battlefield.

Price, George F.: *Across the Continent With the Fifth Cavalry.*

Ronsheim, Milton: *The Life of General Custer;* reprinted in booklet form from *The Cadiz Republican,* Cadiz, Ohio, 1929.

Scott, Major General Hugh Lenox: *Some Memories of a Soldier.*

Seitz, Don C.: *The Dreadful Decade.*

The Teepee Book: Official publication of the Fiftieth Anniversary of the Custer Battle, 1926.

Vestal, Stanley: *Sitting Bull.*

War Department Records.

Wheeler, Olin D.: *The Custer Battlefield;* in *Wonderland* for 1901.

INDEX

ABREU (Colonel): 141.

ACAPULCO (Mex.): California Joe robbed by Mexican officials at, 83.

ADOBE WALLS (Tex.): Kit Carson's battle with Indians at, 140-146; history of old post at, 146; buffalo hunters battle at, 146.

ALDER GULCH (Mont.): 100, 104; claim jumpers at, 104.

ALLEN, EARNEST: 95.

ALLEN'S GOLD RUSH SALOON: fight of dance hall girls in, 219.

AMERICAN FUR COMPANY: 32, 34, 59.

ANDERSON, CHARLES: freighting partner of California Joe, 215-217; killed by California Joe, 217.

ANTHONY (Major): in command at Fort Lyons, 132; moves Cheyennes and Arapahoes to Sand Creek, 132; testimony on Sand Creek massacre, 135.

APACHE BILL (scout): 165.

APACHE CANYON (N. Mex.): 46, 52.

APACHE INDIANS: at battle of Adobe Walls, 143; fight with party under California Joe, 151-154; at Battle of Washita, 175, 190.

APPEARING ELK (Sioux): Rain-in-the-Face claims that he killed Custer, 329.

ARAPAHOE INDIANS: near Fort Lyons, 129; raids on wagon trains, 130; massacre of at Sand Creek, 132-138; at Battle of Adobe Walls, 143; raids on Saline River, Kans., 162; at Battle of Washita, 175; location of village on Washita, 190; surrender to General Custer, 196.

ARMIJO, MANUEL (Mexican Governor of New Mexico): 46.

ARMY OF THE WEST: 45-60; see also *Kearny, Gen. Stephen W.*

BAKER, JIM (Mountain Man): fight with Blackfeet, 36-38.

BARNES, GEORGE: 222.